Perspectives on the Small Community

PERSPECTIVES on the SMALL COMMUNITY

HUMANISTIC VIEWS for PRACTITIONERS

EMILIA E. MARTINEZ-BRAWLEY

NASW PRESS

National Association of Social Workers
Washington, DC

Richard L. Edwards, ACSW, *President*
Mark G. Battle, ACSW, *Executive Director*

First impression, June 1990
Second impression, July 1992
Third impression, December 1995

Library of Congress Cataloging-in-Publication Data

Martinez-Brawley, Emilia E., 1939–
Perspectives on the small community: humanistic views for practitioners / Emilia E. Martinez-Brawley.
p. cm.
Includes bibliographical references and index.
ISBN 0-87101-183-2
1. Community. 2. Community life. I. National Association of Social Workers. II. Title.
HM131.M33625 1990
306.76'2--dc20 90-6439
CIP

Printed in the United States of America

Cover and interior design by Janice Mauroschadt Design
Front cover photo courtesy of Comstock, Inc.

To my mother, who never left the small town.

❧

To Allan, Stephen, and Ewan.

CONTENTS

LIST OF EXHIBITS

CHAPTER 5

CHAPTER 6

FOREWORD

The small community—those towns and villages with populations under 50,000—is of utmost importance to human services practitioners and, consequently, to the National Association of Social Workers (NASW). A large percentage of NASW members practice in small communities. Furthermore, they are educated for practice in the many colleges and universities located in small towns and rural areas. NASW is happy to be publishing this important new book, which offers unique insights into the small community.

Despite the large number of practitioners working in small communities, the small town has been neglected in the professional literature. Human services professionals often are unaware of how issues play out in the small community. A number of myths also exist about life in small towns. For example, for the thousands who fled to rural areas to escape the tumult of the city and to find a sense of community in the 1970s and 1980s, small towns were only a symbol of the trouble-free "good life." Many people perceive small towns as totally homogeneous. The racial and ethnic diversity that exists in small communities is an often unrecognized element in small community practice. The practitioners who must correct these and other myths will find *Perspectives on the Small Community: Humanistic Views for Practitioners* an extraordinarily helpful resource.

The author, Emilia E. Martinez-Brawley, is keenly aware of small communities, as well as sensitive to issues of racial and ethnic diversity. An expert on rural social work in the United States, she has conducted research on rural services in Latin America, Great Britain, the Republic of Ireland, Australia, and Spain. She has presented a number of workshops on approaches to working with Hispanic and rural populations and has published widely in the field.

Dr. Martinez-Brawley's work melds social science theory, practice knowledge, and a broad range of humanistic and literary sources. Her liberal arts perspective, buttressed by very clear analyses of theory and practice, brings a new dimension to the understanding of the complex relationships that exist in small communities.

Introducing humanistic, literary, and journalistic content addresses the mandate of the Council on Social Work Education policy statement that emphasizes the need to integrate professional knowledge with the liberal arts perspective, particularly for baccalaureate students. *Perspectives on the Small Community* represents a clear effort at operationalizing that integration. NASW, which serves as the link between social work education and professional practice, is a particularly appropriate publisher for this new work.

One of the roles of the professional press is to be responsive to the broad interests and diversity of its constituencies. Practitioners across all fields will find *Perspectives on the Small Community* useful as a way of integrating fields of practice in the community context.

MARK G. BATTLE, ACSW
Executive Director
National Association of Social Workers

PREFACE

During the years of preparation of this book, many changes occurred that affected the way in which social workers and other human services practitioners regard the small community (those with 50,000 or fewer people). When I began writing, the centralistic ethos of the 1960s was still prevalent. As the chapters evolved, sociopolitical developments modified those views in positive and negative ways. I have tried to relate to those changes and to acknowledge shifts in the ways in which small communities have been regarded, not only in the literature and the press, but also in the social work field. In 1990, social workers and other human services professionals are more aware of the realities of small towns and more open to the contributions small towns make to the United States than they were during the 1960s. Yet, there is still much that needs to be done as schools of social work prepare students to practice in local environments.

During my years of teaching community theory and practice to generalist social work students, I tried a variety of textbooks to cover essential community content for workers in the human services field. Many of those textbooks were excellent examples of the comprehensive writings of community workers or organizers, and I, as well as my students, derived much useful information from their pages. Nevertheless, the more I worked with books that focused on interventive strategies, the more I realized that students in a human services profession often lack the necessary theoretical background to make sense of the applied perspectives offered in the materials read. More important, the students had not internalized through readings, experience, or social interaction the "idea of community" those books attempted to support.

Most authors of technical community workbooks assume that their readers have fairly sophisticated social science and experiential backgrounds and not only grasp, for example, the intricacies of the debates over the concept of community, but also feel an attachment to the idea of communal life. Given the nature of professional education for human services careers, this assumption is incorrect. Often students in professional programs and novice professionals in social work, corrections, nursing, and teaching seldom have the in-depth social science and humanistic backgrounds that the most currently used community intervention textbooks presuppose. To complicate matters, the accelerated nature of professional curricula makes it difficult for students to fill this gap with social science or humanities readings or life experiences that could broaden their orientation as practitioners.

As I prepared class material and worked with students or practitioners, I became convinced that theoretical concepts from the social sciences must be easily understood and presented in a concise, even synoptic fashion. I also understood that such theory must be interdisciplinary, for much useful information is derived not only from sociology, but also from anthropology, political science, and social and architectural history. Furthermore, I understood that unnecessarily complicated theory would frighten students in professional disciplines who feel that their career choices compel them to prompt action. Enlightened action, they are warned, cannot occur without the understanding of phenomena that theory brings; however, such warnings generally fall upon deaf ears.

For these reasons, I wrote *Perspectives on the Small Community: Humanistic Views for Practitioners*. It is intended primarily to help students and practitioners in the human services professions understand the nature of small-community relationships. Small-town practitioners must have ways of explaining and anticipating community behavior, not just as idiosyncratic manifestations of the folk, but as rational corollaries of the type of unit of social interaction involved. Through a combination of social science exhibits and excerpts from a variety of literary and journalistic works, *Perspectives on the Small Community* is intended to help human services students and beginning practitioners become as close to the small community and village life as those who live in the community.

EMILIA E. MARTINEZ-BRAWLEY

ACKNOWLEDGMENTS

I appreciate the help and support of the Department of Sociology, The Pennsylvania State University, University Park, during the preparation of this book. I appreciate the contributions and comments of many friends and colleagues, including Roy C. Buck, Professor Emeritus of Sociology, who contributed to the development of chapter 4, and Joan Blundall of the Northwest Iowa Community Mental Health Center in Spencer, whose experiences enriched many of my perspectives. I thank Bill Welch and Barbara Brueggebors of *Centre Daily Times;* Ken Fuson of *The Des Moines Register;* Peggy Ritter of Counseling Service, Bellefonte, Pennsylvania; and Pastor Myron Herzberg of Remsen, Iowa, for sharing their thoughts.

I appreciate the help of many small-town people who provided me with clippings as I searched for illustrations on different issues: Malvine Cole, Brother John Hammond, and Hilary Chalmers of Weston, Vermont, and Orval Layton of Lakeview, Oregon. I acknowledge the courtesy and cooperation of small-town newspaper publishers, editors, and reporters who responded to my requests: *Centre Daily Times (Pennsylvania), The Cedar Rapids, Iowa, Gazette, The Black River Tribune (Vermont), Herald and News (Oregon),* and *The Rutland Herald (Vermont).* I also acknowledge the cooperation of newspapers and magazines that cover small-town issues routinely: *The Des Moines Register, The Atlanta Journal-Constitution, Boston Globe, The Christian Science Monitor, Chicago Tribune, The Oregonian, The San Francisco Examiner, Newsweek,* and *U.S. News & World Report.*

I am indebted to Professor Amitai Etzioni, The George Washington University; former governor of Michigan William Milliken; author T. R. Pearson; and Celia Torres and Diane Campoamor, of the National Network of Hispanic Women.

Finally, I appreciate the help of my student teaching assistants. Kirsten Quinn helped proofread various early versions of the manuscript. Julie Parr helped with the library work, read the manuscript, checked references, and provided useful comments, stories, and practice examples. Her work merits my special thanks. I acknowledge the patience and hard work of Debi Welsby, Sheri Miller, and the secretarial staff of the Department of Sociology, The Pennsylvania State University, whose efforts contributed to the timely completion of this book.

Changes in perspective of what is community:

INTRODUCTION

Practitioners who do not have a solid understanding of the theory behind practice principles inevitably will flounder when they try to apply those principles, their interventions reduced to mere attempts to apply a technology. In terms of community practice, the assessments and actions of practitioners who are unable to make theoretical connections, even if correct, lack the substance provided by generalizable explanations. Without an understanding of the community as a theoretical construct, both students of the human services field and practitioners will relate to events in a particularistic fashion, often missing the broad explanatory threads that run behind them. Without a theoretical backbone, discussions of practice in community likely will lack the integrative framework needed to piece together the puzzles and give meaning to isolated occurrences. In the same vein, without a strong belief in or a positive feeling for the communities the professional is supporting, social intervention on their behalf likely will be meaningless.

In what became a classic textbook in the training of many generations of community workers, Murray Ross (1955) stated,

> Just as the caseworker must know a great deal about individual psychodynamics and the process of interviewing, so the community . . . worker must know a good deal about the forces in the community which make for or hinder community integration. . . . (p. 101)

In addition to knowledge about the community, the community worker must have an appreciation for what "community" means to the people involved at both an affective and intellectual level. In this book, references to a "small community" in essence do not mean a community of particular population size. What matters is the nature of the social interaction and sentiment among community residents. As can be seen in many environments, particularly in the United States, a community of as many as 50,000 people can have small-town characteristics.

In relation to the small community, this empathetic stance is not easily developed among human services professionals. Generally, social work and other helping careers have had an urban orientation; the small community, the village, the country, the hinterland, if discussed at all, have seldom been presented in a positive light. The analyses offered by social workers often have dwelt on the more rigid class structure of the small towns or villages or on the problems of depopulation or economic stagnation. One social work student asserted that, in fact, most social work students she knew criticized the ideal of communal life, and certainly, the idea that anyone might derive psychological satisfaction from small-town living. The fear that often is well founded, she added, is that the small community is inevitably prejudiced, intolerant, and rejecting of outsiders. Such intolerance is revealed in the thinking and words of some of the people Fuson (1988b) interviewed in State Center, Iowa (chapter 5), or in the political troubles of Keysville, Georgia (chapter 6). However, is the small town always rejecting? Is it always prejudiced? Is it any more or less rejecting or prejudiced than anywhere else? More important, how committed are human services practitioners to work with the small town and help it change? To be sure, small towns have their share of problems, but it is hard for practitioners to aid their survival if they have no understanding of their strengths or commitment to their continuance.

Occasionally, when students encounter clear explanatory statements of existing phenomena, they are pleased to recognize that theory helps them make sense of the world. If those statements have predictive merit, then their astonishment and delight are refreshing. Of course, students have heard that theory serves to describe, explain, and sometimes even predict a course of events. They have learned this in relation to the natural sciences and have come to accept that there is a certain amount of rigor and prediction in that field. But when a similar state of affairs manifests itself within their ambiguous professional world, the response among learners and novice practitioners is inevitably surprise. For example, social work students never cease to be amazed by the discovery that Ferdinand Tonnies' constructs of "Gemeinschaft" and "Gesellschaft," basic theoretical concepts from sociology, described in more detail in chapter 1, have predictive merit and can be used to understand and anticipate the behavioral style of certain communities and the actions of the residents. The notion of community as an identity-giving unit is a valuable explanatory statement in discussing the behavior of individuals in *place* communities (geographic) as well as *nonplace* communities (that is, professional groups). Students and young professionals can correlate their personal search for social identity with their own community behavior (whether action or inaction). By discovering the personal meaning of theoretical explanations, they come to accept the possible predictive merits of such abstractions, for as Kuhn (1962) discussed in relation to the training of scientists, "the process of learning theory depends upon the study of applications" (p. 47).

Greenwood (1961) indicated that the

> purpose of scientific activity is the description and explanation of nature in all its manifestations. The social sciences . . . describe the highest organization of nature, viz., the characteristics and products of human behavior in the context of culture.

> The end product of the collective efforts of scientists within a given discipline is a system of internally consistent propositions which describe and explain the phenomena that constitute the subject matter of that discipline. This system is called a body of theory. The function of all science is to construct theories about the what, the how, and the why of the natural world. There is some current misunderstanding regarding this function of science, many laymen believing that only philosophers theorize and that scientists "stick close to facts." . . . In this connection it will prove clarifying if I were to distinguish between two levels of knowledge. . . . On the first level are . . . facts called empirical generalizations; on the second . . . are the explanations or interpretations of these facts called theory. (p. 75)

The explanations and interpretations of small-community phenomena, which constitute the core of this book, are theories in the sense that they are based on empirical reality as observed or studied not just by social scientists but by writers, journalists, humanists, and laypeople. Although these descriptive explanations (theories) are diverse and often opposing, they represent the reality of community and the beliefs about community of many participants and observers.

Although it might be difficult to visualize how this kind of explanatory theory can provide practitioners with guidelines for intervention in complex situations, it is evident that the theories in which practitioners believe and the premises and stances they adopt will govern their scientific observations, choice of conclusions, and policy recommendations. Theories influence perceptions and perceptions shape practice.

Not all explanatory statements or theories upon which practitioners act come from the social sciences. If theory can be understood to provide effective ways of comprehending the universe, then many current community dilemmas are explained well by the statements of literary writers, journalists, and laypeople. For example, Thomas Wolfe wrote that "fiction is not fact, but fiction is fact selected and understood, fiction is fact arranged and charged with purpose" (Wolfe, 1929, p. i). For the professional student of communities, it would be a mistake to narrowly interpret theory as solely comprising "positivistic" research findings. *Positivistic* research attempts to capture the "scientific" tradition of viewing research primarily as a means for testing hypotheses (Taylor, 1977). Positivistic research is concerned with measurement, design, and statistical inferences, whereas "naturalistic" research, sometimes called field or qualitative, "seeks to describe the on-going flow and patterning of behavior as it occurs in real life (naturalistic) settings" (Taylor, 1977, p. 120). Philosophy, history, literature, and journalism also can help interpret phenomena and can be useful complements of social science. This book is predicated on that premise.

Social science research has been the primary source of the chapters in part 1 of this book; humanistic, literary, and journalistic sources have provided the illustrative excerpts and exhibits in part 2. Addressing the contributions of novels to community studies, Bell and Newby (1972) suggested that humanistic works, such as John Marquand's (1949) *The Point of No Return*, with hero Charles Gray, often have provided dimensions to small-town life missed by social scientists. For example, Warner, a social scientist who, like Marquand, studied Newburyport, produced the five-volume scholarly series *Yankee City* (Warner, 1963), but missed many of the points Marquand's hero made on social mobility in New England towns (Bell & Newby, 1972). Agatha Christie's (1950, 1963) observations on English village life in her village mysteries and John Mortimer (1984) in *Paradise Postponed* also contributed to community studies.

To feel the pulse of small towns across America, one can learn as much from reading literature as from reading community studies. Zora Neale Hurston's (1935b) *Mules and Men* provided a privileged understanding of life in a small Florida black community circa 1930. Garrison Keillor's (1985, 1987) *Lake Wobegon Days* and *Leaving Home* offered a glimpse of the lives of the residents of a fictional but very real Minnesota town. T. R. Pearson's (1985a, 1987) novels transformed the daily activities of the residents of a small North Carolina town into significant indicators of the reality of provincial life. The narratives of humanists discuss a variety of communal, social, and psychological dilemmas. Particularly in relation to the small community, literature offers an unparalleled pool of relevant descriptions that can enlighten the understanding of small town among human services practitioners.

CONTENT AND OBJECTIVES OF THE BOOK

A major concern in the preparation of this book was deciding which community content from the humanities and the social sciences would help practitioners make sense of the real world.

> What do we need to know about the community which will help those who are concerned about developing a kind of community life in which people feel a sense of belonging, participate in the life of the community, achieve a set of common understandings, and work cooperatively at their common problems? (Ross, 1955, p. 102)

These questions expose a prevailing bias among community practitioners, particularly those who work in small towns and villages. For them, *community* is an identity-giving entity, a personally meaningful sociological unit that relies heavily on the primary interaction of its members. Because of their concern with human relationships, human services practitioners in small towns are naturally oriented toward Gemeinschaft, which is characterized by common understandings, mutual interdependence, and a nourishing sense of personal meaning and participation. Bell and Newby (1972) once observed that behind the objective facade of sociologists who study community "lurk value judgments, of varying degrees of explicitness, about what is the good life" (p. 16). For most proponents of strong community ties, the "good life" is attainable in the intimate small community.

Curiously enough, the more or less explicit value assumptions about the "good life" of the small community are attuned to the cultural orientation of the 1980s and 1990 and thus to the intent of this book. One of the objectives of this book is to illustrate, through the use of literary and journalistic excerpts and exhibits, the strength of communal ties as perceived and reported by those who share in them rather than merely by academics who theorize about them. If the scholarly and lay literature indeed are a cultural barometer, then people are longing for the positive aspects of small-town living, for the supportive milieu of Gemeinschaft. The sense of anomie created by the large impersonal organizations of the early industrial society perhaps has peaked; people have begun an often frantic search for meaningful community. This search fulfills psychotherapeutic as well as social functions. In personal terms, people are looking for intimate community in answer to the external pressures of their complicated lives. Anomie can only be combated by a strong sense of personal interdependence.

Citizens emerging from their hideaways and searching for convivial solutions are flocking in large numbers to the small towns and rural areas not only in the United States but also in many other countries across the industrial world. There has been a resurgence of village life in England and Wales. Even in Scotland, where remoteness often made villages less attractive, people are going back to the Highland and Islands communities they once had abandoned. In continental Europe, where village life was not embellished by the "country squire" tradition of England, people are returning to and reviving abandoned villages. For example, during a recent visit to Catalonia, Spain, the author discovered that many people are refurbishing once-abandoned medieval villages, settling in them, opening businesses, and trying to recreate an intimate environment, often against the odds of diminishing services. This revival does not indicate a lack of concern about depopulation of small towns and villages. On the contrary, depopulation is a prevalent theme both in Europe and America because the village revival often has been, geographically, an uneven phenomenon. But once people can choose where to live, unburdened by the demands of earning a living—as is the case with retirees—the small towns and villages provide the sense of belonging of true communities. This makes small towns all the more deserving of community intervention by social workers so that both the young and old can live in them.

The personal search for community was pervasive enough during the 1970s to have been reported as a new social and demographic movement. The 1980 census (*Statistical Abstract of the United States: 1980, 1981*) documented the growth of many small towns throughout the country. Large numbers of people abandoned the metropolises not for the open country, but rather for small, manageable towns where they could find personal meaning in community. Although the agricultural crisis of the 1980s might influence the migration trends recorded by the 1990 census, the small towns once again have been put at the forefront of study. In those instances where metropolitan growth was recorded by the 1980 census, it was noted that people gravitated to the revitalized older neighborhoods of the inner cities, which resemble the small-town scenario of the hinterland. People gravitated to the small personal communities—the *Neo-Gemeinschaften* (the new, distinct communities of ethnic minorities in the inner cities [Rivera & Erlich, 1981]) of the urban hubs.

The search for meaningful community is pervasive enough to have caught the attention of social scientists and policymakers. Academic interest in small communities has come full circle. In the 1930s and 1940s, sociologists and anthropologists carried out community studies mostly in Gemeinschaft. These researchers once again have returned to those studies, perhaps to gain new insights into their contributions from the perspectives of today. Peter Davis (1982b), the author of *Hometown*, indicated that even the popular mass media have rekindled interest in the prototypical, middle-American town. Apparently, at the moment, the interactional and almost intimate elements of the small community as a place of solace, as perhaps an ideal even more than a reality, are predominating American culture. Although people still suffer from ambivalence about desiring intimacy, investing in relationships, and longing for anonymity, the 1980s seemed to have tilted the scales in favor of strong community ties. Once, movement, migration, and mobility—"the shaping influence of the American national character" (Pierson, 1964)—were pervasive. Currently, the importance of local, small, traditional communities seems to be on the rise. In addition, people in the 1980s who moved were searching for roots, personal contentment, and sometimes collective ideals. In the 1990s, movement will no longer be satisfactory. Although demographic trends can result merely from planning and housing policies, observers' reports all indicate that, beyond policies, people are concerned with the more intangible issues of meaning and quality in their lives. For those people who doubt all other indexes but trust the barometers of the media, recent television series popular on both sides of the Atlantic, such as "The Vets," based on James Herriot's (1985) portrayals of rustic Yorkshire village life, or Bill Moyer's documentary "Marshall, Texas, Marshall, Texas" (1984), which focuses on his own Texan small town, should axiomatically document the search for personal community.

"Local communities" or communities as "primary interaction," by and large, will be the central unit of study in this book. However, nonplace communities or communities as "social categories" should not be disregarded by human services practitioners. It would be narrow and misleading to exclude from study nonplace communities, such as ethnic and otherwise unique groups, and professions (although they can be both, vertical communities or localities). The distinctions between certain communities as social categories (for example, a community of scholars or professionals) and the complex organizations in which these communities generally are organized are tenuous. The boundaries between a "community of scholars" and a "university" as a complex organization are not always clear. In medicine, what is the relationship between the "medical community" and the American Medical Association? In social work, where do the "community of professionals" and the professional associations begin and end? Although practitioners must recognize that nonplace communities provide purpose and cohesion to individuals, they also must confront the fact that the ties that vertically bind people beyond the local setting, along state and national lines, in professional or occupational structures often are bureaucratic and, thus, in a sense, counter to the community spirit—the focus of this book. This book provides human services practitioners who are preparing for or are practicing in small town environments with a useful theoretical scheme and literary and journalistic illustrations for analyzing those communities and for reconciling the opposing perspectives they often must face.

ORGANIZATION OF THE BOOK

This book is divided into three parts. Part 1 contains four chapters that are based on interdisciplinary social science research on important areas of community theory. Part 2 contains two chapters with selected literary or journalistic excerpts and exhibits of the various social science issues discussed. All the excerpts and exhibits in part 2 are preceded by a discussion of the community issues they illustrate. The excerpts and exhibits are in themselves thorough, entertaining, and often captivating illustrations of small-town life. Part 3 brings the material closer to applied concerns. It addresses community-oriented practice and constitutes, in many ways, a practical epilogue.

In part 1, chapter 1 is devoted to discussion of the concept of community and expounds various ways of viewing communities. Chapter 1 serves to clarify concepts essential to the understanding and meaning of the word "community." For example, chapter 1 focuses first on Gemeinschaft and primary relationships; second on basic elements of communal life; third on looking at community as a microcosm; fourth on the influence of history on the physical environment; and fifth on reviewing how single variables can be used to further one's understanding of the concept of community.

The idea of community as a personal solution or community as an answer to anomie is explored in chapter 2. Community practitioners need to understand some of the personal reasons people embrace communal causes. It would be difficult to explain the devoted work of volunteers or the active participation of community members in demanding meetings without an awareness of the personal meaning and satisfaction individuals derive from such activities. Chapter 2 essentially is devoted to providing a sociopsychological understanding of what community means to individuals and illustrating for community practitioners how different people seek different forms of satisfaction through communal relationships.

Chapter 3 focuses on the specific variable of power as a major driving force in communal life. Although the subject of community power, influence, and leadership always has been central to political science discussions, basic concepts from political science and sociology can be particularly meaningful to practitioners in small communities. Models of power distribution in a small town and the relationship between the distribution of power and policy decisions are discussed in chapter 3.

> Nor less I deem that there are powers
> Which of themselves our minds impress;
> That we can feed this mind of ours
> In wise passiveness. (Wordsworth, cited in George, 1904, p. 83)

The power plays among various community actors are crucial in the life of the small community because they affect not only collective decisions but also the way in which people perceive each other, rely on each other, defer to each other in social situations, or are willing to explore common causes.

Chapter 4 addresses the long-standing dilemma of the interrelationship between locality and the larger political or geographic units, an issue that has received the attention of philosophers and government officials. The matter of allegiance to the locality, the region, or the nation has not always been easy to resolve. Can individuals in any meaningful sense belong to vertical communities, that is, those communities beyond locality, or do people only identify with the small unit of Gemeinschaft? The nostalgia of locality and localism coupled with the political mood of the 1980s has given this century-old debate new dimensions. In the field of social welfare, politicians and scholars have persistently debated the relationship among various levels of government. The appropriate role of the federal or central, state, and local governments in relation to all matters of governance, but particularly in relation to social welfare responsibilities, always has been contentious. Practitioners at the local level—which is where practitioners are most likely to find themselves—need to understand the basic premises underlying such controversies. Furthermore, practitioners at the local level need to overcome an often ill-disposed frame of mind toward localities; they need to appreciate local language in its richness. Chapter 4 provides historical and philosophical background for the tensions of the professional and community residents and discusses centralization and localism in an even-handed manner.

Part 1 deals primarily with broad theoretical issues. Part 2 enlivens the theoretical framework with life-like fictional and real-life accounts of incidents in communal life. Few better sources than fiction amply illustrate what social scientists mean when they discuss community as a microcosm of society. Developments in the perception and lifestyles of small towns and villages are explored through the decades. From the protagonists of real and fictional events, the student of community can learn to feel like the people in small towns and villages, empathize with their joys and dilemmas, and perhaps develop a more realistic and yet a basically positive view of nonmetropolitan life. Because social work and other helping arts, products of the industrial world, have never focused sympathetically on small towns and villages, examples of literary and journalistic writings can make a tremendous difference in the practitioners' outlook and in their observational skills.

Part 2, chapter 5, illustrates, through literary and journalistic excerpts and exhibits, the historical evolution of the small town. It provides examples of the community seen as a microcosm of society and shows where one finds information on a small town and how small-town information is disseminated. It also illustrates the current dilemmas of growth and decay in small-town USA, problems that are not dissimilar to those experienced by villages elsewhere in industrial nations. In *The Gentleman from Indiana* and *Main Street*, Booth Tarkington (1900a) and Sinclair Lewis (1920b), respectively, are concerned with societal influences. They ponder the way in which small-town society and values affect the lives of the protagonists. In *Due East*, Valerie Sayers's (1987b) focus is more intimate; she looks at the ways in which the protagonists resolve or do not resolve internal turmoils within their small-town environments. This focus might be a reflection of societal trends: as a culture, Americans in the early 1980s seemed to have moved from looking outward, from being concerned with societal forces, to looking inward, pondering on the intimate forces that propel individuals to continue. Fiction has reflected this change. Social work practice also has been the beneficiary and victim of this societal trend. Increased emphasis on microlevel or clinical intervention attests to the societal concern with individual adjustment; the decreased importance placed on understanding "the collective" as nourishing of individuals and nations points to the shortcomings of the trend. Literary exceptions to this trend are, for example, T. R. Pearson (1985a) and Garrison Keillor (1985), who, in *A Short History of a Small Place* and *Lake Wobegon Days*, respectively, reflected an old-fashioned concern for the external or communal life rhythms of Gemeinschaft; for how people create concerns that are the result of the way in which they perceive and relate to each other. Religion as an important dimension in understanding small-town life also is addressed briefly.

Chapter 6 includes literary and journalistic excerpts and exhibits illustrating village elitism (both long-standing and that of class in the community) as well as examples of democratic coexistence and shared decision making across social groups. It includes excerpts that illustrate that pride and attachment to locality are strong among small-town and village residents. Journalistic excerpts illustrate how provincialism, taken in a positive sense, is still prevalent in many areas of the United States and how it can inspire people to retain the traditions of the locale and to embark on local efforts that aid in the survival of many areas. Chapter 6 examines the realities inherent in governance of the small town.

Part 3 includes one chapter that focuses explicitly on practice. In what sense do human services generalists, particularly social workers, become involved in community? What is the role of social workers in enlisting the aid of communities? How can a better knowledge of the small community help them in their quest? In this concluding chapter, a thrust toward social work practice that is more oriented to the community is proposed. It is recognized that an orientation to the community is particularly important and feasible in certain fields, such as services for elderly persons and children. Nevertheless, consideration of community variables in all fields is underscored. Concerns about lack of anonymity, the nature of confidentiality, and accountability in community-oriented practice are discussed and illustrated with stories from practitioners.

Human services practitioners need to train their senses to discover useful community information hidden in unsuspected sources. The illustrative excerpts and exhibits included in this book will corroborate that practitioners can find invaluable information about the community not only in the social science literature but also in a potpourri of other popular sources. Having perused this book, perhaps students and professionals will see themselves as explorers—explorers who will develop the habit of searching and respecting all information wherever it is found, the patience of dealing with ambiguity, and the desire to pursue alternative insights into the phenomena that surround all people.

PART 1
COMMUNITY THEORY FOR PRACTITIONERS

1

VIEWING THE SMALL COMMUNITY

A well-known student of community has suggested in her work that "trying to study community is like trying to scoop Jell-o up with your fingers. You can get hold of some, but there's always more slipping away from you" (Pelly-Effrat, 1974, p. 1). Although Pelly-Effrat's analogy refers primarily to the sociological research traditions that, at various times, have provided different and often antagonistic perspectives for the study of community, her simile applies to the concept of community itself, which is difficult to define precisely when working with real groups of people.

The focus of this book is primarily on the small community; thus, the definitional task is not as elusive because the parameters are somewhat more circumscribed. Most human services practitioners who work in small towns and villages are dealing with *community* in the sense of a place or location in which an array of activities—social, economic, and political—are carried out. Yet, these practitioners need to deal with communities as microcosms of society. Much like anthropologists, small-town practitioners often view their communities as conterminous with defined territorial and interactional boundaries. Although these boundaries are not absolutely fixed and vary with evolving goals, they are, at least, potentially identifiable for specific purposes. In terms of community culture, practitioners in small towns and villages view their units as possessing unique characteristics, although these communities share in and send messages to the culture at large. In the context of small-town practice, locality as community is still alive and struggling for continued survival.

However, professional practitioners often discover that influences flow in and out of the small community (see, for example, "El Salvador Ambassador to Talk in Weston Friday" and "Ambassador Argues for Salvador Aid, but Weston Remains Unconvinced" on pp. 181–183). Inside and outside institutions are all interrelated and interdependent. What happens inside a local community is determined by and is a determinant of what occurs in the outside milieu. Just as outside forces impinge on local communities, local communities also send their messages or information across to other social systems, highlighting the dynamic nature of the exchange. Particularly in the 1950s and 1960s, proponents of mass-society theory and speakers for the decline of community often dwelt on the complete absorption of the local community by the forces external to it. Mass-society theorists espoused the idea that, with modern transportation and communication systems, the differences between small towns and cities had been obliterated. They also believed that in the modern world, villages and small towns had lost their autonomy, importance, and vitality. For example, Vidich and Bensman (1968), who subscribed to mass-society theory, described the local governing board of the small U.S. town of Springdale (a pseudonym for a real New York State small town):

> In almost every area of jurisdiction the board [of supervisors] has adjusted its actions to the regulations and laws externally defined by outside agencies which engage in functions parallel to its own. State policy, regionally organized fire districts, state welfare agencies, the state highway department—these agencies and others are central to the daily functioning of the village. (p. 115)

Although mass-society theorists of the 1960s have not been as pervasive in their messages, the realities of external bureaucratic forces impinging on the life of small communities is still a problem. The complexities of external economic factors, regulations, and other demands have affected the response of local small-town leaders in the political arena. The erosion of a local leadership is a major concern in the maintenance of community identity.

Vidich and Bensman recognized, however, that external and bureaucratizing forces gained acceptance because there were corresponding forces internal to the village community system that propelled the decision makers in that direction. Vidich and Bensman (1968, p. 199) pointed to the "business, low-tax ideology" of the village leaders, an ideology that provided the necessary internal fit for the absorption of the town by external services. Currently, technical developments and technical demands also have influenced the perspectives of local leaders who, more often than not, have to connect to external sources of funding to live up to expectations in a highly technological world. The dual nature of the message exchange between the small town and the larger outside institutions has been underscored clearly. However, social scientists and practitioners, consumed as they were by the eclipse of community ideas of the 1950s and 1960s, chose not to focus on the complementarity of the small-town–national society message exchange. Instead, they usually chose to stress the demise of local ties.

Internal community forces are not always consonant with forces external to the locality, and vice versa. The preponderance of one or the other at a given point seems to be related to cultural, political, and economic moods that social scientists and practitioners are now beginning to recognize and understand. This pull of internal and external forces constitutes one of the major dilemmas of the small-community practitioner. To deal with this and other dilemmas, human services practitioners need to understand the nature of community relationships and the concepts of Gemeinschaft and Gesellschaft.

GEMEINSCHAFT AND GESELLSCHAFT

Tonnies's Gemeinschaft and Gesellschaft are basic, useful terms for practitioners because they embody a set of community attributes. For human services practitioners, Tonnies's contrasting types of communities provide, unarguably, the most useful analytic tool; and Bell and Newby's explanations of Tonnies's concepts provide the clearest framework to update and apply. Bell and Newby (1972) succinctly introduced and described Tonnies's fundamental concepts as follows:

> If there is a founding father of the theory of community, . . . the label perhaps suits Ferdinand Tonnies more than any other individual. Tonnies's book *Gemeinschaft and Gesellschaft* (usually translated as Community and Society) was first published in 1887. It has provided a constant source of ideas for those who have dealt with the community ever since. (p. 23)

Gemeinschaft

Bell and Newby described Gemeinschaft in the following manner:

> In *Gemeinschaft*, community human relationships are intimate, enduring and based on a clear understanding of where each person stands in society. A man's "worth" is estimated according to *who* he is not *what* he has done. . . . In a community, roles are specific and consonant with one another. . . Members of a community are relatively immobile in a physical and social way: individuals neither travel far from their locality of birth nor do they rise up the social hierarchy. In addition, the culture of the community is relatively homogeneous, for it must be so if roles are not to conflict or human relations to lose their intimacy. The moral custodians of a community, the family and the church, are strong, their code clear and their injunctions well internalized. There will be community sentiments involving close and enduring loyalties to the place and people. . . . (p. 23)

Several behavioral consequences are associated with the Gemeinschaftlich community. *Gemeinschaftlich* ties result

> in a personalizing of issues, events and explanations, because familiar names and characters inevitably become associated with everything that happens. . . . When sociologists now talk about community, they almost always mean a place in which people have some, if not complete, solitary relations. Yet community as originally used [by Tonnies], though it included the *local* community, also went beyond it. It encompassed religion, work, family and culture: it referred to social bonds—to use Robert Nisbet's own key term. . . . (Bell & Newby, 1972, pp. 23–24)

From the perspective of practitioners' current concern with the small community, Nisbet's (1953) social bonds of emotional cohesion, continuity, and fullness are essential aspects to be recognized by human services practitioners. The current search for community that has produced the revival of many small towns and villages, both in the United States and the United Kingdom, is a personal search for emotional support, cohesive networks, and fullness in an individual's life (see, for example, "Getting There" on pp. 120–122).

Gesellschaft

Gesellschaft is the antithesis of Gemeinschaft. Bell and Newby (1972) defined Gesellschaft as follows:

> Opposed to the concept of community was *Gesellschaft* (variously translated as "society" or "association") which essentially means everything that community is not. *Gesellschaft* refers to the large scale, impersonal and contractual ties that were seen by the nineteenth century sociologists to be on the increase, at the expense of *Gemeinschaft*. Here is the central idea that runs through so many community studies: social change is conceptualized as a continuum between two polar types: *Gemeinschaft* or community and *Gesellschaft* or society. For Tonnies, there are three central aspects of *Gemeinschaft*: blood, place (land) and mind, with their sociological consequences of kinship, neighbourhood and friendship. Together, they were the home of all virtue and morality. *Gesellschaft*, however, has a singularity about it; in Tonnies' terms, "all its activities are restricted to a definite end and a definite means of obtaining it." This rationality is, of course, usually seen as a key aspect in the development of western capitalism. Indeed it might be claimed that in *Gemeinschaft* would be found what Max Weber calls "traditional" authority where as *Gesellschaft* incorporates what he would call "rational-legal authority." (p. 24)

Although many sociologists have identified Gesellschaft as metropolis, Tonnies did not necessarily address settlements according to size but rather he addressed the relationships among people in daily interaction. Thus, Rivera and Erlich's (1981) current use of the term *Neo-Gemeinschaft* to describe cohesive ethnic and minority metropolitan pockets is not only correct but also accurate because the nature of people's interaction in those units is similar to the interaction of people in small towns.

Although the personalism associated with Gemeinschaft gave the small community a bad name among proponents of more bureaucratic, rational ties, students of bureaucracy have come to ascertain that the purported rationality of bureaucratic systems is not limitless, but is bound to the integrity and independence of the individuals in the system. Nepotism, favoritism, and personal knowledge are not the monopoly of the Gemeinschaftlich environment. The ecological perspectives on Gemeinschaft community espoused by Louis Wirth (1938) are that population size, density, and heterogeneity combined to produce, for example, in the Chicago of the 1920s, a move in the direction of Gesellschaft.

Although Tonnies's concept of Gemeinschaft was bound to territory, use of the term in a contemporary context stresses just as much the psychological aspects of the ties binding the individuals to the communal unit. Community must be seen not just as a place or geographic locale but as the source from which groups of people derive a sense of personal identity. Using a sociopsychological approach, Clark (1973) suggested that it is neither territory nor function that keeps the notion of community alive; rather, it is the psychological elements that make the community come alive. Clark proposed a considerable reorientation of the study approach to community to free the concept from its strong ties to the strictly sociological elements of "place" and "function." His definition relied on psychological concepts and means, in essence, that "despite all the potential dangers, what has deprecatingly been termed community-in-the-mind must in fact be *the* springboard for any realistic examination of the phenomenon. It is how the members of the group *themselves* feel that is the basic concern" (Clark, 1973, p. 409). Clark's contentions are exemplified by contemporary occurrences. A recent article in *The Atlanta Constitution* described the many clubs that have emerged as the city has become larger and more metropolitan. The idea is to let people feel they belong somewhere, commented the reporter. One psychologist interviewed stated that clubs "help people cope with the largeness of city life by providing a smaller, more human-size community" (Long, 1987, p. 38).

Although perhaps varying in intensity or degree, a certain amount of "community-ness" is apparent in many human groups that share social interaction, regardless of whether they are bound by locale (as are the inhabitants of a town or the workers in a factory) or not (as are an ethnic group or national professional organization or union). Researchers who study towns or villages often find that physical or political parameters are not always conterminous with the boundaries of social interaction. Territoriality or geographic boundaries often must be transcended; however, a difference exists in the degree of cohesiveness and pervasiveness of communal relationships, depending on the extent to which members identify with a territorial area. In some cases, cohesiveness, support systems, and communal identity exist despite the apparent lack and mutuality of their territorial boundaries. In the case of migrant workers, community identity transcends spatial parameters. Despite the focus on the small communal unit with strong sentimental ties and generally with strong territorial ties, Pelly-Effrat's Jell-o analogy is not inappropriate because exceptions to the elements of territory or even sentiment are readily found to obscure one's target and keep one aware of the complexity of the subject.

THE SMALL COMMUNITY OVER TIME: HORIZONTAL AND VERTICAL TIES

People have been fickle in their affections toward the small community, particularly if the community is defined as a town or village where persons not only dwell but find meaning for their private and social lives. Although for decades, both English and American writers have been enamored of small towns and villages because they find solace and felicity in their "community-ness," at other times, they have found the same towns and villages to be divisive, suffocating, and stultifying environments (see, for example, "The Great Harkless Comes Home" on pp. 109–111 and "My Dear, You Really Must Come to the Thanatopsis This Afternoon," on pp. 113–116).

The dialogue about community is a cultural barometer. R.W.B. Lewis (1955), an intellectual historian, suggested that

> every culture seems, as it advances toward maturity, to produce its own determining debate over the ideas that preoccupy it: salvation, the order of nature, money, power, sex, the machine, and the like. The debate, indeed, may be said to be the culture, at least on its loftiest levels, for a culture achieves identity not so much through the ascendancy of one particular set of convictions as through the emergence of its peculiar and distinctive dialogue. (Similarly, a culture is on the decline when it submits to intellectual martial law, and fresh understanding is denied in a denial of further controversy.) Intellectual history, properly conducted, exposes not only the dominant ideas of a period, or of a nation, but more important, the dominant clashes over ideas. (pp. 1–2)

Applying Lewis's barometric gauge, 20th century culture in both the United States and the United Kingdom exhibits clear signs of vitality. Evidence of this vitality is in the clashes over the dominant ideas of small community by scholars, novelists, poets, essayists, historians, social scientists, and preachers, all of whom have entered into this lively and often caustic debate.

Writers in literature and popular works have gone from perceiving, at the turn of the 20th century, the small town or village (the Gemeinschaft) as the only community and the city (the metropolis and its interest groups) as anticommunity, the opposite extreme. During the 1920s, 1930s, 1940s, and 1950s, the city was viewed as the only truly liberating unit of social interaction. During the decades following the 1950s, the pendulum swung again, and the small town, village, and other manageable geographic locales were placed in the position of redeemers of anomie. Although technological, transportation, and mass communication advances might account for some of the popular shift of sentiments, explanations of these pendulum-like mood swings are likely to be less rational and to have more to do with the cyclical nature of history and literary fashion.

Early community studies in the social sciences made value judgments about the virtues and pleasantly predictable patterns of small towns, which generally were viewed as epitomizing community or Gemeinschaft. Bell and Newby (1972) perceptively suggested that "sociologists, no more than other individuals, have not always been immune to the emotive overtones that the word community consistently carries with it" (p. 21). During the first three decades of the 20th century, students of the community in its Gemeinschaftlich sense assumed that Gemeinschaft, at that time only identified with the small towns or villages, was a good thing—its integrity to be guarded, its passing to be deplored. Until the 1950s, the prevalent social science concept was that Gemeinschaft and, therefore, community, was only found in nonurban environments. Urbanism was perceived to destroy cohesiveness, mutuality, and community. As late as 1937, the National Resources Committee in the United States (cited in Nisbet, 1953) commented that

> the urban mode of life tends to create solitary souls, to uproot the individual from its customs, to confront him with a social void, and to weaken traditional restraints on personal conduct. . . . The tenuous relations between men, based for the most part upon a pecuniary nexus, make urban existence seem very fragile and capable of being disturbed by a multitude of forces over which the individual has little or no control. (p. 16)

The notation that the Gemeinschaft was also found in the urban neighborhoods did not emerge until later and still is debated.

Only during the 1940s through the 1960s did social scientists turn to the city and scrutinize its nature to see if elements of community or Gemeinschaft indeed were found within it. Hillery (1969) proposed that the village could axiomatically be labeled "community," and proceeded to view the city comparatively against the community elements found in the village. With regard to the city, Hillery concluded that the village or folk community and city were "variations of the same type of thing as the folk village. The two models are best to be viewed as varying from each other in degree, that is, as an existing continua" (p. 61). This same hypothesis was proposed recently by Rivera and Erlich (1981), who analyzed the flourishing Neo-Gemeinschaft, or ethnic and minority communities of the inner city.

Horizontal Ties

During the 1960s, conceptualizations of community were developed to include, or at least recognize, the impingement of national forces on the local level—an important step in acknowledging the complexities and the systemic interrelationships of various-size places. Perhaps the most influential representative of this school of thought was Roland Warren. Warren (1963) pointed out that "local units" have two distinctive types of systemic ties: horizontal and vertical. "The relationship which. . . [local units] share with each other on the local level . . . constitute the community's horizontal pattern" (p. 237).

Strong horizontal ties clearly were discernible in days past, when fewer complicated industrial patterns of existence and a lesser degree of bureaucratization tended to free the resources and enhance the autonomy of community networks. Much of the popular literature on "place" or local communities highlighted the microcosmic dimensions or horizontal patterns of community existence. A sense of inner control, functional versatility, and mastery of the community's destiny through the development of horizontal relationships was pervasive in the early literature on community.

Vertical Ties

In more contemporary times, horizontal patterns have given way to vertical ones. "The relationships through which [local units] are oriented to the larger society beyond the community . . . constitute the community's vertical pattern" (Warren, 1963, p. 237). Warren questioned whether one could essentially "relate such diverse units as chain stores, branch banks, branch factories, labor unions, churches, schools, voluntary associations, and local offices of state or federal government units to their respective extra community systems" (p. 238). In more theoretical terms, he asked whether there was "a discernible set of relationships to extra community systems which was sufficiently general to be called a pattern of organization" (p. 238). Warren's affirmative answer highlighted the importance of viewing communities not only from the perspective of their microcosmic dimensions (horizontal ties) but also from a macrocosmic perspective (vertical ties). The macrocosmic perspective stresses the dependency of community units to other units in the larger society and the outside world.

In the horizontal community model,

> a number of important community consequences arise from the process of differentiation of interests and association, for in this process, the principal basis for social participation shifts from locality to interest. In the locality type of participation, individuals and families who share the same locality associate in neighborly fashion with others in the immediate vicinity. A unifying basis of interest underlying such association is that of the common locality . . . Such important functions as production and distribution, socialization of the young, social control, and mutual support are performed largely within the locality by such relatively undifferentiated groups as family and neighborhood. . . . [T]he families share a common interest in that they are units of economic production, as in the earlier American preindustrial rural community. (Warren, 1963, pp. 59–60)

In the vertical model,

> the contrasting situation is a differentiation of interests among people in the locality and differential association based on the respective interests. The individual often turns away from other individuals in his immediate locality and associates himself with individuals from other localities on the basis of selective interests. (pp. 59–60)

Warren felt the vertical model was becoming far more prevalent as industrialization and urban growth pervaded the United States.

From a social-welfare perspective, authors quickly supported Warren's position on vertical ties because in the 1960s, human services problems were not perceived to be a local community concern; the idea of vertical ties accommodated the larger role of forces outside the community. In the United States, during the 1950s and 1960s, local decision making particularly in the social welfare field, which had been bound traditionally to county, became more tied to the state and federal institutions. Consequently, local or place communities became particularly vulnerable to the infiltration of outside forces, rewards, and deterrents. Most social workers believed that local communities, although autonomous units, had lost their importance as they became more heavily influenced by the prevailing mores and values of the culture at large, by outside political trends, and by policy actions. Of course, a similar situation had become evident when economic decisions were studied in the industrial world. Community livelihoods were vulnerable to and deeply affected by the decisions of large conglomerates, the demands of the outside markets, and the regulatory powers of national organizations. At least in the eyes of most academics, after the industrial revolution the destinies of local folk became intimately related to the destinies of their nation and, more often than not, to those of the world. However, this relation did not mean that local communities had lost their meaning or importance in the life of most citizens.

Current Considerations

In much of the contemporary social science literature, *place*, undeniably an important dimension of cohesiveness or "community-ness," is not always viewed as a prerequisite of community. Clark (1973) suggested that "to argue that place influences community is a very different matter from assuming that certain geographical units or areas are synonymous with it" (p. 398). Place alone cannot be viewed as the single ingredient of community; however, place is important in contemporary communities.

An examination of the rekindled interest in small towns across the nation reveals that many social scientists are once again agreeing with Hillery (1955). Deviating from recent orthodoxy, these social scientists are suggesting that, for psychological, identity, and practical reasons, community cannot be considered outside the boundaries of Gemeinschaft—vertical ties cannot *build* community. R. Buck (personal communication, October 20, 1982) called this position the 1980 "radical" antidote to Warren and Ross's stance and suggested that "community organization, emphasizing as it does collective autonomy and responsibility, interdependency and individual insufficiency, faces people away from vertical and formalized systems of authority and service." He added that if one "views community as an alternative to emphases on individualism, self-sufficiency and mass society ordered by comprehensive legal, rational authority," then community is, by definition, local. Under this set of presuppositions, community organization is, for Buck, "a strategy for translating vertically sponsored programs into the fabric of day-to-day community life. As community organization matures, the vertical dimension (centralization) gives way to increasing reliance on local autonomy. Funding and other resources are generated close to home, so to speak," with community becoming more of a horizontal phenomenon. Vertical ties are seen, at best, as seed from which community building must be generated.

Buck recognized that problems are inherent in his position. In the diverse American society, the vertical system is strong and often is needed to mitigate the lack of resources and know-how in may local settings. Herein lies the dilemma. Although often necessary, the growth of the vertical system results in further strains—financial, intellectual, and moral—

in the horizontal ties. Both intellectual and moral dimensions must remain strong for cohesive communities to survive.

For small-town practitioners in human services, the consideration of vertical as well as horizontal ties is essential in developing an understanding of how to proceed in certain circumstances. Although some social service projects will quickly capture the local imagination, others might more effectively draw their support from the external ties of the community—the larger society and culture. One of the most delicate assessments a practitioner must make is deciding when to reach for support from sources outside the community, because, as Buck pointed out, vertical ties may weaken horizontal ties. Yet, practitioners often must seek vertical support for funding, expertise, or simply legitimacy. Although most organizing efforts, in the long run, must rely on local support, they at times might be effectively encouraged or expedited by outside trends.

The mutuality of influence and the delicate balance between the local community and the larger society or between the microcosm of the locality and the macrocosm of the nation, and vice versa, become apparent. All communities have an identifiable cadre of local and cosmopolitan influential people (see chapter 3). The local powerful actors will facilitate the horizontal linkages or the intracommunity relationships; the cosmopolitan influential people will be instrumental in making the transition from the local unit to the society at large (that is, the state, region, country, culture, or world). Perhaps, the local practitioner stands at the point where the vertical system meets the horizontal. "This is the point where policy is transformed into action. It is here that the worker must perform the magic of 'taking a recipe and baking a cake' " (R. Buck, personal communication, October 20, 1982). Practitioners face the concrete problems of carrying the unique mark of the community in which the problems arise. Practitioners need to understand the tangible and intangible factors that shape the characters of their communities. They need to be skilled applied ethnographers. They need to be able to see the world and assess its problems as members of their constituencies would, not necessarily to agree with them, but to define clearly the practitioner's point-of-reference in the sociocultural mosaic.

Minimal Essential Elements of Communal Life

The essential elements of communal life are revealed through the lay and the scholarly literature. These elements apply whether practitioners believe that community requires an interactional space or whether practitioners stress non-spatial-elements community. Clark (1973), through his detailed discussions of those elements, concluded that "the strength of community within any given group is determined by the degree to which its members experience both a sense of solidarity and a sense of significance" (p. 409). According to Clark, those essential elements of community flow from MacIver's (1924) early assertions that "life is essentially and always communal life. Every living thing is born into community and owes its life to community" (p. 209). Community is not circumscribed to the sphere of social interactions, but it permeates the visceral and psychological spheres of life. "Community is. . . sentiment," stated MacIver (1924, p. 209); although the term "sentiment" might not be entirely unambiguous, it seems to be the best available to describe the community phenomenon, because it emphasizes the importance of members' self-perception versus that of observers' perception (see for example, "Our Town in 1981" on pp. 123–124, "Arriving in Eatonville, Florida" on pp. 118–119, and "We Won't Roll Over and Die: Hawkeye Is a Small Town Fighting Back" on pp. 143–145).

In terms of the small community, these essential elements of community life are clearly manifested in the interactions of the residents and cannot be ignored by human services practitioners. These elements are solidarity, significance, and security (Clark, 1973). Although *solidarity*, that is, cohesiveness or "we-ness," can be found in large and small units, in place and nonplace community, the degree to which it can be observed in the small town is often more overt. Residents of small towns speak of "We, the people of Clover Hill" or "We, the friends of Township Square" as if there could be no question about the authoritativeness of the "We." A sense of significance must permeate those manifestations of collective behavior that help perpetuate the idea of community. Acts such as public citizen awards, both in towns and communal associations, celebrate the significance of individuals' contributions. Perhaps the search for significance has sparked the current return of hundreds of citizens to the small towns and villages where undramatic and casual contributions to community are counted by their fellow citizens. A sense of security is derived from this mutuality of communal relationships, from the familiarity of the environment, and more obviously, from the affection and support of friends and neighbors (see, for example, "Way Out in the Country, Super Tuesday Much More than a Vote-and-Run Affair" on pp. 204–205).

However, the emphasis on communal behavior has been cyclical in contemporary society and, thus, solidarity, significance, and security often have been hidden behind individualistic strivings. In 1976, Philip Slater wrote a critique of the American obsession with privacy, individualism, and freedom from interdependence he had observed during the 1950s and early 1960s and to which he saw the "flower children" movement of the

1960s responding. Slater pointed out the contradictions and dilemmas that faced the American of the 1950s and 1960s and rendered the average citizen somewhat schizophrenic. On the one hand, Americans pursued competition, success, and material gains; on the other, they sought associations, freshness of air, and communal backyard talk.

> Suburbanites who philosophized over the back fence with complete sincerity about their "dog-eat-dog world," and what-is-it-all-for, and you-can't-take-it-with-you, and success-doesn't-make-you-happy-it-just-gives-you-ulcers-and-a-heart-condition, were enraged in the sixties when their children began to pay serious attention to these ideas. To the young this seemed hypocritical, but if adults didn't feel these things they wouldn't have had to fight them so vigorously. The exaggerated hostility that young people aroused in the "flower child" era argues that the life they led was highly seductive to middle-aged Americans. (Slater, 1976, pp. 10–11)

The seductive elements of romanticized village life to the American middle class probably account for the popularity of British novels extolling its virtues, such as village novels by E. F. Benson (1977), E. M. Delafield (1931), or Agatha Christie (1950, 1963). The recent fascination with James Herriot's (1985) "vet" stories set in the Yorkshire dales illustrates this point well.

To Slater, contradictory streaks in the American character were obvious: individualism was in constant tug-of-war against the desire for community. Slater predicted that the emphasis on individual competition of the 1950s would result in an about-face of philosophy in the 1970s. Currently, many sociologists are predicting that the emphasis on individualism and the relative egocentrism of the early 1980s will bring another about-face in the 1990s. Slater suggested that collectivism has always been "the more usual lot of humans. Most people in most societies have lived and died in stable communities that took for granted the subordination of the individual to the welfare of the group. The aggrandizement of the individual at the expense of his neighbors was simply a crime" (Slater, 1976, p. 9).

Slater (1976, pp. 8–9) identified some of the natural desires of people that are or should be satisfied through communal ties. One is the desire for "community"; that is, solidarity or cohesiveness—the wish to live in a total and visible collective entity. Another desire is for engagement, that is, significance—the wish to confront one's surroundings and find the meaningful extensions of one's ego. Another desire is for dependence, that is, security—the wish to satisfy and be satisfied.

The most pervasive common elements of community are not just the product of social scientists' empirical observations but have been stated by philosophers and observers of the human condition. These elements probably can be best realized within the parameters of the small environment. Many of the excerpts in part 2 highlight those essential elements of communal life.

THE DISCIPLINARY ORIENTATION OF COMMUNITY CONTENT

A review of the literature on communities shows that writers, journalists, philosophers, and social scientists have tried to isolate the concept of community and have struggled with its ramifications in an enormous and often unmanageable array of works. For students of small communities, the following three ways of viewing community practice by various social scientists are of paramount importance:

1. Communities seen as illustrative microcosms
2. Communities seen as result of physical, historical developments
3. Specific variables seen as the focus of community research

Communities as Illustrative Microcosms

For generations, anthropologists have studied communities and conducted ethnographic research in primitive villages and other environments. In the anthropological tradition, and probably because of the nature of field observations, the anthropologist has tended to identify community with a place or location in which a whole array of activities—social, economic, and political—are conterminous with territorially defined boundaries. Pelly-Effrat (1974) suggested that among writers of this orientation exists "claim (whether or not it is explicit) that the community under study represents a microcosm of the total society or some important segment of the society" (p. 6).

Sociologists also have followed this approach in the study of communities. In the United States, this orientation was prevalent in the 1920s when Lynd and Lynd (1929) published *Middletown*. Community as a microcosm of the society at large has been one of the respected research traditions of anthropology and sociology (see, for example, "Arriving in Eatonville, Florida" pp. 118–119). This approach has been popular among British sociologists—Williams (1964) and Pahl (1966) both shared in this orientation. With an anthropological bent, Frankenberg (1957, 1966) produced a number of landmark studies about a small town in Wales and about British communities. He emphasized that special activities such as weddings and christenings bound the communal microcosm. In addition, architects and urban planners using this approach have studied communities, particularly "planned" or "utopian" communities. The very idea of a planned or a utopian community is imbued in the belief that community can be potentially a self-contained microcosm. Although communities have been studied as microcosms, they still can be influenced by outer community forces. Practitioners have learned that planned communities and utopias often survive or fail because of outside stresses. However, the emphasis of those who look at communities as microcosms is on the potential of inside forces to illustrate, in reduced scale, the gamut of human experiences, whether economical, political, or psychological.

Unfortunately, community studies in sociology have been unduly maligned and criticized when the sociological investigation turn quantitative. Ruth Glass (1966) labeled those studies as "the poor sociologist's substitute for the novel" (p. 148), and, as Bell and Newby (1972) reported, "Ruth Glass' criticisms went further than this. She also castigated community studies for their 'innumeracy' " (p. 13)—a lack of figures that bothered the budding scientific sociologists. Yet, community studies had extraordinary humanistic and scientific merit. They read like novels, a quality not to be perfunctorily dismissed; they documented social history and provided accessible blueprints for professional practitioners to follow in their studies of specific communities.

Community studies in sociology were criticized because of their holistic approach—their tendency to describe all aspects of life in the towns studied, a tendency that greatly curtailed the possibility of making statistical inferences or generalizations. However, it is precisely this tendency of community studies to view communities holistically and as microcosms of human interaction that renders them useful to human services professionals, in the same fashion that novels can teach a great deal to community practitioners. Many of the best and most lively descriptions of individual communities (fiction and nonfiction) have come from the literature: Mark Twain's (1900) *The Man Who Corrupted Hadleyburg*, Lewis's (1920b) *Main Street*, Marquand's (1949) *The Point of No Return*, and Lyford's (1962) *The Talk in Vandalia*. Good prose and valid information are not mutually exclusive.

The notion of community as a microcosm of society and the merit of good prose in community study currently are being reviewed and illustrated by non–social scientists. For example, Keillor's (1985) *Lake Wobegon Days* painted a microcosm of human existence. Searching for a community where he could find a variety of social dimensions on which he could base his novel *Hometown*, Peter Davis (1982b) visited the chief of the Demographic Statistics Branch of the Population Division of the U.S. Bureau of the Census. Davis recounts the following dialogue:

> Tell me [he said to the chief], where can I go to combine categories of social research with techniques of storytelling? Where I can observe activities the way an anthropologist might, as Robert and Helen Lynd did in *Middletown*, and then tell about them

> as Sherwood Anderson did in *Winesburg, Ohio*. Stories of marriage and morals, work and leisure, politics, crime, punishment, religion, caste and class. Stories of real people using not only fact but fantasy, not only information but impression, attitude, legend—diverse tidings that disclose particular truths in a community. (p. 10)

After much thought and search in the catacombs of the Bureau of the Census and those of his mind, the leading demographer responded:

> "You have to find a place," he [the demographer] said, "big enough to have everything its people need and small enough so you can figure out what the hell is going on." The town should be northern enough to be industrial, southern enough to have a gently rural aspect, western enough to have once been on the frontier, eastern enough to have a past. No single integer can ever contain the whole, but it can contain processes that reflect those other integers. (p. 11)

The tendency to theorize that urbanization destroys the folk community and that to find community as a microcosm one must avoid totally urbanized centers undergirds traditional community studies. Redfield (1941) exemplified this tendency in *The Folk Culture of the Yucatan* and, as Bell and Newby (1972) criticized, framed his questions so that it appeared that folk societies were necessarily and always more organized than cities. However, social workers and other human services professionals have not suffered from Redfield's tendency. On the contrary, folk (small) communities, until recently, held no interest for human services professionals, who tended to focus on urban community dynamics. Recently, however, local communities have become more interesting and appealing to human services practitioners, who felt their dynamics merited closer scrutiny. Political, economic, and demographic forces, as well as the rebirth of volunteer and self-help local efforts in the provision of social services, have helped expand the interest of social workers and other human services generalists beyond the impersonal parameters of Gesellschaft into the strong networks of Gemeinschaft (Conklin, 1980).

However, communities still are found in Gesellschaft. Frankenberg (1966) aptly documented those communities in some British urban estates, and Rivera and Erlich (1981) discussed them in relation to the urban Neo-Gemeinschaften. As Frankenberg (1966) suggested, "Size is not the key. Community implies having something in common. . . . Those who live in a community have overriding economic interests which are the same or complementary. They work together and also play and pray together. Their common interest in things gives them a common interest in each other" (p. 238). Often, at least for the purposes of study, it is easier to find oneness and complementarity in the small units. Thus, social science examples of community as a microcosm have tended to focus on small towns.

Many of the selections in this book clearly illustrate that writers have perceived various place communities as microcosms of society. Inasmuch as human services workers emphasize the interconnections among the political, economic, educational, and social segments of community life, they too support the perception that communities are microcosms of the total human experience. Research of the community as a microcosm tends to be holistic—it not only examines the interplay of many community forces, but also stresses the interaction of all the forces on the stage of community life. It is "after 'reality' described and analyzed as 'totality' (i.e., interrelationships between the various segments of community life) . . . [It is] stressing a certain style of research, of direct observation and reporting" (Bell & Newby, 1972, p. 17). Viewing community as a microcosm of society implies selecting, albeit by default, a naturalistic or field-based research method of emphasis and an interdisciplinary orientation.

Communities as Physical and Historical Developments

Social workers more so than other professionals are aware of the relationship between individuals and their culture. Generalist social workers must confront the intertwining of psychological and cultural variables as determinants of the lifestyle, the choices people make, and the patterns of activity individuals follow. The same connection exists between communities and their culture (*culture* interpreted to include people, places, sense of time, and other processes). Arensberg (1955), an anthropologist, hypothesized that "communities seem to be basic units of organization and transmission within a culture. They provide for human beings and their cultural adaptation to nature the basic minimum personnel and the basic minimum social relations through which survival is assured and the context of culture can be passed on to the next generation" (p. 1143).

For Arensberg, as for many others, a correspondence between cultural constructs and the physical form of specific communities exists:

> Mumford demonstrated that for each cultural advance in European life, a new form of the city emerged. The medieval borough around market and cathedral, urban counterpart of the manorial village, expressed the high Middle Ages; the baroque capital of parade avenues, palaces, and *places d'armes* mirrored the absolutist national states, the sooty tangle of factory and slum and the residential segregations of the withdrawn squires on the hill in mill towns and mill cities matched the industrial and railroad age. Each community town (here "city") was unique just as the age, which the anthropologist calls "culture", was unique. . . .
>
> We can thus expect American culture, in its many subcultures of region and age, to show similar correspondence in forms. (p. 1144)

Arensberg proposed an early ecological perspective of local communities. He suggested that the historical background and the social relationships of particular groups during particular periods became explicit in physical variables, that is, in the shapes or forms communities take throughout the land. For Arensberg (1955), the American New England town illustrated the principles of his theory:

> The eminent colonial historian Wertenbaker accepts the derivation of the New England town from the manorial village of the champion country of East Anglia, whence most of the Puritans came, a derivation established by Homans. In East Anglia, the village in turn was a local specialization of the open-field village of the North European plain. It was brought into newly opened Fenlands by Angles and Saxons from the Elbe mouth and was of a settlement pattern, village type, and agriculture quite different from that of once-Celtic western Britain and even from that of nearby once-Belgian and Jutish Kent. Nothing prevents inventors in a New World from elaborating, adapting, formalizing already familiar, even unconscious, heritages. In fact, that is the way anthropology tells us most cultural evolution (*anglice* "invention") proceeds. The urbanizing Puritans rationally planning new settlements in the wilderness were elaborating ancestral cultural materials and, as we shall see, every other American pioneer community did likewise. (p. 1148)

A similar thesis was proposed by architectural analyst Darley (1978) in her study of British villages. She viewed "villages of vision" from a contemporary planner's perspective. Her descriptions, just as those of Arensberg's, illustrated the relationship between the history and beliefs of the founders or planners and the layout of the community:

> In 1861, as Saltaire took form in its valley outside Bradford, George Cadbury took over the family tea and coffee firm. He had spent much of his spare time working in Sunday Schools and had a Quaker conscience for the welfare of others and an unusually clear sight of what needed to be done to improve life for his employees.
>
> However, it was not until later, when the firm moved out into the countryside to a new large factory, that the situation offered itself for a real advance, not merely in the smaller details but for a change in environment. The essential difference between Cadbury's plans at Bournville and others, before and after, was that they were designed not merely as improved *industrial housing*, but as improved housing—equally suitable for office workers as for packers in the chocolate factory. The planning was revolutionary; low density suburban villa development was the starting-point with large detached housing replaced by various cottage forms, both terraced and semi-detached. . . .
>
> Physical fitness was one of Cadbury's prerequisites for a contented employee . . . enormous emphasis is laid on groups of men doing press-ups and women doing gentle gymnastics. . . . Cadbury [also] thought that employees could achieve a measure of independence and self-sufficiency, as well as health, by cultivating their own vegetables, and he rightly felt that gardening was the perfect antidote for repetitious work. (pp. 137–138)

An understanding of the historical development of communities in particular areas is valuable. The choice of building material and the distribution of buildings in the landscape all tell about the identity of the community and the life of its members. Regional differences, in these instances, can be important.

A corollary of the physical distribution of people are *centers*—loci of interaction for people in the community (Freilich, 1963). Freilich, an anthropologist, suggested the identification of centers to facilitate the study of human interaction in "primitive communities."[1] A *primitive community*, an anthropological construct, is a type of interactional system that, according to Freilich (1963), is unique in the following ways:

- in terms of using a set of geographic points (centers) as loci of interaction
- in having a given set of associational groups meeting at such centers
- in developing a local interaction culture based on information collected at such centers and distributed primarily to members of the community (p. 122)

Experience in local communities (whether small towns or city neighborhoods) suggests that the same notion of center can be useful for assessing interactional patterns in small communities, not only in nonindustrial societies but in the industrial world (see, for example, "Arriving in Eatonville, Florida" on pp. 118–119). For example, in one farming town, the "locals" meet every morning for their breakfast at the coffee room of a local hotel. The businesspeople of the downtown area frequent the coffee shop in the early hours. They have their breakfasts before opening stores or offices at 9 a.m. The farmers meet in the same coffee shop at 9:30 or 10 a.m., when they come to town to complete their business dealings or do their shopping. Obviously, the coffee shop is an important community center; practitioners who wish to establish relationships in the community would be well-advised to use it. Likewise, in small Pennsylvania towns, fire halls are important and powerful centers where people congregate to discuss community issues and make decisions. In the United Kingdom, there is no better center for taking the popular pulse of communities than the local pub. Cafés or bars frequented by small town locals play the same role in towns and villages in the United States. Churches, markets, schoolyards, pubs, and coffee shops all can be centers that facilitate the practitioner's

[1] The term "primitive" is not one this author would select. It is used here to describe a construct and not to make a value judgment on development.

assessment. Human services workers often lack the influence that guarantees community backing for their endeavors. An intellectual as well as a sympathetic understanding and appreciation of the nuances of local settings can greatly enhance their perspective and broaden their sphere of action (see, for example, "Services" on pp. 162–165).

Variables as the Focus of Community Research

In addition to those social scientists who have primarily used the ethnographic or field observation approach and who have studied community as a microcosm, there are those who have followed a more specialized approach that emphasizes a single variable or a complex of related variables. This approach assumes that although many variables appear in community, they are not all equally salient in all communities. Thus, some communities might be particularly fruitful arenas for studying community power, others might be propitious settings for examining social needs, and still others might make excellent terrain for analyzing decision making. This more particularistic approach to the study of communities often gives the neophyte practitioner the impression that, for those investigators, community is not a holistic or integrated unit but the juxtaposition of distinct variables of unequal weight.

The study of single variables in communities, an approach that is more aligned with the positivistic research tradition, has been another common research approach among sociologists and political scientists. Hunter (1953), for example, looked at his city of study from the perspective of its power structure. He examined its *elitism*—the pyramidal distribution of power and decision making in the community, in which there are a few influential people at the top of the power structure who influence decisions in many spheres of life. Political scientists such as Dahl (1961) who isolated *pluralism*—an urban pattern of decision making in which there are many influential people who are on equal footing in the community strata but who only influence decisions in their own specialized areas of operation—in contrast to Hunter's elitism also have related to the variable of power within communities. Wellstone (1978), in a more recent study of Rice County, Minnesota, criticized the lack of democratic pluralistic decision making in small communities. However, studies that focus on democratic decision making through majority rule often fail to see the consensual elements of decision making in small towns. In the past, leaders often spoke of consensus when what they really had was the approval of the elite only. Current consensus tends to reflect broader participation, even in small towns. For positivists, more comprehensive pictures are attained cumulatively, through the analysis of specific variables. Although not a positivistic study, Wellstone's work highlights the single variable of power, searches for its distribution within a rural community, and explains how it can or cannot be upset.

Pelly-Effrat (1974) warned that it is more fruitful to conceive of community as a "multidimensional ordinal variable" (p. 21)—that is, several factors compose a community. In attempting to understand community through studies that emphasize specific variables, practitioners should keep Pelly-Effrat's admonitions in mind, and not be mislead into thinking that the single variable under consideration is, alone, representative of the "community-ness" of the social unit being analyzed. It is important for human services practitioners to study power, authority, and influence within communities. The implications of these notions for service delivery are obvious and fundamental. Yet, community practitioners must remember that although community decisions might be based on power relationships, not all community actions or behaviors are. History, traditions, idiosyncrasies, beliefs, prejudices, geographic, and environmental factors all converge and influence community situations and the outcomes of communal events.

INGREDIENTS FOR ASSESSMENT

Practitioners can seldom afford to subscribe to single definitions. They need to look at their small towns and villages from at least six perspectives, asking many questions to determine the ingredients for assessment.

First, is the community-of-mind conterminous with a locality or place, and if it is, what are its parameters? The importance of locality cannot be underestimated or overestimated. "Community-ness" cannot be imposed on localities because it develops through the exercise of relationships through time.

Second, what are the systemic ties of the community? How strong are the horizontal or local ties in the political, economic, educational, service, and other fields? How affected is the community by external forces (vertical ties)? Because the small-community practitioner might need to strengthen the horizontal ties, particularly in the helping fields, it will be important to determine specific areas of social interaction where such efforts are likely to be more fruitful. Such a determination might require identifying the strongest horizontal ties or the weakest vertical ones.

Third, how does the community rate in terms of cohesiveness, engagement, and interdependence among its members? What does the sense of belonging do for individuals in the community? (Consider solidarity, sentiment, and significance.)

Fourth, how holistic are the communal relationships? Are the communal activities encompassing a view of the community as a microcosm? If so, what kind of a picture can be painted of this microcosm?

Fifth, how has the particular community developed through the centuries or the decades? How evident is the local or regional mark in its development? How unique is its background? Are its physical characteristics congruent with the current patterns of interaction of its members? Additionally, what are the salient community centers? How are those centers regarded by the people in the locality? Are they viewed as legitimate or marginal? Can the professional, particularly if an outsider to the community, become a participant in one or more of those centers?

Sixth, what are the specific salient dimensions or variables? For example, are power relationships so obvious or important that they deserve special study? Are there salient patterns of social class interaction? In most local communities, power and class relationships can be strong.

Practitioners must consider these salient ingredients when assessing the nature of their small communities and identifying the pull of forces that will affect their interventions.

2

Community as a Personal Solution

Searching for Identity and Meaning

Modern individuals are plagued by anomie and disorientation. Having lost much of the feeling of control over their destinies, modern people are struggling with their sense of selfhood. "Surely the outstanding characteristic of contemporary thought on man and society is the preoccupation with personal alienation and cultural disintegration" (Nisbet, 1953, p. 3). With varying degrees of sophistication, all people ask, Who am I? What is the purpose of my being? What is the meaning of my existence? In their quest for answers and solutions to the puzzles of their lives, people turn to community, because their broadening preoccupation with insecurity is accompanied by a growing regard for the merits of membership in community. Increasingly, individuals of the late 20th century are seeking to escape the freedom of individualism and secularism that once propelled many to the metropolises. Nostalgia has become a major theme of American society. "It is plainly a nostalgia, not for the greater adventurousness of earlier times but for the assertedly greater community and moral certainty of the generations preceding ours" (Nisbet, 1953, p. 31).

People turn particularly to community because the family is perceived to be weakening and becoming more remote from each person. Because of the processes of civilization and industrialization, the family is growing smaller, less orthodox, less encompassing, and less capable of satisfying individual needs. Roszak (1978) lamented the apparent contradiction of the reduction of the family unit in a world where all other societal institutions are expanding:

> I began . . . with the lament that our world has become "too big." But there is one institution that has become too small, and that is the family. It has wasted away to the bare minimum and is desperately in need of expansion. In fact, this is not an exception to our thesis: it is a corollary. Things have gotten too big at the expense of basic structure. Some of these structures—the neighborhood, the village, the community

> of work—have simply been driven into the ground as obstacles to big system efficiency. The most basic structure of all, the family, lingers on. It remains a biological necessity. . . . The family is tolerated—but only in its most denatured, nuclear form. It might be an axiom of our thesis: the bigger the industrial apparatus, the weaker the family. The one subtracts its human resources from the other. . . . (p. 152)

The family also is becoming less permanent and more transient because of the pressure of modern living. Although permanency is not a virtue per se and should not be made a social fetish, chronic impermanency results in anxiety, and, as a result, people experience a disquieting feeling of loneliness and disconnectedness. Thus, in our contemporary world, the smaller the family becomes, the more individuals search for purpose and meaning in the larger collective, in contrived groups, and in artificial or utopian communities.

Alternative arrangements that take the place of Gemeinschaft have been flourishing for a variety of people. For example, for many of the old and the young in search of community, shopping malls have become *the* community. Even judicial controversy has arisen over whether malls are private property or part of the community like any park, airport, or downtown square. For many people, shopping malls are the only community they experience. Keyes (1973) wrote of what he found in a shopping mall named Whitman, which he describes as "an honest to goodness community dominated by kids but not limited to them" (p. 120):

> The heart of this community wasn't the dip-in-and-outers, the dilettantes who only showed up on Saturday. The real Whitman community was the people who hung out there virtually everyday, and had for years, the people with some commitment to the place.
>
> One widow, seventy-eight years old, has her breakfast every morning at 10 in [a mall department store], then [sits] around on the benches before having some milk at 1 and returning to an empty house. She'd been coming to Whitman for four years, and really enjoy[s] the kids. . . . They tell jokes and sit around. And the kids return their affection.

Individuals often find that a variety of "contrived" environments become their community and fulfill a need where family might not exist or might have failed. A recent article in *The Atlanta Constitution* mentioned interest clubs as a way to help "people cope with the largeness of city life by providing smaller, more human-sized community" (Long, 1987, p. 38). Keyes (1973) commented that "an ideal community would be like a good family: the group from which one can't be expelled. Or like Robert Frost's definition of home—"the place where when you have to go there, they have to take you in" (p. 168). One of the reasons for the success of modern therapeutic communities such as Weight Watchers or Alcoholics

Anonymous is that people may err, but when they return to the group, they are in community. They are at home; they are taken in; new pacts for responsibility are drawn and past ways forgotten. How many people can do that in their own families? People search for personal communities, hoping that in community they might find others who will accept fully their strengths and foibles. In turn, people are prepared to accept the strengths and weaknesses of others. Human services practitioners must understand the forces that propel individuals to participate in communal activities. Practitioners who work with groups or clubs will see these artificial communities as fulfilling the roles that natural communities once played.

Human services workers can learn valuable lessons from the "patch system" that has been tried in Britain. Over the past decade, many British local authority social services departments have advocated the decentralization of services to small units called "patches," wherein generalist workers attempt the "fusion of statutory work with voluntary action in the community" (Hadley & McGrath, 1980, p. 1). Within the basic (and compared with the United States) more comprehensive framework of the British welfare state, "community care" (Walker, 1982) or "community social work" (National Institute for Social Work, 1982) are being revived. In principle, community social work supports and enhances the personal and identity-giving role of the community. A true patch should be a communal unit that has been identified as meaningful for residents and workers. Patches cover areas as dissimilar as rural Herefordshire and inner city London, but their rationale includes

> the abandonment of existing assumptions about the automatic superiority of the large-scale bureaucracy as the principal model of organization, and readiness to explore more statutory services and community care, decentralized, flexible structures; a broader more open definition of professionalism which has room to recognize the full potential of lay workers . . . ; acknowledgement of the present contribution and future potential of the community to provide a whole range of services for itself; the right of local communities to share in decision-making about service priorities and methods of provision. (Hadley & McGrath, 1980, p. 10)

The patch worker recognizes that the community offers itself as a personal solution and meaningful environment for many and is willing to capture this recognition and apply it in his or her work. Although patch work is not necessarily viewed as a panacea for the social services generalist, the concept begins to recognize the central role of community in the life of service workers and recipients alike. With the patch model, human services workers can no longer remain the "anonymous persons from county hall, dropping in from outer space" (Jones, 1980, p. 16).

People find meaning in their social role within communities; they find meaning in the participatory responsibilities. "The more we retreat into homebound self-sufficiency and isolation," said Darley (1978) of the London Courtland Institute, "the more we hear of the 'the community' " (p. 9). People who are not anomic are busy, active, coping, living, winning, or losing but never disengaged. People who are not anomic find meaning in helping the larger collective; they find meaning in being helped or cared for by those with whom they share community. In fact, community often takes over (or is sought to do so) what once were solely individual or familial cares.

Parents are recognizing the community's role in their personal lives and are recognizing and accepting community functions that, at other times, would have been deemed intrusive. The community is being viewed, sometimes appropriately, sometimes inappropriately, as a psychological answer or a personal solution. In a recent television interview with parents who had joined a "tough love" group as an answer to their child-rearing problems, one of the participant fathers emphatically asserted, "Parents do not raise children, communities do" (Donahue, 1982). The enormous growth of support groups, from farmer's support to La Leche groups for young mothers, attests to the communal needs for well-being that cannot be met by individuals.

Providing another illustration of this search for personal support from the collective, Keyes (1973) wrote about W. H. Auden on the occasion of the poet's return to Oxford:

> W. H. Auden recently left New York City and returned to England, to Oxford. The British poet said that he regretted leaving his adopted home of more than two decades, but explained: "It's just that I'm getting rather old to live alone in the winter and I'd rather live in community. Supposing I had a coronary. It might be days before I was found."
>
> At Oxford, he said, I should be missed if I failed to turn up for meals. (p. 145)

Keyes suggested that for him, as for Auden, the attainable community is "the place where it is safe to be known" (p. 145). That kind of community has the advantage of being plausible in a variety of settings, from a village to a town, from a commune to a bar or church. Keyes continued his comments on Auden's actions:

> Auden fingered what, for me, is the minimum criterion of being in community, of being known: that my absence, as well as my presence, be noted. . . .
>
> Such a community is more than many of us have—a place where we're recognized as a unique name, face, and set of quirks. Where we can go everyday and be sure of finding familiar faces.
>
> But there's that next level, the one Auden mentioned, of also being missed when absent. (p. 145)

Perhaps Auden's level of "counting," of making a difference to others, inspires persons to seek community in a variety of ways (for example, "Our

Town in 1981" on pp. 123–124). Some old-time residents of the megalopolis seek Gemeinschaft in their neighborhood. Others flock to the small town searching for that personalized sense of being missed when they do not show up at an affair, of knowing the daily cadences as they go about doing routine activities (see, for example, "It's a New Day in State Center, but What Will Life Be Like at Dusk?" on pp. 130–136 and "Lack of Teamwork Hinders State Center's Fight to Survive" on pp. 137–141). What millions want, reported a recent *Newsweek* article, "is a piece of the simple life: friendly, slow paced, basic, safe, a return to community on a human scale" (Morganthauw et al., 1981, p. 27). Other individuals join communes or utopian collectives wherein they share beliefs or philosophies and where they sometimes find, in the communal effort, their lost sense of self, the personal "salvation" they seek.

COMMUNITY AS A PSYCHOSOCIAL "SALVATION": THE UTOPIANS

The idea that community could spell salvation is not new. The term "salvation" here is used metaphorically to mean deliverance of an individual or group from psychological or social destruction, or preservation of the person or the group from danger, loss, or difficulty. Although "salvation" here is not used in any religious sense, communities often have given some individuals the same support religious beliefs give others. Page Smith (1963) suggested that the New England covenantal community, perhaps the cornerstone or model of American communities in other regions, represented a truly religious experience, not just in the dogmatic sense, but in the sense of feeding the inner lives of its members. Such a community

> was intensely communal in that it turned inward toward the interior spiritual life of the community; it was, however, remarkably dynamic, creating surpluses of human energy that were discharged increasingly against an intractable environment. (p. 12)

The combination of potential for individual fulfillment and external, pragmatic viability laid the success of the covenantal community as a personal solution for those who embraced it.

Centuries after the decline of covenantal communities, the community as a personal solution was expressed in the themes of the philosopher Josiah Royce, one of the great American idealists.

> Royce came to his concern for the great community by his own Western experience as a child and young man growing up in the Gold Rush Town of Grass Valley, California. Apparently, the violence, the deceit, the crime, and the greed [of

> individuals he encountered as a young man caused Royce enough irritation to set his thoughts on constructing] a theory of community by which men could live not only in peace with one another, but in service and personal creativity. (Allemand, 1976, p. 48)

Royce proposed that "only the consciously united community . . . can offer salvation to distracted humanity and can calm the otherwise insatiable greed and longing of the natural individual man" (Royce, 1916, p. 49).

In more contemporary times, a number of utopian communities motivated by similar philosophic considerations emerged:

> Many were religious, but many others were secular in the ordinary sense of the word. . . . the Mormon community, one of the strongest and tightest . . . had a great deal of communal ethic in it, and still does. (Nisbet, 1953, p. 103)

The American utopians had their antecedents in Europe. Darley (1978) recognized the difficulties and failures experienced by many Britons in their quest for the perfect community. She also recognized that, within limitations, many of these quixotic seekers of community were gratified in their dreams and provided realizable blueprints for not only architectural but also for sociopsychological communities:

> The theorists whose writings abounded with schemes veering from the hare-brained to the potentially workable fell foul of many obstacles and the higher the aims of the community builder, the further they might fall. . . . many of the ideas lay dormant and in a more advanced social climate could be readopted. Advance was very slow. . . . Industrial experiments were often merely marginal improvements, concentrating in early days on better education and facilities than the norm. Inevitably each step advanced the standards and gradually the aspirations of the social reformers were realized.
>
> Allied to the comparatively simple aims of improved housing and conditions came the far more complex theories of environmental community reform. . . . Effecting revolution in environment, was one way to influence future living conditions. All idealists of varying persuasions, they set precedents and provided practical examples of workable communities which had immense influence abroad and in this country. (p. 11)

Kanter (1972), a student of visionary communal movements in the United States, provided yet a broader review of the historical search for community. She suggested that utopian communities have been the response to three forces: religious, politico-economic, and psychosocial. Religious communities often emerged as a result of separatist and Pietist sects seeking closer contact with God and each other. In the past,

> spiritual ideals [for such groups] were preeminent. Communism was adopted at times only through economic necessity to permit the community to retreat to its own territory to live and practice together. Often these groups coalesced around a single charismatic figure. (p. 4)

Examples of such utopian experiments were the Shakers, Amana, and Brook Farm.

Current religious communities such as the Hutterian Brethren and many communities founded on Eastern mysticism can be analyzed using Kanter's explanations. Although many Old Order Amish communities in, for example, Pennsylvania, Ohio, Indiana, and Iowa, are not utopian in the conventional sense, they do represent a continuation of successful earlier communal experiments, now translated into a way of life for the group. Collective efforts intertwined with religious beliefs related to the nonuse of machinery have been successful in helping Old Order Amish communities survive and succeed in these hard times for modern agriculture (Logsdon, 1986).

Another type of utopian community emerged out of politico-economic concerns because of increasing dislocation and poverty in the wake of the Industrial Revolution. Like the religious communes, it was inspired by the social creed of reformers who sought "in the small socialist community a refuge from the evils of the factory system" (Kanter, 1972, p. 5). Places such as New Harmony (1825–27), the Wisconsin Phalanx (1784–1850), and Brook Farm (1814–47) were inspired by the social philosophies of idealist reformers Horace Greeley, Robert Owen, Charles Fourier, and Etienne Cabet.

A large number of modern communes also are the result of psychosocial forces. These communities reject society's emphasis on achievement and material gains and seek to provide their members with a place to grow, experience intimacy, and realize their potential. For the truly utopian groups, all modern institutions are considered "sick" and "are felt to be instrumental in promoting the neurotic behavior at the root of our most pressing social problems" (Kanter, 1972, p. 7).

Initially successful but rather short-lived communal settlement efforts became part of the widespread American quest for community as personal solution of the 1970s and 1980s. Unfortunately, what are personal solutions for some people are personal offenses for others. For example, a group of followers of the Bhagwan Shree Rajneesh, an Indian sect that settled in the village of Antelope, Oregon, apparently offended many of the citizens. The Rajneeshees outnumbered old-time residents 65 to 35 ("Guru Follower Has Edge in Oregon election," 1982, p. C8). This group of newcomers clothed in sunset colors frightened the old-time, mostly retired citizens of Antelope. Having exhausted the usual measures—zoning laws, building permits, the courts, and even a referendum to dissolve the city—to keep the newcomers out, the old-timers finally decided to abandon the village to the new group. The Rajneeshees captured, through elections, the office of mayor and a number of city council posts. They voted to change the name of the town. In 1985, the leader of the Rajneeshees encountered serious trouble and emigrated to escape legal entanglements in the United States. During subsequent legal proceedings, followers voted to change the name of the town back to its original name in an effort to patch up relationships with the locals. Although the conduct of such modern communities concerns many citizens, their cohesiveness, strength, and, frequently, their economic success is a serious issue for study.

The notion that these alternative communities or "new Gemeinschaften" are personal solutions is clearly highlighted by those who perceive them as performing functions once carried out not just by communities but by families:

> Scaling down the industrial leviathan means building bigger families—or rather bigger households. It is not more children we need in families, but more family we need in the life of every child: more adults to share the home and participate in parenting the young. And such families are being built, as experimental models with many shapes and under many names. We hear them spoken of these days as communes, collectives, rural homesteads, ashrams. . . . (Roszak, 1978, pp. 152–153)

Roszak (1978) evaluated these new communes as follows:

> We are living through a period of exuberant communitarian experimentation, one of the great episodes of the Utopian tradition. . . . The fluidity and variety of experimentation is immense, and it moves on many fronts at once, challenging our concepts of child rearing and sex relations, work and property, authority and freedom, privacy and participation, consumption and distribution. . . . (p. 153)

However, he cautioned that "one has to be tentative, not simply because the communes are new and untested (not all of them are) but because our society at large and many communitarians themselves, no longer possess a fixed standard of success and failure to work by" (p. 153). An example of abuses of this search for community as a personal solution occurred in the Reverend Jim Jones's community in Georgetown, Guyana, where fanaticism led to the suicide/massacre of hundreds. Unfortunately, in the American heterogeneous culture, many of those who search for meaning in new and sometimes esoteric communal experiences may be seeking personal meanings or identities they have never before experienced. Unlike societies in Israel or China, American society has had little experience with communal alternatives such as kibbutzes, whose founders also were builders of a community at large.

Although the search for community as a personal solution shares many of the characteristics of the utopian movements described by Kanter and Darley, the search involves not only communes or utopias but ordinary towns and villages across the United States. People who have now joined the search for personal community are not only intellectuals, social philosophers, utopian supporters, or religious mystics, but also average citizens—insurance salespeople, entrepreneurs, teachers, farmers, and civil servants. The search for personal meaning in community is widespread all over the industrial world (see, for example, "Our Town in 1981" on pp. 123–124).

COMMUNITY AND SIZE

Community as a personal solution apparently can only be found in an intimate unit. Even during the early 1960s at the height of the national captivation with large-scale systemic linkages and vertical communities, community residents identified with their local community, as is shown in Lois Dean's (1967) study of five midwestern towns:

> From the social-psychological point of view, most Americans do not live in "the nation" or "the total society"; they live in towns and cities. . . . For most Americans, then, their local community of residence still constitutes the microcosm in terms of which the national community is comprehended and evaluated. (p. 6)

Gemeinschaftlich ties cannot materialize in large environments. Keyes (1973) described this problem for Americans:

> The benefits of small scale have been ignored too long by Americans. . . . A manageable size has been considered irrelevant to the quality of our human institutions. The convenience of collected resources, the efficiency of long assembly lines, large hospitals, schools, and factories have taken priority. One analysis of a variety of writings on America found that love of size, of bigness, was something generally agreed upon as unique to this country. It has a lot to do with our loneliness.
>
> We may have come "together" to fight World War II; Texans may feel an intense relationship to their state and when I went to see the Rockets play basketball, I felt very much a San Diegan. But such feelings of "community" are all in the abstract, and generally pass. The other members don't know me, nor I them. (pp. 173–174)

The need to identify with a manageable communal unit is not just an American phenomenon. In Britain, although local differences might appear to be less pronounced given the small size of the country, any keen observer of human nature will quickly discover that, at least from a psychological viewpoint, people from the North of England identify with the North country, people from London are clearly Londoners, and Scottish and Welsh people relate not only to their nations but also to local areas in their countries. The lore and pride of nation, region, and locale are beautifully illustrated by a story told frequently in the Outer Hebrides of Scotland and carefully recounted by Finlay Macdonald (1983):

> I grew up with the legend that the Good Lord made the world in six days, and despite what people like Charles Darwin and David Attenborough have had to say on the subject that's the way that the bit of me I like best likes to believe it. If only for the tail end of the legend which goes on to say that when God was resting, as everybody should, on the seventh day, he suddenly discovered that he had completely forgotten to use one last handful of jewels which he had meant to place in some exotic area like the Caribbean. However, rather than break the Sabbath more than was necessary, he just opened a window in heaven and threw the jewels out without even bothering to watch where they fell. Some cynics claim that he still doesn't know but that, in fact, they strung themselves out along the north-west coast of Scotland forming the long line of islands now known as The Outer Hebrides.
>
> I was born in the second island from the top. At least we call Harris an island, and even the Post Office calls it "The Isle of Harris," but, geographically, it is only a tall mountain range which separates it from what is called, also inaccurately, the Island of Lewis. Be that as it may, a Harrisman is a Harrisman, and a Lewisman is a Lewisman, and neither would have it differently! (p. 6)

Recently, scholars, environmentalists, and economists have discussed the advantages of manageable size from an ecological perspective. In 1967, Dean studied five communities with a definite orientation toward the value of vertical community linkages for economic growth. Despite this orientation, her findings supported the viewpoint that if place community is to act as a personal solution, there is bound to be an optimum size beyond which the community cannot grow because psychological ties are lost. Human services professionals have been caught between commitment to the local, cohesive community unit (the "philosophy of community") and professional training that has emphasized the merits of vertical linkages to larger and more resourceful systems. Social service workers, in many ways, have questioned the community of manageable size because, unfortunately, the equation has read:

small community = insularity, discrimination, nonservice ideology

However, for human services workers to understand and be effective in the localities in which they work, they must transcend their own stereotypes and dispassionately scrutinize the relationship of size to viable human communities (see chapter 4). They must realistically recognize the limitations of small communities and inventory their strengths. Seldom can human services workers successfully attack the discriminating practices of small towns if they discriminate themselves or view those towns negatively.

Dean (1967) believed the degree of personal meaning derived from the community unit to be related not just to size but to the corporate organization of the community. She identified the following three types of corporate structure:

1. Local form, in which the linkage is largely one-way, from the local to the national system. The national community serves largely as a market for locally produced goods.

2. Unit form, which comprises communities with plants of large corporations in which final or complete products are prepared or manufactured. Products are sold both locally and nationally. Business leaders interact at the national and local systems.

3. Lateral form, in which plants produce specialized units of national products, generally assembled somewhere else. Ties are primarily at the national level. Business leaders' local interactions are likely to be token (pp. 8–9).

Of these three types, only the local form rendered a community with high levels of local-system cohesiveness that could approach the degree of intimacy required for personal solutions. Although the local form of corporate structure resulted in a degree of community economic isolation, social insularity, and moralism, "River City," as Dean called her local form example, was said to constantly voice familial sentiments. "One big happy family" is how many leaders described River City, and as Dean (1967) commented, "Sticky as it may be," there was no question that the sentiment was genuine (p. 72). However, small insular communities, although a solution to disconnectedness and anomie, do realistically limit freedom—the Gopher Prairie syndrome—a matter well illustrated, for example, in the excerpt from Valerie Sayers's (1987c) *Due East* (see "Services" on pp. 162–165). Yet, many people will gladly trade social freedom from constraints for intimacy and personal belonging.

Nonetheless, decentralization and manageable size are prerequisites for building personal communities wherein individuals can find the sense of significance—an important element in combating anomie. Large communities are not intrinsically bad, but, as E. F. Schumacher (1973) contended, for every kind of activity or endeavor there is an appropriate scale.

> What I wish to emphasize is the duality of the human requirement when it comes to the question of size: there is no single answer. For his different purposes man needs many different structures, both small ones and large ones, some exclusive and some comprehensive. Yet people find it most difficult to keep two seemingly opposite necessities of truth in their minds at the same time. They always tend to clamor for a final solution, as if in actual life there could ever be a final solution. . . . For constructive work, the principal task is always the restoration of some kind of balance.

> Today, we suffer from an almost universal idolatry of giantism. It is therefore necessary to insist on the virtues of smallness—where this applies. (If there were a prevailing idolatry of smallness, irrespective of subject or purpose, one would have to try and exercise influence in the opposite direction.) (pp. 65–66)

What might be an efficient type of structure for economic gains in the modern industrial world might be an altogether meaningless or counterproductive unit when individuals are interested in seeking personal or psychosocial solutions to their existence.

If what people are seeking is community as a personal solution, it becomes apparent that their disconnectedness is not going to be remedied in large units wherein they will continue to experience a lack of personal significance. Rather, it is in the smaller units that people probably can achieve recognition and social support. However, if the limitations community places on an individual's freedom result in his or her unhappiness and estrangement, then a community that is a small unit is not the solution. Human services workers need to identify the community that might represent their client's personally manageable and meaningful unit. Because the community of child welfare workers is geographically dispersed, and the heterogeneity of culture and mores extends beyond one area, child welfare workers cannot capitalize on community resources or enlist any population in their efforts. A recent study of preferences for personal social services among farm families addressed the issue of location (Martinez-Brawley & Blundall, 1989).

> Assuming that the family decided to consult a professional helper or social agency, [family] members were asked to discuss their preferences for location of the agency. A helpful hint was given: would you prefer it to be inside or outside your local community? . . . Community appeared to be defined according to parameters within which farmers need not feel powerless or second class.
>
> Overall, most families stated that they would prefer an agency within their local community. . . . [They] did not want to drive more than 30 miles. In relation to the specifics of the locale, most people expressed a preference for multiservice type buildings, suggesting that no one would then know why the family (or person) was going into the building. (p. 518)

Professionals cannot in a vacuum calculate the size of a community and provide a generalizable prescription, but, as Schumacher advanced, in practice, they can learn to trust their intuition or clinical judgments.

The issue of the appropriate size of a city has fascinated philosophers and planners through the centuries. Ebenezer Howard, precursor of the English and perhaps even the American New Towns movement initiated in the late 19th century, struggled with the notion of size and offered his blueprint for the ideal "Garden City." In his perspective, Howard wanted to create a Garden City that would combine the best elements of city and country; he proposed the maximum number of 30,000 people to inhabit a nucleus of 1,000 acres surrounded by an agricultural belt of 5,000 (Petersen, 1968, p. 160). Other philosophers and planners from Josiah Royce, the 19th century idealist thinker, to Benton MacKaye, the 20th century conservationist, struggled with the ideal size of cities. Perhaps the lack of successful prescriptions further attests to the validity of Schumacher's proposition that people really do not know what is right, although, at least in relation to community as a personally meaningful unit, experience has shown that for most people the community unit should not be too large. "A real community for me," wrote Keyes (1973), "a safe one, can't be comfortable with too many members. There's definitely a limit to the size of the group in which I can feel comfortable" (p. 175).

Qualitatively, the sense of personal identity derived from communities of a manageable size is different from the sense of identity that can be derived from other, larger units, such as professional or ethnic communities. The Gemeinschaft gives individuals inner direction. However, the community of interest gives individuals direction in relation to others; it addresses the outer image. At the level of the Gemeinschaft, people become familiar with each other's quirks (see, for example, "It's a New Day in State Center, but What Will Life Be Like at Dusk?" on pp. 130–136, "A Pretty Girl" on p. 151, and "Talk at the Gas Station" on pp. 151–154). Each person's identity becomes recognizably public and lives are shared experiences in all their facets. The following story told by Keyes (1973) illustrates how public identities can become:

> I wrote the final draft of this manuscript in a little California town called Comptche. To call Comptche a town is a presumption. Downtown consists of one small store and post office. . . . Comptche's few score residents are scattered on outlying farms.
>
> Though I'd find it hard to live here the year round, several things impress me about Comptche. The store owner asks for no I.D. to cash a check. She knows who I am. Though the post office is tiny, and the postlady anything but a model of brisk efficiency, I find myself far more sure than in the city that she will get my letters where they're going. The postlady knows me, my name, where I live, why I'm here, and the fact that I'm always getting magazines Postage Due. I get a much greater feeling of trust from that than from the brisk professionalism of the vaguely familiar faces at one of six counters of my post office in San Diego.
>
> One time, a sign appeared on the post office bulletin board saying: "The wedding is on for July 21st." The next day that sign was down and another had taken its place, reading "The wedding is postponed till July 28th." Nothing more. *That's* being known. (p. 173)

In the community of interests, only one aspect of people's lives is shared with the collective—each person becomes known in a single-dimensional way (for example, by professional accomplishments and benevolent deeds).

In Gemeinschaft, each person becomes known for the sum total of his or her idiosyncrasies.

Post offices have been notoriously accurate barometers of the heartbeat and connectedness of communities. They have been centers through which individual members become known to their community. These identity-givers on occasion have demanded loyalty from community members. In the following case (Margolis, 1980), a local post office demanded unqualified support, and community members reciprocated, putting their "cash" on the line:

> The rural post office frequently helps to reduce isolation and sustain community. Such connections are far from abstract. When the residents of Lemont, Pennsylvania, opposed a plan to move their post office from the town's center to its outskirts. . . , so strongly did the citizens of Lemont feel about the location of their post office that when push came to shove, more than 300 of them donated $8,000 for work the contractor had already undertaken on a new objectionable site; it was the Postal Service's price for calling off the project. (p. 28)

Because they are small and individuals are known, personal communities often make serious demands on the citizenry. Despite these demands, people continue to search for communities of a "manageable size." The communities that have grown and continue to grow, as reported by sources for national statistics and by the press, are small rural towns with accessible economic resources, such as high-tech industries or proximity to metropolitan centers where work is available. Although people might resign themselves to work in impersonal environments, they still prefer to live in highly personalized ones.

PAROCHIALISM AND SIZE

Because size is an important variable in the maintenance of personal solutions, community members often will keep outsiders at bay. Perhaps the rejection of outsiders by small-town dwellers is based on an intuitive knowledge and desire to keep the numbers small to avoid a loss of local identity. The tension between "insiders" and "outsiders" in small communities often gives meaning to much social interaction. The tension must be seen in functional as well as dysfunctional terms for both the individuals and the group (see, for example, "Our Town in 1981" on pp. 123–124). To maintain community, even the most progressive individuals safeguard size and manageability.

Minority communities, for example, often are cautious of newcomers and outsiders, just as much as majority communities often are of minorities.

Although those people who have been ostracized might not themselves ostracize outsiders, all communities safeguard themselves from outside forces impinging on the communal unit (see, for example, "Arriving in Eatonville, Florida" on pp. 118–119 and "It's a New Day in State Center, but What Will Life Be Like at Dusk?" on pp. 130–136).

Students of the "commune movement" of the late 1960s and 1970s noted that many of the communes that survived in a somewhat permanent fashion protected themselves from "permanent intruders." Berger (1981) described this behavior in a somewhat typical rural California commune:

> The Ranch is not the kind of commune that is easily accessible or open to anyone who wants to crash—as, for example, Morningstar Ranch was, a place whose very openness and accessibility brought it widespread publicity (and disaster) in the early phase of the commune movement. . . . The Ranch protects its privacy rather well. . . . Although the signs at the gate to its access road are not encouraging ("No Trespassing"), visitors may be welcomed if they are friends of someone who lives there, or even friends of friends, but they are generally not welcome to stay for very long at least not without considerable discussion. (p. 24)

Similar exclusionary practices exist elsewhere. For example, in an article about the rebirth of small towns across America, Reese and Malamud (1981), two *Newsweek* reporters who noted a 32-percent growth in the population of Peterborough, New Hampshire, between 1970 and 1980, reported that

> the influx of people has forced the town to grapple with the question of growth. Partly due to the persistence of newcomers, Peterborough adopted zoning laws in 1970. Now, says Paul C. Cummings Jr., 67, publisher of *The Peterborough Transcript*, one of the two town newspapers, "No board has more life-and-death power in the town than the planning board." As a result, Peterborough has no flashing neon signs, no McDonald's and it retains the look and mood of a Grover's Corner. But Peterborough's slow growth policies have a less fortunate consequence: most housing is too costly for those who hold jobs in the area. (p. 28)

The dilemma is real—the town is trying to protect its size. The very characteristic that makes the town desirable also makes it rejecting. Town clerk Stella Sumner said that those who come to Peterborough are "searching for peace and quiet. They want closeness, sense of belonging" (Reese & Malamud, 1981, p. 28). Yet, to maintain this quality, which is the greatest asset of the town, the conflict between newcomers and old-timers might be exacerbated.

The parochial ways of small communities can be supportive or rejecting. New arrivals in Gemeinschaft prize the tangible sense of concern that is common to many. "This place has all the qualities of a small town. You smile at people and they are supportive," reported a newcomer to Crested Butte, Colorado (Morganthauw et al., 1981, p. 29). Others have recounted similar experiences. A couple who moved to an upstate Pennsylvania farm struggled through the bitter winter with meager resources but learned respect for the taciturn compassion of their neighbors who, in their own quiet and reserved way, responded to emergencies no matter how they felt about the newcomers. On the other hand, many more newcomers have observed how "neighborly courtesy doesn't always mean acceptance" and some migrants to small towns find themselves ignored and end up being resentful. "In Crested Butte, the town's cadre of older Croatian miners keeps its distance from the big-city arrivistes, and older newcomers can be hard on still newer arrivals" (Morganthauw et al., 1981, p. 29).

Unfortunately, parochialism is unavoidably viewed in negative terms. Although *parochial* simply means belonging to a parish or a locale, *parochialism* has come to mean narrow in scope and in spirit. Yet, a parochial attitude can include pride of place, which is an essential dimension in a healthy community. Examples of the positive and negative aspects of the parochial attitudes of small town folks are found in Fuson's "It's a New Day in State Center, but What Will Life Be Like at Dusk?" (pp. 130–136). On the positive side, State Center, Iowa, survived because of the pride of place of its inhabitants. On the negative side, the town suffered the consequences of the negative parochialism of the past. Because of the town's fears about outsiders (particularly racial minorities) decisions were made that hurt its finances. A positive corollary reported by Fuson was that the town dwellers themselves recognized the inherent problems and consequences of past discrimination.

Community in its most manageable size and Gemeinschaftlich dimensions presents social work practitioners with a philosophic dilemma. Although professional practitioners value openness, free access, and the routine welcoming of outsiders to existing social institutions, inevitably they are faced with making decisions that are exclusionary. Practitioners exclude people from services when the organizations can no longer absorb new arrivals efficiently. Practitioners withdraw support from those perceived to be the strongest clients when numbers grow overwhelmingly large. At the community level, when commitment to the survival of the unit clashes with the practitioner's inclusionary philosophy, he or she must be prepared to make considered judgments that are not inspired by arbitrary whims or discrimination but by pluralistic values. In the future, efficient professional intervention might be determined by how supportive practitioners can be of diverse groups in their unique searches for belonging and personal solutions. Social workers might well have to become interpreters of the ideal of community and advocates of the satisfaction of community building.

Social work does not have a proven record of success in helping build nurturing communities. For example, social workers have not been able to successfully get old-timers to welcome newcomers, or to relieve the distresses of the displaced. In efforts to be helpful to newcomers and the distressed, social workers perhaps have disregarded old-timers' fears and have aggravated antagonisms and created battles of will in which no one, in the end, could win. Perhaps as professionals, social workers might be more successful by acknowledging a community's desire to maintain some sense of collective control. This acknowledgment does not mean condoning the prejudicial exclusions of certain groups or the capricious monopolizing of certain resources. Rather, it means that social workers must become cognizant and realistic about the limitations of growth. As environmentalists have contended, one need not be for or against growth, but attuned to the idea of responsible growth—a concept social workers have tended to disregard in their professional enamoredness with vertical ties. Growth is often counterproductive to community sentiment (see, for example, "Lack of Teamwork Hinders State City's Fight to Survive" on pp. 137–141). However, social workers slowly are realizing that meaningful community ties are not imposed from without or willed by well-meaning practitioners. They are built slowly by "average" folks and require much personal nurturing and investment. Community, in the modern world, is a complex evolving and active concept that defies many existing assumptions and, consequently, requires constant reinterpretation.

COMMUNITIES AND FREEDOM

Just as manageable-size communities enhance a person's sense of meaning, belonging, and social support, they also demand a much greater degree of conformity and impose broader restrictions on one's freedom. People are the product of generations that have rebelled against the restrictions of community. This desire for freedom has become part of the very fiber of people's lives; yet, it also has resulted in the anomie people now seek to remedy.

Although current local communities might not be as extreme in their parochialism as Lewis's (1920b) Gopher Prairie or Sayers's (1987b) *Due East* (see discussion in chapter 5), they still are strict—the smaller the size, the stricter the rules that control the behavior of community members. Much of the struggle between insiders and outsiders in Gemeinschaft concerns issues of authority. By virtue of their experience in given settings, old-timers claim a degree of deference, respect, and adherence to prevailing codes of behavior that newcomers are often unwilling to grant. Even in permissive atmospheres, the situation often exists. For example, some of the communes that emerged in the 1960s disbanded precisely because of tension between community and conformity. Many of the early commune members wanted to share the "joy" of community but wanted also to give full expression to their individual freedom. With few exceptions, the reality was that the communal activity limited individual freedom. Communal activity necessitated adjustments and accommodations. "To deny the relations between community and conformity, to call them two different things," wrote Keyes (1973), "is to make community that much more difficult to achieve" (p. 182).

For many generations now, people have been conditioned to hold fast, at least intellectually, to a philosophy of ideas of individualism, believing that happiness can only be found in release from ties, in what people erroneously perceive as complete freedom. Nisbet (1953) documented how many 18th and 19th century liberal reformers forced an almost artificial dichotomy between individuals and society:

> The demands of freedom appear to be in the direction of the release of large numbers of individuals from the statuses and identities that had been forged in them by the dead hand of the past. A free society would be one in which individuals were morally and socially as well as politically free, free from groups and classes. It would be composed, in short, of socially and morally *separated* individuals. . . . Freedom would arise from the individual's release from all the inherited personal interdependences of traditional community, and from his existence in an impersonal, natural, economic order. (pp. 226–227)

Freedom as complete release from ties is not a viable alternative, because it denies part of the human condition. "An individual," wrote Slater (1976), "is a motley collection of ambivalent feelings, contradictory needs and values, and antithetical ideas. He is not, and cannot be, monolithic, and the modern effort to pretend otherwise is not only delusional and ridiculous, but also acutely destructive, both to the individual and to society" (p. 36).

Contemporary studies in social psychology and the experiences of millions have revealed that people cannot be self-sufficient in social isolation, that their "nature cannot be deduced simply from elements innate in the germ plasm, and that between man and such social groups as the family, local group, and interest association there is an indispensable connection" (Nisbet, 1953, p. 229). The philosophy of individualism might have been an answer at a time when societal institutions such as the family and the community required that individuals hold on to tradition and conformity. Currently, however, the main psychological malaise apparently is not a suffocation of belonging but an overwhelming lack of belonging. Individualistic incentives—whether to increase production, to improve the human condition, or to free one's time—become important only in the context of meaningful social relationships. John Dewey (1930) wrote a generation ago that individualism often "ignores the fact that the mental and moral structure of individuals, the pattern of their desires and purposes, change with every change in social constitution" (p. 81). According to Dewey, it would be absurd to suppose that the ties that hold individuals together in religious, political, artistic, domestic, or educational organizations are merely external. For Dewey, such ties affected the mentality and character of individuals, enhancing their disposition. Dewey saw negative conformity not as the result of too much communal interaction but rather as the result of an inner void. "Conformity is a name of the absence of vital interplay; the arrest and be numbing of communication. . . . It is the artificial substitute used to hold men together in lack of associations that are incorporated into inner dispositions of thoughts and desires" (pp. 85–86). Yet, he saw a positive side to conformity when he suggested that "conformity is enduringly effective when it is a spontaneous and largely unconscious manifestation of the agreements that spring from genuine communal life" (p. 87).

Small towns often are accepting of and find a special social role for the nonconformist member—the town's eccentric. In Tilling, E. F. Benson's (1977) fictional "picturesque" village somewhere in the south of England, the very strength of one of the characters known as "Quaint Irene" was that she was a gifted young painter who wore breeches and close-cropped hair and smoked a pipe. T. R. Pearson (1985a) humorously described the "peculiar" characters of his small North Carolina town with acceptance and even pride. He told of the advancing eccentricity of one community member:

> That was the day Miss Pettigrew stopped being just peculiar. She'd been peculiar ever since I'd heard of her and ever since I'd known what being peculiar meant, but now, when folks spoke of her they would say she was Not Right, which was an advancement of a sort. The town of Neely had seen a blue million peculiarities in its history, but those among its citizenry who were genuinely not right were rare and cherished. (p. 10)

"Individualism," wrote Slater (1976), "is rooted in the attempt to deny the reality of human interdependence" (p. 34). However, Slater noted that interdependence frees rather than enslaves; it enables one to find personal solutions.

In their daily work, human services workers may observe that the more a person fears being affected or controlled by or interdependent on others, the more that person suffers psychologically and socially. Those people who pathologically fear being governed or who, like adolescents, react adversely to the mere idea of dependence, feel such a degree of helplessness and need for dependence that they often require more governing, control, or care—often the case with institutionalized individuals. At all three levels of community living—the city, the neighborhood, and the family—individuals encounter restrictions on their freedom (Zablocki, 1971). Individuals are aware that belonging and "community-ness" might, in the long-run, represent curtailment of freedom as a release, but not necessarily curtailment of their social potential. The fullest potential of human beings is realized in associations and communal efforts. Even the blossoming of organized religion speaks of people's desires to strengthen the associative aspects of creed. The endurance and meaning of many religious groups cannot be divorced form the sense of earthly security and meaning they are able to provide. Their communally oriented messages and rituals help ease the individual's sense of isolation and provide ways of validating communal traditions.

Human services practitioners need to recognize that although those who are now seeking Gemeinschaft might intellectually understand and recognize the restrictions that communal living will place on them, at a deeper, affective level, they have difficulty comprehending what those limitations mean for each member's individualism. To be "in community" is to know and be part of other people's lives. More often than not, community members seek knowledge without malevolent agendas. For those people who have grown used to anonymity, the realization that others can curtail their behavior may be difficult for them to face. Commenting on Peterborough's newcomers, *Newsweek* (Reese & Malamud, 1981) quoted a native: "The biggest problem for many newcomers is simply adapting to Peterborough's old fashioned ways. . . . In a small town you cannot always speak your mind" (p. 28) or remain unidentifiable. For better or for worse, one's private actions are, in a general sense, communal actions. "The Peterborough Transcript," reported *Newsweek* (Reese & Malamud, 1981), "now lists births to unwed mothers along with marriages and deaths—while the town's annual report includes those who fail to pay their taxes" (p. 28).

Social workers have not always been trained to understand, be sympathetic to, and, appropriately respond to these freedom-impinging aspects of life in small communities. The education of practitioners has either ignored the real demands that community membership places on social workers or has been generally critical of the restrictions of such membership. Education of human services workers has wanted to recognize community but has failed to acknowledge the personal consequences of living in real communities on a day-to-day basis. In addition, the individualistic emphasis of education has taught students to react negatively to community demands. In a sense, the current trend toward Gemeinschaft and practice in local units has caught professionals by surprise; they often are unable to respond appropriately to what, in essence, are natural corollaries of practice in community. Some rural practitioners are aware of these dimensions. From them, social workers can learn what it means to practice in community:

> Social work in a rural setting offers the practitioner a variety of delights and difficulties because of the visibility of both client and worker. . . . The mental health center, where I have worked for 1 1/2 years, averages 300 cases per year. To give an idea of what that means for visibility of client and practitioner, when I went to a son's Little League game, I found three children on his team who were known to me through the clinic. As the season wore on and my family and the client's families spent evenings at the ball park together, the usual professional image was impossible to maintain. In a small community, we are, above all, neighbors. (Fenby, 1978, p. 162)

The sharing process involved in real community living can enhance the social worker's credibility as a human being. However, for those who persist in surrounding professional relationships by evasive mystique, practicing "in community" is not likely to prove satisfactory. Being in community represents a modification, if not a curtailment, of the degree of freedom for both the social worker and client. Yet, the understanding and sharing that both parties experience by their mutual communal experience can enhance the professional relationship and the degree of satisfaction the social worker and client derive from the contact.

It would be impossible for a social worker truly invested in community sentiment to maintain the traditional distance between social worker and client, an arrangement often dictated by bureaucracy. The current emphasis on service delivery at the local level necessitates that social workers demystify for the neophyte the nature of the professional relationship. The current demand that human services workers work with the community and use volunteers and community members requires that these workers look closely at the impositions on people's freedom that this model represents. Fenby (1978) illustrates what working in community really means in practice:

> Just as neighbors are often my clients, so also I am often theirs. When I go to a shop or for professional advice or to see my child's teacher, I am quite likely to run into someone I know as a client. The roles are reversed. Now I am the seeker and they are the helpers. Because of this, it is virtually impossible to maintain the role of the omnipotent therapist. (p. 163)

This very impossibility makes the nature of the professional's role in community all the more demanding.

However, community demands are not only positive; they also are negative. The public disclosures of private matters, the gossip, the prejudgments are a reality and an inevitable part of what people encounter when they seek to live and work in "personal" communities. Yet, a community's curtailment of an individual's freedom is similar to a social workers' curtailment of a client's self-determination. Both concepts, freedom and self-determination, exist not in a vacuum but within the parameters of social demand and gregarious coexistence aided and abetted by local cultural norms and values.

OCCUPATIONAL/PROFESSIONAL AND RACIAL/ETHNIC COMMUNITIES

Other levels of community at which people partially satisfy their need for identity and significance are the occupational/professional, affiliational, and racial/ethnic communities (or "communities of interest"). The nature of the relationship between local community and other structured communal units has interested scholars for many decades. In terms of the affiliational community or community of interest, for example, Simmel (1950) studied secret societies and extreme political parties; Zablocki (1971) studied the relationships of members of the Bruderhof, a religious sect then in its third generation. Other social scientists have explored the unique ties that bind members of churches (Riesman, 1955), labor unions, and businesses. These scholars have found that communal linkages must be translated, qualified, and changed in analyzing communities that are dispersed within the larger society. In essence, one must focus on vertical linkages while still characterizing and addressing the sense of significance and identity generally derived from horizontal ties.

The analysis of the more unusual forms of communal units is outside the scope of this discussion. The focus instead is on the professional/occupational and racial/ethnic communities, which are the communities most likely to attract the attention of human services practitioners. A professional community, according to Goode (1957), is

> community without physical locus, and like other communities with heavy inmigration, one whose founding fathers are linked rarely by blood with the present generation. It may, nevertheless be called a community by virtue of these characteristics: (1) Its members are bound by a sense of identity. (2) Once in it, few leave so that it is a terminal or continuing status for the most part. (3) Its members share values

> in common. (4) Its role definitions vis-à-vis both members and non-members are agreed upon and are the same for all members. (5) Within the area of communal action, there is a common language which is understood only partially by outsiders. (6) The community has power over its members. (7) Its limits are reasonably clear, though they are not physical and geographical but social. (8) Though it does not produce the next generation biologically, it does so socially through its control over the selection of professional trainees, and through its training processes it sends these recruits through an adult socialization process. (p. 194)

These characteristics also apply to racial/ethnic communities, except for characteristic 8, because racial/ethnic communities produce their next generations biologically and are unable to choose or train their members in any selective sense. The development by schooling among certain groups is generally the result of natural child-rearing practices and seldom an adult-socialization process.

For many people in modern society, occupational/professional and racial/ethnic communities constitute a source of identity and significance and community as a personal solution. Many observers have viewed community of interest as a poor substitute for other forms of communities that, consequently, were seen as doomed. However, because community in its more tangible and traditional sense of Gemeinschaft is anything but dead, these other communal units can be viewed in a different light because they offer types of rewards that differ from those of the intimate Gemeinschaft. It is perhaps at the local level that the affiliational community offers its members the most. Although generally most members of a racial/ethnic group or an occupational/professional body would identify with an affiliational community on a national or even worldwide basis (for example the worldwide Jewish, black, Hispanic, medical, or social work communities), it is at the more circumscribed level of the region or the immediate locale that identity ties are strongest. For example, although individual Jews will express solidarity with the worldwide Jewish community, they are likely to be more concretely identified with the Jewish community of their particular area, because it provides a more tangible system of supports than the Jewish community in the abstract. Even within the parameters of a closely related group, Hispanics or Latinos in the United States, for example, have tended to identify themselves with particular regions of origin (for example, Puerto Ricans, Mexicans, Colombians, and Cubans). They have developed their most cohesive community sentiments that way, a matter of political concern for those who see the need for broad unity of subgroups in attaining political goals.

In relation to the affiliational community, Freeman (1973) wrote that despite what authors have said, those people who joined the women's rights movement were not people "atomized and isolated" from intermediate structures between the family and the nation, but rather were those who participated in intermediate communication networks—in communal networks.

> The most serious attack on mass-society theory was made by Pinard. . . . He concluded that intermediate structures exerted mobilizing as well as restraining effects on individuals' participation in social movements because they found communication networks that assisted in the rapid spread of new ideas. (p. 41)

Historical data corroborate the existence of communal intermediate ties, at least in the United States, among the precursors of the women's rights movement who met at Seneca Falls in 1890.

An individual's sense of identity is nourished through a number of concentric spheres of "communal participation." At the most global level, a member might experience some sense of community as he or she identifies with the goals and images of a worldwide or national group. At a narrower level (for example the state or region), a member might express solidarity with yet another more meaningful and tangible set of symbols and aspirations. At an even more circumscribed level (for example the local area), a member's community sentiment and identity are translated into a personal set of rewards and obligations. A Hispanic or Latino American in the United States, for example, experiences different degrees of collective identity at the national, regional, local, and specific subgroup levels. Although that person might enhance his or her sense of identity as he or she embraces membership in the national Hispanic or Latino community, he or she might gain further support from shared experiences at the regional level (for example, Mexican Americans in the Southwest), or at the local or subgroup levels (such as Chicanos in San Jose, Puerto Ricans in New York City, Cubans in Miami, and Colombians in Washington, D.C.). Likewise, black people would identify with various West Indian or Caribbean communities. Local, regional, and national groups represent sources of strength and identity, but the degree of binding at the communal ties varies with the level and consequent intimacy of the interaction.

Traditionally, social scientists have viewed participation in the affiliational community as antagonistic to participation in Gemeinschaft. They have seen individuals who have fervently cultivated their ties to communities of interest as evidence of a decline of other forms of community. For example, Zablocki (1971) lamented that

> for many people, the neighborhood or home town has given way to the community of interest. With the automobile and the telephone, it is probably easier for people of common interest to find one another, and spend time together, than ever before in history. Such communities of interests are a kind of intentional community, but they

> fall short of satisfying the human need for communal relationships. For one thing, an individual characteristically belongs, not to one, but to a number of different communities of interest. Since relationships between members of such interest groups tend to be sequential and transitory, their members tend to avoid becoming deeply dependent on one another. Another problem stems from the fact that communities of interest often have no physical center or boundaries. . . . This sort of community lacks any sense of permanence beyond the motivations of individual members. Under such circumstances one would not expect to find the kind of friendship and belonging that comes from the sharing of pains and pleasures over a long period of time. . . . The major problem seems to be finding some way to . . . rid themselves of some of the surplus freedom with which their senses have been overwhelmed. (pp. 293–294)

Some of Zablocki's concerns are probably well-founded—for example, many people, unable to find psychosocial solutions for their anxieties in more intimate communal forms, might seek the substitute of the community of interest. However, participation in one or many communities of interest can be seen as complementing (rather than supplanting) an individual's membership in Gemeinschaft. The thousands, according to the 1980 census (*Statistical Abstract of the United States: 1980*, 1981), who have flocked to small towns and villages probably are members of a variety of affiliational, occupational/professional, and racial/ethnic communities; yet, they still seek the ties of solidarity and significance that more likely are found in intimate, traditional, multi-interest groups.

When the now rejected notions of the "melting pot" in American society were in vogue, strong identification with racial/ethnic communities was seen as a threat to successful engagement in other more "normative" types of communal units. Symbols of identification, such as language and rituals, among members of racial/ethnic communities were discouraged, and dual belonging in the ethnic and the local community was suspect. Many members of ethnic groups lived in ethnic Gemeinschaft, thus bypassing altogether the issue of biculturality, because their radius of personal commitment was that of the community of residence alone (see "Getting There" on pp. 120–122). However, having been rejected, racial/ethnic groups often used their shared sense of hardship as a tool for building the cohesive protective communities their members required for survival. Just as the outside world frowned upon contacts with members of ethnic pockets, attempts by members of ethnic groups to make commitments outside the group also were regarded with reservation (see, for example, "It's a New Day in State Center, but What Will Life Be Like at Dusk?" on pp. 130–136). "Hillbillies" huddled together in the safety of special neighborhoods or bars; Hispanic or Latino Americans had their barrios; black people, their "harlems," or rural pockets or urban confines.

As American societal emphases have shifted in the direction of recognizing and appreciating pluralism and diversity, people have begun to recognize that membership in racial/ethnic communities, similar to membership in the community of interest, need not exclude members of a particular group from sharing in building of community with diverse people. Today, people must rise to the challenge of building meaningful, accepting communities within pluralistic structures, a need that transcends the boundaries of the United States. The enhanced sense of racial/ethnic consciousness of all groups should be used to help build nurturing, yet diverse communities. The Gemeinschaften of the 1990s can be tolerant of outsiders, yet remain manageable in size. They must recognize unique cultural traditions, yet be open to enrichment. It is perhaps in the achievement of these complex goals that human services practitioners who are well prepared to understand communities can play a facilitative role.

COMMUNITY: A BALANCING FORCE FOR ANOMIE

Communities provide meaning, a sense of belonging, and well-being among people. A positive sense of community is seen by sociologists and psychologists as a balancing force for anomie, the sociological disease of contemporary individuals. The enormous growth of support groups—from farmers' groups to mothers' groups—attest to the need people have for finding units of social interaction that take on community responsibilities when "natural" communities do not offer support. The larger the unit of social interaction in which people live their daily lives—such as large cities—the more people seek intimacy and solidarity from groups that recreate the natural community environment. Although the typical inhabitant of megalopolis might find it difficult to explain, many contemporary individuals are willing to trade their free and anonymous environments for the greater warmth of the more restrictive small community.

People have searched for community as a psychological healer or personal solution. Utopians have created artificial communities on religious, sociopolitical, or philosophic grounds. Some utopian experiments—the Amish and the Amana, for example—have been successful. Others have been fraught with problems and tensions resulting from the influx of outsiders into unsuspecting and unprepared small towns. Community as a personal solution apparently can only be found in an intimate unit. Many towns have attempted to protect their size and thus have discriminated against outsiders. Although protection of size does not justify exclusivity, social services practitioners need to understand the threat that the influx of outsiders might represent to many small-town residents. People are threatened not only because of their parochial views but also by the loss of community that results from expansion.

Human services practitioners have known for a long time that small communities enhance people's sense of well-being, meaning, and participation, but also curtail the freedom of their inhabitants. Small-town dwellers surrender some of their individual freedom for a sense of significance. A positive relationship exists between belonging and conformity. Yet, the paradox is that small towns and villages, although they demand conformity, have been known to tolerate eccentricity or peculiarity. Eccentrics often have played important social roles within the structure of relationships in small towns.

People also can satisfy their need for identity in occupational/professional and racial/ethnic communities, which enhance the sense of meaning and significance of their members. Although vertical communities have not been the object of study, they are important in terms of the local scheme. Generally, people who belong to large racial, ethnic, professional, or other types of vertical communities identify with local units that fulfill their need for identity and belonging.

3

POWER, INFLUENCE, AND LEADERSHIP IN THE SMALL COMMUNITY

The study of specific variables in communities has been a common research approach among sociologists. Power and decision making, the central themes of this chapter, are two such variables that have been pivotal in a number of community investigations. For decades, social scientists have been fascinated by the potential of researchers of community power to identify other community characteristics. The most classic example was perhaps Hunter (1953), who sought to understand "Regional City" (thought to be Atlanta, Georgia) through his investigations:

> I shall be using the concept of community as a frame of reference for an analysis of power relations. This is done because of a strong conviction that the community is a primary power center and because it is a place in which power relations can be most easily observed. (p. 11)

Social workers and other human services providers have learned that a thorough knowledge of people and structures that promote or interfere with community decision making is essential to their understanding of community units and to their professional functioning. Thus, the study of power, influence, and leadership is at the core of the preparation of community practitioners. In the small communities across the United States, an understanding of the intricate pattern of power relationships is a prerequisite for effective practice.

OVERVIEW OF THE BASIC CONCEPTS

A distinction should be drawn between *power*, the abstract capacity, the potential to affect the course of events in particular communities, and *influence*, the concrete, operational capability of actually swaying the course of specific actions. For many years, the study of community power and influence was obfuscated by researchers' confusion between the two concepts. In the late 1960s, a number of students of community clarified their meanings. "Power refers to potential but not necessarily exerted influence. Influence is conceived as the making of decisions that cause change" (Magill & Clark, 1975, p. 35). *Powerful actors* are people who have the potential to exert influence, *influentials* are people who do exert influence, and *leaders* are people who exert influence by mobilizing others to join in their causes (see, for example, how Carol Kennicott eventually decided to mobilize Gopher Prairie through the lady members of the Thanatopsis Club in "My Dear, You Must Really Come to the Thanatopsis This Afternoon" on pp. 113–116).

> Leadership refers to a complex process whereby a relatively small number of individuals in a collectivity behave in such a way that they effect (or effectively prevent) a change in the lives of a relatively large number. (Freeman, Fararo, Bloomberg, & Sunshine, 1968, p. 189)

Although powerful actors, influentials, and leaders can be the same people, the attributes of power, influence, and leadership do not necessarily have to be embodied in the same individuals. Whether the same people are identified as powerful and influential and carry out the charismatic leadership role in a given instance indicates the degree of elitism or pluralism in a particular community. Certain approaches to the investigation of power holders in a community, for example, *reputational studies*, tend to help identify powerful actors; others, such as *decisional studies*, tend to render information on community influentials and leaders.

In his study of power, race, and privilege, Wilson (1973) proposed the use of two similarly distinctive terms for the concepts of power and influence. They were "power ability"—what here is called "power"—and "active power"—that is, "the actual exercising of influence by Group A over Group B such that the behavior of Group B is modified in accordance with the wishes of Group A" (Wilson, 1973, p. 15). The influence or active power of one group over another is not simply the result of the overt efforts of the influential (superordinate) over the subordinate or controlled group. The behavior of subordinates (whether individuals or groups) can be modified simply by what they perceive to be the influentials' power ability or command of power resources:

> Broadly defined, power resources have to do with the properties that determine the scope and degree of the group's [the superordinates' or influentials'] ability to influence behavior. These properties could include high social status, reputation for power, capability to bear arms, control of political office, control of mass media, wealth and land ownership. . . . Generally, inducement and persuasion resources are applied by groups that have placed themselves in a position whereby they can often influence another group without resorting to threats or penalties (i.e., constraint or pressure resources). (Wilson, 1973, p. 16)

A group can have influence because it is perceived to have power or access to power resources. This perception may reinforce existing patterns of power distribution, a situation that often exists in small communities where perceptions are widely and easily divulged. Saul Alinsky (1971) observed that power is not really what a group has but rather what its enemies think it has, thus stressing the complicated relationship between power, the abstract capacity, and influence. That power and influence are affected by public perceptions is a fundamental point human services workers need to understand. Inertia on the part of workers, clients, or community members is often related to their perceptions. If a group perceives itself as noninfluential, it is rarely possible for it to muster enough energy or to tap enough resources to take action. Often the social worker in the community must modify perceptions as an encouragement even to modest action.

An example of the effect of public perceptions is the film about the black experience—"The Autobiography of Miss Jane Pitman" (Columbia Broadcasting System, 1974). In a moving scene depicting the return of young Jimmy to the black church of the small Louisiana town of his parents during the early Civil Rights struggles of the 1960s, the viewer is confronted with two clearly different perceptions of the power black people could exert at the time. As Jimmy assertively addresses the small congregation, the issue of perception of power becomes highlighted. The congregation's apparent lethargy, a result of historical experiences and perceived powerlessness, is contrasted with Jimmy's strident calls for action, a result of his different perception of the group's capabilities even under those oppressive and traumatic circumstances. The recent blossoming of groups such as Mothers Against Drunk Drivers (MADD) also is the direct result of small, unobtrusive groups developing the feeling that they can organize and make a difference.

Conservation and ecology groups are other examples of influential groups. In one small village, a former powerful mine owner and current landfill operator attempted to sell additional, strip-mined land for landfill waste disposal sites. To complicate matters, the former mine owner was reputed to have been a benevolent employer; citizens of the town felt grateful to him because of his actions when the coal industry was suffering. In early attempts, a group of ecologically minded citizens were able to stop the sale not because they held much power in the town but because they were able to activate enough verbal people to be perceived as a powerful threat. They were able to become influential. However, such displays of influence can be short-lived, particularly if the group is perceived to be ad hoc. In the same village years later, the former mine owner, fueled by a long period of economic depression, revived the issue of the expanded landfill sites. The task for those citizens who influenced the decision to stop the first sale was to regroup. People or groups who influence decisions without being part of the power elite often are forced to become watchdogs.

PRACTITIONERS AND SMALL-TOWN POWER HOLDERS

Just as social workers must play a role in highlighting the potential influence various groups can exert through a variety of means, from voting to forming coalitions, they also must recognize any extraordinary, undue optimism that results from their own political naivete. Human services workers usually are deeply committed to the democratic process and can easily miscalculate the influence of the franchise in community change. Although in democratic societies power (in the sense of potential to influence) exists in the franchise, actual and particularly long-lasting influence might result from, for example, powerful lobbies that do not necessarily represent "majority" views.

Even sophisticated political scientists have assumed that two parallel, equally forceful systems of power and, consequently, of influence exist. One is based on wealth or command of resources and one on votes. These assumptions often have proved erroneous, and empirical investigations have concluded that "nothing categorical can be assumed about power [or influence] in any community" (Polsby, 1960, p. 476). Piven and Cloward (1977) supported this conclusion:

> In the 1960's the dominant pluralist tradition was discredited, at least among those on the ideological left who were prodded by outbreaks of defiance among minorities and students to question this perspective. In the critique that emerged it was argued that there were not two systems of power, but that the power rooted in wealth and force overwhelmed the power of the franchise. The pluralists had erred, the critics said, by failing to recognize the manifold ways in which wealth and its concomitants engulfed electoral-representative procedures, effectively barring many people from participation while deluding and entrapping others into predetermined electoral choices. The pluralists had also erred by ignoring the consistent bias toward the interests of elites inherent in presumably neutral governing structures, no matter what the mandate of the electorate. (pp. 2–3)

Piven and Cloward (1982) also examined the historical explanations for this situation, which they saw as the peculiar U.S. democratic/capitalistic puzzle:

> The great anomaly arises in the United States, for nowhere else did the working class have so little political power, and yet nowhere else were its formal rights so extensive

> at so early a stage of capitalistic development. This is the puzzle that demands explanation. How was it possible for capital to triumph, and to triumph so fully, in the context of the most fully developed democratic laws in the world?
>
> The men of property who set out to create a new government following the revolution were as apprehensive as their English counterparts to the threat to property posed by mass enfranchisement. (p. 70)

According to Piven and Cloward (1982), the answer for the founding fathers was elaborate organizational arrangements in the newly founded representative government:

> The wondrous intricacies that resulted are familiar: an elaborate arrangement of checks and balances . . . intended to check what Hamilton called the imprudence of democracy . . . indirect elections . . . and the outright denial of the franchise to women, the unprotected, Blacks and Indians. (p. 72)

Without embracing necessarily a particular ideological position, human services workers must be at least familiar with the ways in which the power of the franchise has been curbed through the centuries, from old-fashioned coercion and fraud in electoral politics, to the more subtle and sophisticated practices of high-cost election procedures, to powerful lobbies that, in the end, minimize party or philosophical differences of the elected leadership.

Although researchers have documented a significant increase in the number of women who can be identified both as politicians and power actors, generally women influentials were found in traditionally nurturing or expressive issue areas (health, welfare, human rights, and the environment). Studies by Bell, Hill, and Wright (1961) and Constantini and Clark (1973) documented the existence of fixed sex roles in rural communities, which determined the lower participation of women at least in the political leadership. A more recent study by Bokemeier and Tait (1980) accurately clarified the distinction between politician and power actor, with the power actor possessing a broader and more varied role in the decision-making process. Although these researchers document that the prospect for the increase in women power actors is excellent, small communities in particular are slow to operationalize changes and to substitute social attitudes (see, for example, "New Democracy Tries to Take Root" on pp. 185–186).

Although more women have gained access to important positions in the health and welfare arenas and a number of business and political offices have opened up to them, many small communities have not yet significantly assimilated women in the established decision-making ranks (see, for example, "Where Governing Is 'Women's Work' " on pp. 205–208). Many female social workers or human services providers might experience difficulty interacting with power figures who do not share their convictions and commitments to gender equality.

Wilson (1973) suggested that a group's command of power resources or a group's ability to influence "should be considered in terms of their liquidity, that is, the extent to which they can be deployed or mobilized to exert influence" (p. 17) in a particular situation. Some resources can be deployed easily and quickly for particular purposes but not for others. For example, during the Civil Rights struggle, the legal machinery of the National Association for the Advancement of Colored People was (and still is) an effective resource to be deployed to win civil rights court cases (Wilson, 1973, p. 17). The same resources, for example, might not be influential in a boycott of products of companies that discriminate. Thus, influence is particularistic; abstract power, or power ability, is affected by perception and assumed to be broader in scope.

In this sense, people and human services workers in small communities are at both an advantage and a disadvantage. They are at an advantage because they often can mobilize more readily through town meetings, petitions, and open forums to influence particular decisions. They are at a disadvantage because the influentials are often the same people as the powerful actors (see, for example, "Mountaintop-Area Citizens Question Plans for Landfill" on pp. 197–198).

In a small town, support or opposition to a particular issue might have broader consequences than expected for the human services worker or administrator because he or she will be seen as supporting or opposing the individuals involved in the decision and not just the decision itself. For example, in one small university town, the powerful actors who represent the university's perspective on environmental or developmental issues are the same people who sit on the hospital board, make decisions for United Way allocations, and so forth. Their influence on particular issues cannot be divorced from their broader effect or place on the power structure. However, human services workers should not become passive or paralyzed from influencing small-town decisions. On the contrary, the key to success in small-town political interventions is a heightened awareness of the interconnections of people in Gemeinschaft. Those who make decisions know that the same awareness is required of them if they are to remain influentials.

In addition, the amount of leverage or influence a particular group may have on a given issue will depend on the circumstances that surround the process (Piven and Cloward, 1977). A group's influence will be determined minimally by how crucial the group's contribution or withholding is to others in the community. A group that provides noncrucial services, for example, can seldom influence outcomes through withholding services; those providing crucial services can. For example, a strike by teachers is less likely to be influential than one by nurses. Another determination of a group's influence is how realistic the issues at hand are in terms of gaining concessions. Because influence is particularistic, the narrower the issue the more feasible the concessions vis-à-vis the overall community equilibrium. For example, a group of human services workers is more likely to influence county commissioners about the use of a public swimming pool by retarded people or by a group of delinquent youths than it is to obtain, at once, the use of all public recreational facilities for the same group. Realistically, social change is more likely to be incremental than all-encompassing or radical. Particularly in small towns and rural areas, the value base of the population militates against all-encompassing and sudden changes. Although more applicable to protest movements than to the influence desired by human services workers, influence also depends on a group's (or person's) ability to protect itself from reprisals. It is hardly beneficial to gain influence in one area only to have to make immediate, costly concessions in another.

Although power is distinct from influence, and leadership is a corollary of influence, the three are interactive in the reality of community events. Although these concepts (particularly power and influence) often, at least for study purposes, are considered separately, practitioners must consider their complementary nature in effecting community outcomes, particularly in the small communities. Social workers have concluded that even the most undramatic community intervention has potential for affecting the way in which community decisions are made and might be perceived as impinging, positively or negatively, on the interests of various community groups. The development of a cooperative day care center in a small community, for example, might be viewed as affecting the business interests of middle-class day care or nursery school entrepreneurs, who might have had a monopoly on the provision of such services. On an even smaller scale, the decision of a worker, supervisor, or administrator of a child welfare agency, for example, to purchase day care from one entrepreneur versus another can represent threat or support for existing community power and leadership groups. Yet, these are not dramatic interventions, but rather daily occurrences in the field.

All community practitioners, whether directly involved in community projects or indirectly involved in community life through the lives of the individual clients they counsel, quickly learn that they must be familiar with the power and decision-making structures of the communities in which they function. Disregard or inattention to the power ability of community actors can result in damage to the outcome of specific projects and in curtailment of the human services worker's capacity to effectively mobilize community resources. Such damage occurred in many small towns across the country when community mental health centers, for example, began the movement toward deinstitutionalization. Because of lower property values in small towns, large homes in need of renovation were earmarked for halfway or transitional facilities for mentally ill or retarded people. Many power actors in small towns often organized opposition to such moves either because of personal interests (property values always being a concern) or because they had not been identified and coopted in advance by the human services administrators, who often miscalculated the scope of influence of such power actors.

In small communities, social workers and human services practitioners need not be active organizers to come in contact with the powerful, with influentials, and with leaders of communities. Social and human services workers often will be involved in agencies whose boards are examples of the power, influence, or leadership structures of their communities. Human services workers in small communities will invariably find themselves persuading, collaborating, coopting, or perhaps opposing community leaders in relation to social services decisions. Perhaps social workers might find themselves initiating proposals that then might be followed to fruition by community leaders, while the human services practitioner becomes the energizer, harmonizer, or expediter of the project. Social and human services workers must be able to identify and appraise the presence and position of power actors in the community whether they be friends, marginal observers, or foes to the social work cause.

Social workers as professionals often find themselves in the position of being "special interests" in small towns. The advent of the social worker as an entrepreneur or private practitioner has resulted in many problems with vested interests in small towns. Awarding contracts for psychotherapy to mental health providers, training contracts in child welfare, or foster care contracts to entrepreneurial groups that sell foster care to public agencies all have become areas fraught with the tensions of vested interests. The public sector social worker who is related to the entrepreneurial contractor for his or her agency is not unusual. Pressure and favoritism among professionals in the competitive arena are relatively new phenomena that practitioners, administrators, and public service watch groups need to be aware of and avoid. Moral persuasion on behalf of clients or groups will not be convincing in small towns if local officials or other power holders know that the professionals have been guilty parties in surrendering to the pressure interest groups.

MODELS OF COMMUNITY POWER: ELITISM AND PLURALISM

Scholars who have investigated the structure and function of communities in relation to power and decision making primarily have come from the sociology and political science disciplines. Unfortunately, their findings have not always agreed. From a pragmatic stance, it is important to understand the contributions of various models and viewpoints. Many early community studies, although not directly concerned with the power structure, recorded lasting observations on the leadership patterns of small towns. *Middletown* (Lynd & Lynd, 1929) and *Middletown in Transition* (Lynd & Lynd, 1937), the two famous studies of Muncie, Indiana, by a team of early sociologists, were seminal to the development of community studies in sociology. Although these books have been criticized by more contemporary sociologists for lack of a well-ordered theoretical structure (Bell & Newby, 1972; Madge, 1963), the Lynds introduced observations on how power functioned within the structure of the small town. In *Middletown in Transition*, the Lynds observed the pervasive influence of a single family in the town:

> After ten years' absence from the city, one thing struck the returning observer again and again: the increasing large public benefactions and the increasing pervasiveness of power of this wealthy family of manufacturers whose local position . . . is becoming hereditary with the emergence of a second *generation of sons*. (Lynd & Lynd, 1937, pp. 74–75)

Although the Lynds showed that many of the points of control were public spirited, that they often revealed a family's willingness to help with local problems, and that leadership and control often would be forced upon the family by circumstances (or public perceptions), it was apparent to the Lynds that the lines of leadership and control were highly concentrated (Bell & Newby, 1972, p. 88). The structure of power in Muncie was clearly visible.

The Lynds also observed the changing nature of the power elite. These observations continue to be valid:

> Every American city has its successful businessmen, but the American success story has been kaleidoscopic in recent years. Local giants, the boys who have grown up with the town and made good, have shrunk in stature as rapid technological changes, the heavy capital demands of nation-wide distribution, and shifts in the strategic centers for low-cost production in a national market have undercut the earlier advantages of location, priority in the field, or energy; and as Eastern capital has forced them out or bought them out and reduced them to the status of salaried men, or retired them outright in favor of imported managements. One can classify American small

> manufacturing cities into two groups: Those in which the industrial pioneers or their sons still dominate the local business scene, and those in which "new blood" has taken over the leadership; and it is likely that a census would show today a numerical predominance of the second group among cities containing major industries. (Lynd & Lynd, 1937, p. 76)

However, the term "power structure" was not actually coined and used broadly until 1953 when Floyd Hunter, a political scientist, published *Community Power Structure* (Hunter, 1953). Since that time, numerous studies of power have been conducted by sociologists and political scientists. The many studies have not necessarily contributed to the conceptual clarity of the problem: terms such as "power," "influence," "leadership," and "decision making" often have been defined imprecisely. Yet, what has emerged is a clear demarcation between proponents of two models or explanations of how power, influence, and leadership are distributed in communities. These two explanatory models, elitism and pluralism, are useful tools of understanding for small community practitioners.

Elitism

Proponents of *elitism* (Hunter, 1953; Lynd & Lynd, 1929, 1937; Piven & Cloward, 1977; Vidich & Bensman, 1968) suggest that power and influence are highly centralized in communities. For the elitists, power resides in the hands of a few individuals or groups who are directly or indirectly involved in decisions simply because the scope of their personal or group interest is so pervasive that it is almost impossible for them to be indifferent to any decision. This was the situation of the "X Family" in *Middletown in Transition* (Lynd & Lynd, 1937). One of the Lynds' informants said at that time:

> If I'm out of work I go to the X plant; if I need money I go to the X Bank, and if they don't like me I don't get it; my children go to the X college; when I get sick I go to the X hospital . . . my wife goes downtown to buy clothes at the X department store . . . I get help from X charities; my boy goes to the X YMCA and my girls to the X YWCA; I listen to the Word of God in X subsidized churches . . . and if I am rich enough, I travel via the X airport. (p. 74)

Although the situation in many contemporary small towns is more subtle—that is, the YMCA and YWCA are not likely to bear the name of their main benefactors, the bank also might have a more neutral name, and the charities might only be indirectly aided by the X family or families such as through the United Way—nevertheless, chances are that the main actors or leaders in these organizations will be members of a small group of influentials. Old-timers in small towns often can readily discern that although the names of board members of banks, United Way, YMCA, or YWCA might not all be the same, they often are related by marriage, club membership, or other institutional connections (see, for example, "Our Town in 1981" on pp. 123–124). As early as 1935, the Lynds had seen those interconnections:

> In view of the tightening of social and economic lines in the growing city, it is not surprising that the type of leisure time organization which dominates today tends, in the main, to erect barriers to keep others out. (Lynd & Lynd, 1937, p. 312)

In 1976, the Center for Program Effectiveness Studies of the University of Virginia undertook a close replication of the Lynds' second Middletown study. In a third Middletown study, Caplow and Chadwick (1979), using much more sophisticated methodology, found that in the Middletown of the 1970s, occupational prestige was still unequal, although the number of people belonging to white collar and professional occupations had increased. These authors found an increase in the average level of occupational prestige of the town's population as a whole. This increase was explained by the increase in white-collar occupations in Middletown and the decrease in blue-collar occupations since the Lynds' studies. Although the lack of equalization of occupational prestige indicated the persistence of elitism in the structure of small-town power, other indicators should be considered. Caplow and Chadwick found that there had been considerable equalization in relation to patterns of daily living. Working class and business people had come closer together regarding issues of housing quality, marital adjustment, and educational aspirations for their children, issues that are not directly related to the existing distribution of power but do speak in favor of an improved quality of life for all.

Although the new elitism of small communities (particularly in the growing or thriving small town) might be slightly more participatory (with a larger number of leaders or with a cluster of corporate leaders), chances are that even the shrewd practitioner may have difficulty identifying with the community power actors. Visually, elitism is often represented pyramidally; the broad base of the pyramid symbolizes the larger participation at the lowest levels of the decision-making structure; the narrower top of the pyramid represents the power or decision-making elite. In contemporary times, small-town elitism could perhaps be best represented by a truncated pyramid (Figure 1).

Until recently, the literature often suggested that two types of elites existed in communities—one based on wealth and one representing the electoral process. Currently, researchers are less prone to separate the two,

Figure 1.
Elitism

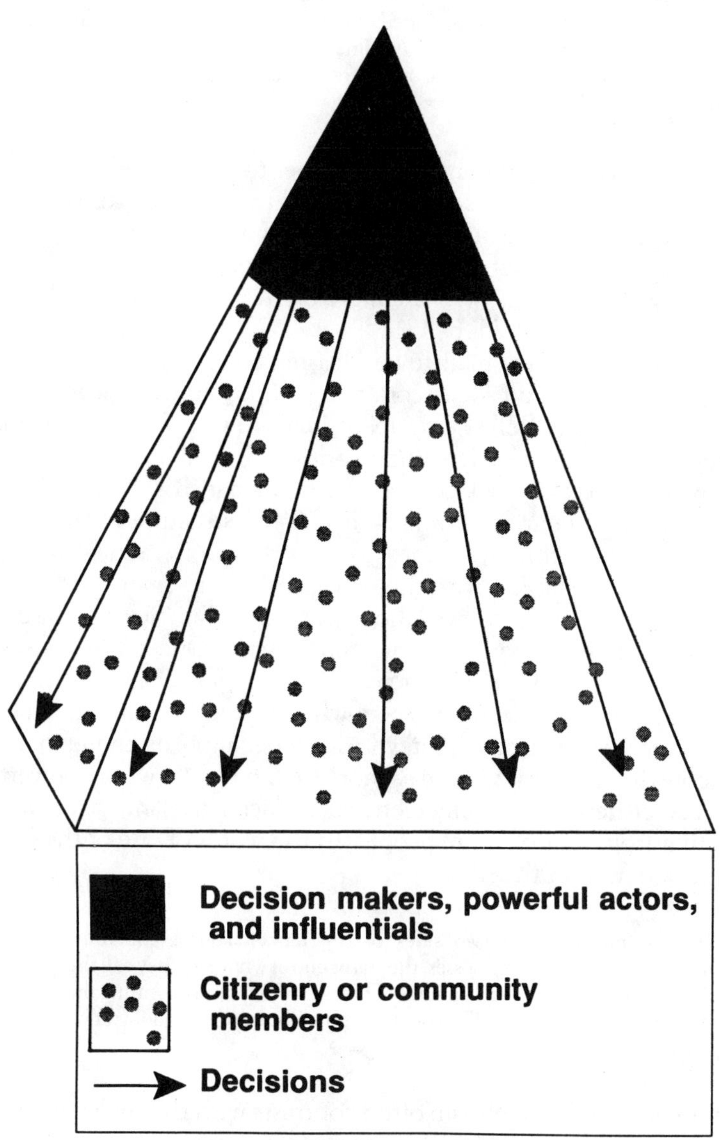

because they often are found in close interaction at the upper levels of the pyramid:

> The interlocking, duplication and overlapping of leadership roles tend to channel community policy into relatively few hands, and it results, at the level of the personalities of the leaders, in some degree of community coordination. That is, a wide range of community activities are coordinated simply because a small number of individuals are engaged in a wide range of leadership positions. (Vidich & Bensman, 1968, p. 258)

It is useful for the small community practitioner to note that the degree of interaction of the power actors has been found to be related to the size of communities. Comparative studies have found that smaller towns tend to have more centralized patterns of decision making. Thus, the smaller the town, the fewer "the leaders, who are more often in agreement with each other" (Magill & Clark, 1975, p. 38).

This phenomenon of small-town elitism is discernible across small towns of varying racial and socioeconomic composition. A recent documentary film (Stekler & Bell, 1985) about small-town politics in the rural South depicted power and leadership struggles in the small Louisiana town of Tallulah, a 75-percent-black community in the parish of Madison. The film showed the ascendancy of a black leadership structure in the town. Although that leadership was not based entirely on money, and its ascendancy had to do largely with the struggle of black Americans for the franchise, the filmmakers showed how the economic ties to powerful interests affected the behavior of elected leaders. One of the elected officials, a black veterinarian, was viewed by many of the black citizens as too conciliatory with the white farmers who made up his clientele. The other elected official, a black barber who depended more on the support of his black constituency, was viewed as more tied to ideology than powerful interests. Yet, citizens saw the emergence of a black leadership structure as not dissimilar from that of white people. In the words of one of the town dwellers interviewed in the film,

> The power is split here on two sides of the fence. You've got your white southerners . . . who are your big bosses, the status quo or whatever they call them. On the Black side of town, you have a handful of Black politicians just running the town. They are all in the status quo and if you don't go with the status quo, you've got to buckle down.

This picture of small-town elitism often contrasts with that of larger cities with more decentralized or pluralistic power structures.

Pluralism

Although the philosophic conflicts between elitists (or power structure proponents) and pluralists (Anton, 1963) cannot be justly summarized here, for the pluralists, the identification of decision makers is more fluid and changes with various issues. *Pluralism* is visually represented by a circle within which a number of small circles, or loci of decision making, are found (Figure 2). Thus, the pluralists would not speak of a single-community power structure but of various loci of decisional control:

> The first and perhaps most basic presupposition of the pluralist approach is that nothing can be assumed about power in any community. If anything, there seems to be an unspoken notion among pluralist researchers that at bottom *nobody* dominates in a town so that their first question to a local informant is not likely to be, "Who runs this community?" but rather "Does anyone at all run this community?" (Polsby, 1960, p. 474)

The pluralists object to the sociological hypothesis of a fairly stable and stratified distribution of power. They insist that power is tied to issues and that "issues can be fleeting or persistent, provoking coalitions among interests groups and citizens, ranging in their duration from momentary to semi-permanent" (Polsby, 1960, p. 476).

A major objection to the idea that power is only "issue-bound" can be found in the realization that not all issues do become public issues and that individuals or groups can control the nature of the issues about which the decision making will be public. Can people safely

> ignore the possibility . . . that an individual or group in a community participates more vigorously in supporting the nondecision-making process than in participating in actual decisions . . . ? (Bachrach & Baratz, 1962, p. 949)

Without disregarding the problems inherent in the pluralist approach to the study of power or overlooking the possible biases of the elitists, the understanding of both perspectives will help practitioners ask the right questions. Both perspectives have influenced the ways in which people search for power actors in communities.

ONE-PERSON, TIGHTLY KNIT, SEGMENTED, AND DIFFUSED POWER

Several "power structures" correspond roughly to various points of the elitism–pluralism continuum. Powers (1967a) defined the power structure in small towns as an "identifiable interaction pattern composed of power actors who may relate to each other in a number of different ways" (p. 156). The following patterns of interaction emerged from Powers's proposals:

Figure 2.
Pluralism

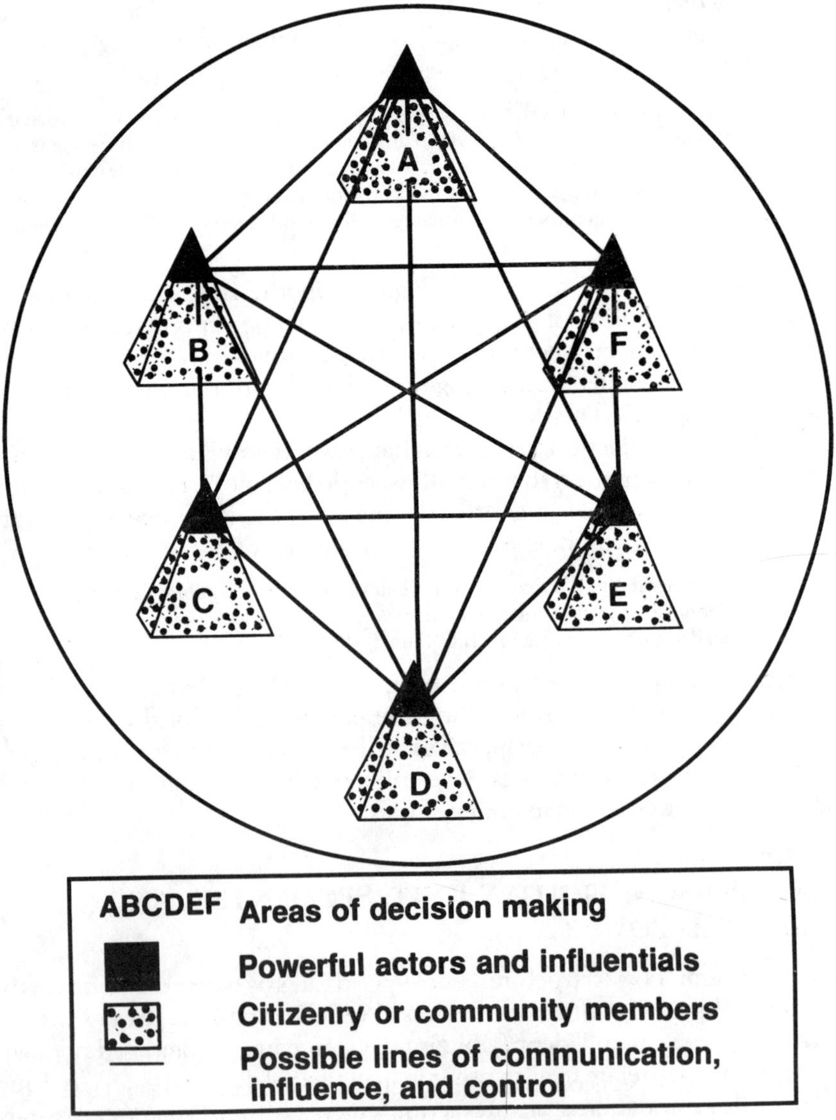

A
B
F
C
E
D

ABCDEF Areas of decision making

Powerful actors and influentials

 Citizenry or community members

Possible lines of communication, influence, and control

one-person power structure, tightly knit group, segmented power structure, and power pool or diffused power structure.

In the *one-person power structure*, the power centers on one individual or family who has dominated the community for generations. Such a person or family might be surrounded by "lieutenants" who carry out decisions. This type of power structure was more common in the past than in current small towns. The *tightly knit group* is closer to the modern elitist community with a truncated but elitist structure. The *segmented power structure* refers to divisions of power within an elitist structure. For example, there might be a Democratic and a Republican elite; or a Catholic and a Protestant elite; or a labor and a managerial elite. The *power pool* or *diffused power structure* is closer to the pluralistic model:

> With this more or less loosely-knit group there is some specialization by issue areas. All of the power actors do not act in concert on every issue. For example, only a few will be at the core of issue A. Similarly, three or four may be at the core of issue B. Only one or two may be involved in both. (Powers, 1967a, p. 156)

However, regarding the diffused power structure in small communities, Powers (1967a) warns that

> many communities appear to have a diffused power structure in which the power actors form a loosely-knit structure from which particular individuals are drawn into the core of specific issues—with some overlapping or linkage from one issue to another. This does not mean that all power actors in the "power pool" will always agree. There may be rather well-defined cliques within the pool, with little, if any, overlap. Logically, one could define as a possibility such complete specialization by issue area that no overlap occurs and thus there are as many separate power groups as there are issue areas. Such a situation has not been found in any community study of social power. For one reason, there is often a common set of resources (capital, credit control, mass media) crucial to nearly every major issue. These resources are often controlled within a community by one individual; that is, there is one newspaper or one bank. As such, there will be some overlap in the individuals involved in different issue areas. (p. 159)

The general opinion among students of small communities is that a power elite probably will be identifiable. This power elite will more likely be a group of influentials who closely interact on many issues rather than a single family. The visual representation of a truncated pyramid describes the modern elitist small town (Figure 1).

CHARACTERISTICS OF COMMUNITIES, POWER DISTRIBUTION, AND POLICY DECISIONS

In a broad, philosophical piece related to the role social scientists can play in policy decision making, Etzioni (1989) suggested that the "me first model" of the social sciences is too narrow and is becoming outdated as people approach the 21st century (see, for example, "The 'Me First' Model in the Social Sciences Is Too Narrow" on pp. 172–175). Etzioni proposed a model of policy development that considers the welfare of the community. Magill and Clark (1975) offered advice to social workers in relation to influencing policy decisions that affect the welfare of people in communities. These authors conceptualized a continuum drawn according to the socioeconomic characteristics (or level of socioeconomic development) of communities. Centralization and decentralization of power and decision making were identified as corresponding to various points on that continuum. Thus, although elitism and pluralism remained significant theoretical alternatives in the Magill and Clark model, the application of those concepts to actual communities involved variables related to size and economy.

Because human services workers involved in organizing projects cannot always conduct their own power studies in each community, they should consider certain information derived from previous research:

> If a formal comparative study is impractical, the results of past studies relating socioeconomic characteristics to centralization should be helpful. Cities [communities] are likely to have more centralized power and decision-making structures if they:
>
> - are small in population;
> - are economically nondiversified (there are few employers and types of employment);
> - do not have competitive political parties or many voluntary associations;
> - have a city manager (and no mayor or a weak mayor);
> - have nonpartisan elections;
> - have at-large electoral constituencies. (Magill & Clark, 1975, p. 40)

Mennaghan (1976) analyzed more than 80 social science studies to examine the correlation between community characteristics and power structure. Although Meenaghan's methodology was more empirical than that of Magill and Clark, their results were surprisingly coincidental. Mennaghan identified five variables he found associated with power distribution in communities and suggested that community workers attempting to determine the patterns of power in a community initially concentrate on these variables.

> The empirical findings show that many of the hypothesized relations between specific variables and types of power structure are not confirmed and should not be stressed in attempts to ascertain patterns of community power. There are, however, seven variables—region, extent of absentee ownership, number of political and economic groups, degree of competitive-conflict, and instances in which the study focused on public and recurring issues—that were found to be significantly associated with the type of power structure. These are variable on which community workers can rely in initial attempts to determine the patterns of power. (Mennaghan, 1976, p. 129)

In concrete terms, Meenaghan's findings would suggest, for example, that a southern community is more likely to have an elitist distribution of power than one in another region of the country; that a community with a high degree of competing economic/business or industrial interests is more likely to be pluralist; and that a community with a high number of varied political groups is also more likely to be pluralist, whereas locales where business competition is low or where political homogeneity is high tend to be elitist.

Other investigators do not necessarily agree with Meenaghan's statements on regional variations. For example, Curtis and Jackson (1977) studied the community forces that shape social stratification across six different American communities. They found that although social rank and displays of social status were common in all communities, they were not necessarily more marked in southern than in midwestern or other locations. The recent changing patterns of population distribution as well as the effects of central government and court decisions on the life of small towns has significantly narrowed, but not obliterated, the ability to make generalizations on the power structure based on geographic location alone. Consequently, practitioners perhaps should focus more on the other variables suggested by Meenaghan to help them identify and understand the power structure of their communities and view generalizations on geographic location with caution.

Practitioners are interested in the power distribution of communities inasmuch as it affects social work practice or human services policy decisions.

> The type of power structure that prevails in a community will often influence social work decisions about strategies of intervention. If, for example, power is held by an elite, the intervention might include locating vulnerable points in the power structure, organizing the disenfranchised and powerless, recruiting resources from outside the community, and mobilizing the elite. In communities where the sources of power are pluralistic, intervention might be directed at educating the various leaders about their respective areas of power and at developing and using coalitions. The usefulness of ascertaining the distribution of power before adopting a strategy of intervention makes it desirable to be able to infer the type of power structure from other, more obvious characteristics of the community. (Meenaghan, 1976, p. 126)

Human services workers must attempt to anticipate the degree of support or opposition leadership is likely to offer on a specific issue. Workers must examine the scope (narrow or broad) of the changes sought.

> If more fundamental changes are being sought, involving new conceptions of what is important or right, it is hard to avoid dealing with leading members of the power structure as well as with lower-level or more specialized decision makers. (Magill & Clark, 1975, p. 39)

The more controversial the policy outcome, the broader the support it will require to see it materialize (see, for example, "Our Town in 1981" on pp. 123–124).

A public good decision in a small town, for example, will generate more support than a fragile or controversial decision. Consider the public good decision to clean up the water supply. The clean water consumed by group A is also consumed by group B. Theoretically at least, group B has nothing to lose if group A succeeds in implementing a clean water policy. However, even such apparent public good decisions can represent hidden threats. For example, do suppliers of alternative clean water (for example, bottled-water merchants) oppose the policy change? What is the weight of the possible gains of the policy versus its costs? An example of a fragile decision might be the construction of a bypass around a small town. Although such a decision may benefit some interests (such as trucking), it might take away resources from others (such as small downtown businesses). In the social welfare arena, a public good decision might be the establishment of a Senior Center downtown, particularly in an aging small town. Most citizen groups would see themselves as being potential beneficiaries of the facility. A more fragile decision would be a halfway house for mentally ill people or a residence for homeless people.

Whether a community is elitist or pluralist, the nature of the change sought will affect the tactics used by human services workers.

> If the pattern of power is elitist, the worker can examine the probable relationship between the issues relating to change and the interests of the elites. The worker attempts to determine whether the changes will be compatible, neutral, or incompatible with the interests of the elites. So long as these issues are not apt to be perceived by the elites as incompatible with their interests, the worker has justification for inferring that the practice strategy should be collaborative. In this situation, the worker can assume the general role of enabler or facilitator and emphasize the more traditional practice tactics of education, consciousness raising, and joint action. The potential resources for and objects of such tactics might well be select members of the elite, who are disproportionately capable of achieving changes. (Meenaghan, 1976, p. 129)

However, when the nature of the change of policy proposed is incompatible with that of the elites,

> it is essential to identify the resources—actual and potential—of both sides and thus to calculate the probability of engaging in successful conflict. Useful in identifying resources will be state and regional regulatory agencies, public funding requirements, state laws, and the influence and power of state and national organizations. Such extra community resources are especially relevant to conflict strategies in elitist communities, since elites tend to have their disproportionate power precisely because of the resource patterns within the community and the resulting citizen apathy. (Meenaghan, 1976, pp. 129–130)

In pluralist communities, the human services worker will need to assess whether the change or policy sought is compatible or incompatible with the influentials in the specific issue area. For example, in terms of day care policy decision, who constitutes the leadership in that particular issue area? How do they feel about the proposal? What are the broader networks that might be affected? If the worker discerns compatibility with the leadership in the particular issue area (and benefits for interlocking interests), he or she likely will engage in collaborative strategies with that leadership. If there is disagreement or if the policy proposed is incompatible with the leadership in the issue area, the worker may need to rely on conflict-resolving strategies. However, in pluralist communities as in elitist ones, "the more the practitioner moves toward a noncollaborative strategy, the more he/she needs to focus on organizing the sustaining interest groups" (Meenaghan, 1976, p. 130).

Conflict in small towns is always a two-edged tactic. Memories in small communities are long and conflictual relationships often transcend single issues. Although conflict cannot always be avoided—and perhaps should not always be avoided—practitioners must carefully calculate and judge its consequences. What are the interest groups that favor the policy or change? How broad is their sphere of action in community decisions? What are the interest groups that oppose the policy or change and how broad is their sphere of action? The small-community practitioner, like a city practitioner, will need to elicit the necessary information and publicize issues so that individuals, organizations, and groups can assess their interests in the light of such information; forge coalitions with elements of the community to maximize power resources; educate powerful individuals in relevant specialized areas; and engage, if necessary, in negotiations and bargaining to achieve conflict resolution if conflict emerges (Meenaghan, 1976, p. 130). The ways in which the processes of information giving, education, and coalition building will be carried out will differ in small communities. At this point in the change process, the human services practitioner will test out his or her informal communication networks in the small town as well as his or her abilities to reach out and coopt, directly and indirectly, the influentials.

IN SEARCH OF POWER ACTORS: THREE APPROACHES

Various social scientists have proposed a number of ways of identifying the power actors or influential members of communities. Powers (1967a) advised that

> research has shown that certain individuals in every social system—family, community, organization, and the like—can and do influence the decisions or actions of others. Often a community social action project fails because key people in the community power structure were not recognized or appropriately involved. The change agent, such as the Extension worker or teacher, who has a basic understanding of social power and who can identify the individual "power actors" in the community, can enhance his chance for success in social action efforts. (p. 153)

Although traditionally, each of the most common approaches may have represented the perspectives of particular disciplines or particular scholars and may have rendered a particular type of leadership, consideration of various approaches is more likely to provide a balanced picture of the power structure of communities. Furthermore, every community's power structure is always in some state of transition (see, for example, "Village Life—In Crisis or Clover?" on pp. 128–129). The rate of transition, the solidarity or diffuseness of the power actors, and membership in the power structure may vary considerably from one community to another and within a given community over time. A community power structure is a dynamic social system and, as such, needs to be studied from various perspectives. Three basic approaches to the identification of power actors in communities that emerge from the literature are the (1) reputational, (2) positional, and (3) decisional.

Reputational Approach

In *Community Power Structure*, Floyd Hunter (1953) formulated a technique for identifying the power structure of his "Regional City" (presumably Atlanta, Georgia). Hunter's method, the *reputational approach*, involved asking informants in the city to identify the powerful individuals. The basic assumption underlying this method was that "reputations for influence are an index of the distribution of influence" (Wolfinger, 1960, p. 634). Hunter concluded that a small number of businesspeople and professionals constituted the power elite of Regional City. Informants had identified, through "reputations," people perceived to be powerful in most situations—power actors rather than influentials, although in highly elitist and in many small communities, the two often overlap.

The reputational approach provides a basic tool for the identification of powerful actors. It is particularly useful in towns and villages where people's actions tend to be more public and accessible to open community scrutiny. Even informal chains of information or "gossip lines," if used with caution, are useful in telling practitioners how community members perceive the power distribution. Human services workers are cautioned against disregarding obvious or commonsensical sources of information simply because the information cannot be "scientifically" validated. The judicious evaluation of the opinions of long-time community residents, of local newspaper people, and other keen observers of the towns and counties across American are useful and important, although perhaps unconventional, sources of information.

The reputational approach should help practitioners formulate a list of powerful actors in all fields, different fields, or just the human services field. Small-community practitioners should compile lists in a variety of fields of action because such lists often will show the interconnections of influentials and help the practitioner avoid potentially costly errors of tact. Powers (1967b) suggested that

> in this approach, most often used by sociologists, a list of community power actors is obtained by asking a number of knowledgeable community residents to name and rank those persons reputed (perceived) to have the most social power. Usually information is sought on several issues (such as health, education, and industrial development) which may have arisen within the last two to five years.
>
> The reputational approach usually involves two major steps. The first step is to interview several knowledgeables (sometimes called a panel), obtaining their perceptions of who are the influential persons in the community. These data are then summarized and at the second step, all the persons who have been named two or more times, for example, are interviewed to obtain their ranking of the persons already named. Each is given the opportunity to add others they perceive to have equal or greater social power than they have. Social scientists have labeled this two-step procedure and variations of it the "snowball" or "cobweb" technique. The study of social power by this reputational technique may identify past, present, or anticipated power. (pp. 239–240)

Although several scholars have criticized Hunter's method, it has continued to be used as a useful (if not perfect) index of community power.

Positional Approach

Another approach often used in the identification of powerful actors is the study of the civic and business leadership of a town, or the *positional approach*. People, such as the mayor or bank president, who occupy key positions within the town's structure are identified as having positions of power. In the social service arena, influential policy boards often are positionally constructed. Thus, the United Way board or the community mental health boards, for example, often have in their ranks the mayor of the town, bank presidents, chamber of commerce leadership, and local corporation executives. Generally, the names of those people in the positional structure of small towns who are more than mere figureheads also will appear on reputational lists. However, even leaders who are only figuratively powerful actors cannot and should not be disregarded because, if not their influence, their opposition to community decisions can have serious consequences (Powers, 1967b).

Decisional Approach

In the 1960s, Robert A. Dahl (1961) and Edward C. Banfield (1961) studied decision making in New Haven and Chicago. They concluded that pluralistic structures existed in the cities of study. For pluralists, power means participating in decision making. As a result of their studies, Dahl and Banfield developed the *decisional approach*, which identifies influentials.

> This [decisional approach], most often used by political scientists, is sometimes referred to as event analysis. Basically, the researcher determines the persons actually involved in several community issues that have occurred recently—or preferably are in process at the time of the research. Persons "involved" are those making public statements, voting to do something, attending meetings, and the like. The major shortcoming of the technique is that it does not search out persons acting "behind the scenes." In addition, the opportunity to observe several community issues covering a wide range of interests is difficult to come by—even for the researcher with time, energy, and money. Furthermore, such a procedure would tend to reveal more implementors of decisions than initiators of decisions. While implementors are important to the ultimate outcome, they do not play the key role of legitimation. (Powers, 1967, p. 240)

Using the decisional approach, small-town practitioners should study news items, reports, features, and editorials of local newspapers. Usually, local newspapers follow town, county, and regional decisions and identify the individuals involved in those decisions and describe their roles. The major problem of the decisional approach involves the decisions that can never be scrutinized or studied:

> All forms of political organization have a bias in favor of the exploitation of some kinds of conflict and the suppression of others because *organization is the mobilization of bias*. Some issues are organized into politics while others are organized out. (Schattschneider, 1960, p. 71)

Using All Three Approaches

The three approaches have been favored differentially by proponents of pluralism or elitism. The pluralists scrutinize single issues so that various power actors or leading groups are likely to emerge. Pluralists tend to criticize the reputational approach on the grounds that reputed power is not the same as actual power. Pluralists also tend to criticize the positional approach to the study of power, because they believe it discloses authority or leadership rather than power. Unlike many sociologists who tend to accept authority as a form of power (Loomis, 1960; Powers, 1967a), political scientists often take pains to distinguish between the two concepts:

> While authority is closely related to power, it is not a form thereof; it is in fact, antithetical to it. In saying this, we reject both the traditional definition of authority as "formal power" and that which conceives it as "institutionalized power."
>
> To regard authority as a form of power is, in the first place, not operationally useful. If authority is "formal power," then one is at a loss to know who has authority at times when the agent who possesses "formal power" is actually powerless. To say that Captain Quegg continued to have authority on the *USS Caine* after he was relieved of his command by the mutineers is to create needless confusion. (Bachrach & Baratz, 1970, pp. 32–33)

On the other hand, sociologists' notion of authority as formal power can be useful in explaining many of the incongruous measures and mandates often issued by outgoing administrators or politicians who exercise their "formal power" long after they have ceased to influence their subordinates or constituents.

Students and new practitioners should attempt to apply all three approaches to the identification of power actors in their communities and draw parallel lists of key actors identified according to each approach, thus constructing a rudimentary barometer of power actors. If a leader's name appears with regularity in lists drawn according to the positional, reputational, and decisional approaches, then the social services provider can safely surmise that the particular actor is likely to exert influence in an array of decisions and in a variety of areas. Similarly, if certain names appear to be confined to one type of action or to a single area of influence, it might be likely that those individuals have a more circumscribed arena of influence. However, as with all rudimentary barometers, the practitioner should not conclude that a name not appearing in any list divests that person of all influence.

INTERNAL AND EXTERNAL INFLUENCES ON POWER ACTORS

Sills (1975) suggested that "all community groups, including those concerned with providing a service or promoting mutual help are likely to come up against, and have to reckon with, the exercise of power in their locality" (p. 24). For example, groups will confront power actors in carrying out basic steps such as obtaining planning permission or seeking material or human resources. In addition to the locally based power holders, most powerful bodies inside a locality also operate from outside. Warren (1963, 1978), who subscribes to a systemic perception of the community similar to that of Sills or Vidich and Bensman (1968), suggested that

> varied studies of status in the macrosystem . . . lend support to the importance of considering local power structures as largely determined by position in the macrosystem and suggest the inadequacy of power structure studies that consider the macrosystem as a largely peripheral issue while concentrating on the internal dynamics of the specific local community. The new manager of the important local branch plant of the national corporation almost immediately finds himself exercising inordinate influence on local situations, not because of any locally generated adulation, but because his position as dictated by the national system gives access to important resources, which can be utilized for positive or negative sanctions vis-à-vis other local actors. . . .
>
> It needs stressing that in virtually every aspect of local community activities, important organization linkages to parts of the macrosystem are operative whether this linkage be through religious denominations, professional associations, company branch subsidiaries, branches of federal and state government, labor unions, or whatever. . . . (Warren, 1978, p. 432)

According to Warren's perspective, local groups are seen as interconnected to externally based organizations that must be considered in any power analysis. Strong horizontal and vertical ties exist among community decision makers. Vidich and Bensman (1968) stated that political leaders "not only point up the boundaries of the actual jurisdictions of political units but also indicate the significant linkages and combinations within local government and the political agencies of the wider society" (p. 222).

Whether community members feel positively or are critical about the encroachment of external forces, they cannot afford to deny reality (see, for example, "Mountaintop Sewer Woes a Catch 22" on pp. 199–200). External forces must be analyzed and assessed for their potential to exercise or influence community control. Perhaps it behooves practitioners to heed MacKaye's (1962) advice:

> These forces are neither "good" nor "bad" but *so*. And they do not stand still, but flow and spread as we have told. Can we control their flow before it controls us? Can we do it soon enough? . . . What instructions can we issue to our modern day explorer (whether technical or amateur) to guide him in coping with this modern-day invasion? (p. 209)

Sills (1975) constructed a model of community power holders that includes a listing of externally and locally based powerful actors found within most community settings. Although the exact names of certain local or nationally powerful groups might differ, local and nonlocal powerful actors can be identified in most U.S. communities. Sills suggested that the local power structure should be seen as comprising externally and locally based organizations and local officials and political party leaders. Externally based organizations include national or multinational groups who may have local subsidiaries, investment property and contracting companies who conduct business from a distance but put considerable pressure on local authorities, national newspaper chains that control and editorially influence local papers, national and state governments that influence and control local fiscal and administrative decisions, and national and state legislators who might support or oppose local decisions. Locally based organizations include large local firms that sponsor local projects (the community might feel indebted to these firms); small local firms that are always prepared to form coalitions to protect themselves and their interests; and other large institutions such as universities, trust funds, or churches that are landowners and that have special tax or other advantages. Local officials and political party leaders are those people who minimally possess one essential tool or resource, that is, the control of both the content and flow of important information on local matters (Sills, 1975, pp. 24–28).

Human services professionals must recognize the influence of these internal and external forces in the small community. In recent years, many small communities have been affected, for example, by issues of growth and development in which various forces have played a major role. For instance, the price of housing in many small towns is related to the availability of affordable units. Outside builders and investors often are involved in deciding where and how many units to build. Local firms and local landowners often have opposing perspectives because of conflicting interests. Local officials are vulnerable to both internal and external influences.

LOCAL AND COSMOPOLITAN INFLUENTIALS

Human services practitioners need to understand the types of influentials and leaders that are found in small communities to help them assess whether a particular individual, identified as an influential, is likely to be interested in espousing, for example, a local social service cause or project or whether he or she is more likely to be involved in an issue that transcends the local community. Which type of influentials will be responsive to local problems and concerns and which type will not? Whom should the local practitioner tap or coopt to help legitimize micro or macro causes? (For examples of the two types, see "It's a New Day in State Center, but What Will Life Be Like at Dusk?" on pp. 130–136 and "Lack of Teamwork Hinders State Center's Fight to Survive" on pp. 137–141.)

Two types of influentials are effective in the local community, but each possesses different orientations and spheres of influence: (1) the locals and (2) the cosmopolitans (Merton, 1949, 1957). These terms do not refer to the regions in which interpersonal influence is exercised; rather, they refer to the nature of the issues the two types of influentials will espouse. According to Merton (1957), the town or village is essentially the local influential's world; he or she is only marginally interested in the outside world; local issues are his or her sphere of action. The local influential is essentially parochial in scope of interest and activity. The cosmopolitan, on the other hand, although an influential in the local community, looks at the outside world with keen interest and regards himself or herself as an active member of a larger society.

The behaviors of the two types of influentials vary markedly. The local influential is more thoroughly "adapted to the community" (Merton, 1957, p. 395) and usually is not interested in expanding his or her influence outside the local community. This type of influential has made his or her mark in the locality and is interesting in staying. Personal contacts legitimize and help a local influential to establish himself or herself and give him or her political, business, and other types of support. Local influentials are truly Gemeinschaftlich in their style of operation:

> They crowd into those organizations which are largely designed for making contacts, for establishing personal ties. Thus they are found largely in the secret societies (Masons), fraternal organizations (Elks), and local service clubs—the Rotary, Lions, and the Kiwanis. . . . Their participation appears to be less a matter of furthering the nominal objectives of these organizations than of using them as contact centers. (Merton, 1957, pp. 398–399)

The local influential might become a local political figure but seldom will run for national office. He or she is likely to espouse causes that are public and acceptable. For example, the local influential will support the local Red Cross Blood drive or the Kiwanis Pancake Day to secure funds for good causes but seldom will spearhead a local sex education project or campaign to get the local hospital to provide better services to welfare mothers.

Cosmopolitan influentials also belong to various organizations and espouse causes because their region of influence is still the local community. However, the nature of those causes and organizations vary from that of the local influentials. Cosmopolitan influentials join professional societies and espouse causes where special knowledge and skills are required. They are interested in organizations because of their functions, rather than because of the people they are likely to meet.

Although neither educational level nor occupational status distinguishes local and cosmopolitan influentials, other characteristics differentiate the two types. Merton postulated that local influentials are long-time residents of the community. Their relations with people have typically helped or hindered their escalation in the ranks of the town's influentials. They usually have worked their way up the ladder of influence, which generally has been a slow process. Townspeople generally have known the local influentials' strengths and limitations. On the other hand, cosmopolitan influentials usually are outsiders to the community who have arrived with some skills, knowledge, and status. They have gained acceptance more quickly among the town's influentials. They often transfer their status from their prior positions to the new community. Cosmopolitan influentials were found in many of the fast-growing small towns of the 1980s. They are the cadre of professional or company executives who seem to have taken their place in the power structure of small towns with greater speed than many local influentials have; thus, cosmopolitan influentials often will be resented by the local influentials.

Many professionals, including human services workers, will experience the same dilemmas the cosmopolitan influential faces. Although they might be quickly accepted in the structure of the town, they need to be sensitive to the concerns of the local influentials. Human services professionals need to be aware that "the cosmopolitan influential has a following because he knows; the local influential because he understands" (Merton, 1957, p. 403). Merton (1949) believed the "impersonal welfare worker" could never become a local influential. Merton's assertions stressed the problems of maintaining strictly bureaucratic interactions within the context of small communities. Forty years later, social workers have discovered the problems intrinsic in relying only on bureaucratic interactions in small communities; yet, although a few human services practitioners actually may have modified their practices and currently might favor a practice approach sensitive to the interconnections of insiders, generally, Merton's analysis still applies. One of the most debatable issues affecting the approach to social work practice in small communities is the extent to which human services practitioners can and should become local influentials. It is essential that human services practitioners be aware of their styles—the implications of a particular style of personal relationships are very marked in small communities.

PRACTITIONER AWARENESS

Social scientists have studied power as a separate variable in the microcosm of communities because by understanding how power is distributed, they often have learned about other community characteristics.

Likewise, practitioners who are interested in community projects or community interventions in small towns must be aware of how decisions are made, who makes them, and how the powerful and influential members of the community often are intertwined into closely knit circles.

The theoretical distinctions among power, influence, and leadership often are obliterated because power actors, influentials, and leaders are frequently the same people. Practitioners must be aware that in most modern small communities, although the power distribution is often elitist, what is found is no longer a perfect pyramid—a single individual or family involved in most decisions—but a truncated pyramid, with a close-knit group of influentials who are involved in the decision making.

Practitioners who are attempting to secure legitimacy for their projects or to coopt influentials into their causes need to be able to identify the influentials as local or cosmopolitan to determine how these types of influentials will fit into those causes. Practitioners also need to make lists of reputational, positional, and decisional power actors and decision makers in the small communities to keep a finger on the "pulse" of the small town.

4

Locality and Localism Reconsidered

Emilia E. Martinez-Brawley with Roy C. Buck,
Professor Emeritus of Sociology, The Pennsylvania State University

Casual observation would suggest that despite modernization, the daily round of life for millions of people is carried out in relatively small, circumscribed, and local settings. For the modern nonmetropolitan dweller, it may not be an overstatement to conclude that a 15- to 20-mile radius around one's home encompasses the space of one's daily activity. With the possible exception of the commuting suburbanite, it may well be that the more urban one's residence, the more one's radius is reduced. In the context of helping people, physical proximity is an undeniably important variable. Experience in the field of social work has shown that in helping people resolve daily problems, sophisticated expertise often is much less important than physical proximity.

Technological advances, urbanization, and corporate industrialism have encouraged *place release*—that is, conditions of daily life wherein natural or constructed space and environment play limited roles in ordering interpersonal relationships or in contributing to the social and psychological sense of personal and collective well-being. *Localism*—pride of place or the state of being concerned with locality—sometimes is viewed as an obstacle to furthering intergroup understanding because of its emphasis on boundary, "we and they" labeling, and provincial anticosmopolitan spirit. On the other hand, place release is the mark of modern cosmopolitan lifestyle. Although thinking exclusively in local terms might be anticosmopolitan and might deny the interdependence of the world, the new localism that community workers can support is not of that nature.

Confusion and often disdain for local (often labeled "regionalistic") ties have occurred not only in the social sciences but also in literature. For example, Hobbs (1985) discussed how the works of writers often were dismissed by critics and publishers as being regional (or local):

> While critics of regional literature assert that an author preoccupied with Kentucky (or another rural area) ignores Athens and Rome, its advocates argue that Athens and

> Rome can only be reached through Kentucky, Nebraska, or Yoknapatawpha. As one partisan puts it, regionalism is not "an ultimate in literature, but . . . a first step. . . ." The coming to close knowledge about the life of a region in which [the writer] lives is a first necessity for sound writing, even as knowledge of oneself—"know thyself"—is also a first necessity. (p. 87)

Little can be universal that is not rooted in a recognizable locale. Certainly, action is always related to one's surroundings. The localism that nourishes communities today and strengthens helping ties is captured in the slogan "Think globally, act locally."

In times of need and particularly in crises, the lonely elderly person or the anxious parent may benefit more from the ready support of a neighbor than from the expertise and sophistication of the remote professional. To the extent that these observations and conjectures are valid, perhaps ways should be found to capitalize on localism and reduce its negative consequences—too much attachment to locale may narrow people's horizons and have negative consequences in caring for certain groups—and entertain the possibility that the relationship between cosmopolitanism and localism is not necessarily futile. A key proposition guiding the perspectives of human services workers is that cosmopolitanism and localism may exist in complementary relationship supporting individual sense of well-being and the common good. That healthy localism, while enhancing pride in community, need not be exclusionary is another basic premise in the reconsideration of provincial spirit and locality.

PROBLEMATIC INTELLECTUAL STATUS OF LOCALISM

Students in the human services field generally are required to take a wide spectrum of social sciences courses. Often, courses are limited to general surveys and introductory content. Emphasis is on trends, generalizations, macrodemographic summaries, definitions of concepts, and thumbnail sketches of theoretical perspectives. Courses in statistics and research methods generally involve data sets of a demographic character and emphasize drawing judiciously worded conclusions and recommendations for further study. Throughout this experience, students are urged to embrace the value of generalization and be wary of specifics and concreteness. Students are warned against citing personal experience and observations as valid data. Over time one's home, neighborhood, and community fade into the background and one takes on the abstract, rational, and professionally certified views of instructors, textbooks, academic journals, and professional publications.

There is, however, an inherent paradox in this approach. Although concrete daily experiences are discarded as too specific and invalid, scientific scrutiny focuses on small segments of reality. The careful social scientist focuses not on cosmopolitan or universal experiences but on the local experiences of particular groups. In a recent essay, O'Brien (1988) discussed how 19th century intellectuals rejected cosmopolitanism as inherently anomic: O'Brien quoted the warnings of the 19th century French historian Jules Michelet:

> What can be sadder than to sink and never be able to rise again by an act of will? From being a Frenchman [one] falls to the level of a cosmopolitan, of just any man, and from there to the level of Mollusk! (Michelet cited in O'Brien 1988, p. B1)

Despite warnings, 20th century scholars have continued to be wary of local perspectives. Instead, as the 21st century approaches, scholars need to reexamine somewhat dispassionately their fears of attachment to locality.

Because of academic antagonism toward local perspectives, student exposure to community in all its ramifications is often minimal. Local government often is relegated to a week of lectures in an introductory political science course. Courses in community often are viewed as marginal to more mainstream "clinical" study and as contributing to general education objectives, a broadened view of social realities, or the maintenance of a social work community tradition that no longer exists. In the social sciences, instructors who teach community-oriented courses often are viewed by their peers as overly "humanistic" and not analytical. Students may be advised to steer away from community courses because of their alleged lack of utility and overall irrelevance.

Yet, many human services workers spend significant proportions of their careers employed in small and often quite rural communities—thus, community courses are useful. Unfortunately, workers and especially neophytes who have been intellectually and technically nurtured in a university environment that perhaps was inimical to localism and rural and rustic customs and traditions may suffer cultural and intellectual shock and a compelling sense of incompetence as they move into practice. Work demands in small municipalities may be such that perspectives and specializations neatly compartmentalized in courses and curricula tend to blend, losing clear-cut identity in the course of daily work.

During a recent visit to Catalonia, Spain, one author was asked to lead a training session for social work practitioners newly assigned to serve rural and small communities in a fairly traditional province. One of the major concerns of the practitioners was that life in the small communities they were to serve often was antithetical to what had been described in their urban courses. Practitioners found that, as human services workers, they had to approach work matters as personal interactions, that people would perform tasks for others as "favors" to the worker; for example, a neighbor might check on a particularly belligerent or disliked elderly person as a "favor" to the agreeable new worker. Social workers had been taught that in the bureaucratic world, formal arrangements freed them from personally taxing commitments. Yet, the social reality in which these young workers found themselves was different. The social reality of the small community anywhere often does not correspond with the descriptions of community life practitioners are offered by mainstream scholars in professional programs (see, for example, "Village Life—In Crisis or Clover?" on pp. 128–129).

Perhaps even more of a problem to young professionals is the stark awareness that they have been socialized to the language, norms, and values of their profession and age-status cohort to the extent that they may have become blind and deaf to the rich, varied, and intricate cultural mosaic that characterizes daily life in the small community. As Edelman (1977) pointed out, "Linguistic reference engenders a 'reality' that is not phenomenologically different from any other reality" (p. 35). The antiprovincial reality created by academic language may have become the reality future human services practitioners believe in and the only reality they are open to or able to perceive. If local communities were thought of negatively in a school, the novice practitioner, finding himself or herself in a small community, may perceive it as such. The practitioner may have difficulty searching for and identifying local strengths and enjoying contact and meaningful dialogue with local people. Although the professional and somewhat ironic antiprovincialism of academic language may have served younger workers well during years of formal schooling, it often is ill-suited to the work demands in small communities where old and young, rich and poor, schooled and unschooled work, play, worship, love, and quarrel in a different common idiom—spoken and unspoken language, lore, and custom.

BEYOND THE ECLIPSE-OF-COMMUNITY PERSPECTIVE

Human services workers caught up in the pressures of day-to-day work, bureaucratic routinization, and entrenched administrative power often have little motivation or incentive to keep up with advances in the social sciences or humanistic disciplines. Communication between academic disciplines and human services organizations is underdeveloped and often fraught with nit-picking and occasional prejudice. Human services workers and social scientists, more often than not, go their separate ways linked with little other than ad hoc and intermittent perfunctory professional cooperation and exchange. Perhaps nowhere is this predicament more evident than in the case of community organization and development workers and social scientists specializing in the structure and processes of day-to-day community life.

Community as an object of study "comes and goes" in social science research as theoretical and methodological orientations change over time (Stein, 1960). Early research was devoted to identification of natural communities. Following was a period where eclipse-of-community and mass society constituted major themes. Finally, and currently, theoretical conjecture and research rediscovered community and its attendant attributes of territoriality and localism. Before 1950, sociologists who studied communities as a microcosm of society searched for, found, and mapped such microcosmic communities. They emphasized the concepts of "natural community" as an outgrowth of interaction limited by space and consciousness of kind, or the cohesion among people who share history, values, and so forth. The pioneering Chicago sociologists of the 1920s and 1930s who studied urbanization, bureaucratization, and social disintegration in the cities came from small-town backgrounds. Locality-bound communities provided a framework of reference for their studies; thus, the city was analyzed from the perspective of local or natural communities within it.

> The urban community turns out, upon closer scrutiny, to be a mosaic of minor communities, many of them strikingly different from one another, but all more or less typical. Every city has its central business district; the focal point of the whole urban complex. Every city, every great city, has its more or less exclusive residential areas or suburbs; its areas of light and of heavy industry, satellite cities, and casual labor mart. . . . Every American city has its slums; its ghettos; its immigrant colonies, regions which maintain more or less alien and exotic culture. Nearly every large city has its bohemias and hobobohemias, where life is freer, more adventurous and lonely than it is elsewhere. These are the so called natural areas of the city. (Park, 1952, p. 196)

Natural communities proved to be a popular perspective of human services workers. These communities offered a practical base for organizing self-help programs and servicing people in need. Additionally, historical information showed that these locality-bound theories of community had inspired some of the early 20th century studies that led to significant social reform.

Whether "locality-bound" theories of community were of the community-as-microcosm or of the natural community variety (Pelly-Effrat, 1974), from a sociopsychological perspective, the theories emphasized the idiosyncratic and identity-giving nature of territorial boundaries and localism. However, in the decades following World War II, individual alienation, eclipse of community, and the rise of mass society were major themes used to interpret the findings of community research (Stein, 1960). Vidich and Bensman's (1968) study of "Springdale" in upstate New York addressed the constraints that mass society places on small towns. However, their earlier edition of the study was misinterpreted widely. They commented on these misinterpretations in their 1968 edition:

> As teachers and occasional lecturers we have been forced to counter the attitudes of superiority that students and other sophisticated urbanites have too easily adopted toward the residents of Springdale, whose community only accidentally happened to become the object of our study.
>
> We have observed that the urbanite and the student of sociology are remarkably insightful when it comes to understanding the structure of psychological defenses that apply to the rural dweller. We have also observed, however, that this insight and knowledge of the Springdalers' defenses frequently serves as a source of support for the urbanite's and the student's own defenses. By assuming a snobbish and condescending attitude toward the Springdaler, the urban sophisticate implies that the situation of powerlessness does not apply to him. (p. ix)

To the extent that large organizations and the manifestations of mass society have eroded community identity and rendered individuals anomic, the small-town resident and the urban dweller both have been affected. Yet,

> though [the urban dweller] faces the same problems of powerlessness, he finds it hard to disidentify from the agencies of dominance because he shares the same geographical and cultural milieu of the agencies and institutions which dominate him. However, like [the small town dweller], if the [urbanite] too is to assert his identity or individuality, he must develop defenses that will allow him to cope with the situation. Because the modern urban condition does not provide him with an independent cultural tradition, his defenses cannot be those of the Springdaler, who at least feels he is connected to the values of the nineteenth century. The urban dweller has had to invent a new set of defenses which consist of the cultivation of "privacy," of "leisure," of "style" and of culture. (Vidich & Bensman, 1968, p. x)

The strength of these defenses today cannot be denied. The cult of "privacy," of "leisure," and "style" of the young and rich is evident everywhere.

The *eclipse-of-community perspective* offered a favorable climate for methodological and theoretical perspectives centering on bureaucracy and complex organization and demographic analyses. This perspective purports that individuals are caught up in rationally organized formal structures and governed by formal procedures and rules over which they as individuals have little influence. Certain categories of individuals with similar attributes (specialization) exist in isolation from institutional and cultural norms. An understanding of complex organization (bureaucracy) and demographic information composed the core of social science knowledge for students following the eclipse-of-community period.

The eclipse of community perspective emphasized Warren's Great Change, "a complex division of labor and system of social stratification and organizational networks characteristic of urbanized mass society [that had inundated] local communities" (Richards, 1978, p. 568). Although this was the prevailing perspective during the 1960s, critics pointed out its severe limitations. Even those who agreed that vertical integration had taken place in small communities pointed out that this was not really a great change, but a situation that in varying degrees had existed throughout the decades in the life of American small towns. American small communities have always experienced forces integrating them with the nation as a whole. However, Richards questioned the mass society popular belief that integration always was superimposed on small communities and that any degree of it resulted in loss of autonomy:

> [The] historical role of vertical integration in sustaining rural communities leads to questioning the thesis that continuation of or even increases in those ties necessarily bodes ill for the future autonomy of small towns. A diversity of agricultural, industrial and governmental ties to urban society may now assure these communities of greater latitude in decision making than when villagers were totally at the mercy of urban farm commodity markets. (pp. 571–572)

The apparent hold that mass society theorists had on interpreting social phenomena would not last. During the late 1960s and 1970s, a period of rediscovery of community emerged. The social unrest loosed across the land spurred the imagination of a small enclave of social scientists; works of varying degrees of intellectual rigor centered on a romantic search for community and ways to combat mass society theory and to restore "human scale" to daily life. This was a period of experimentation with alternative lifestyles and a renewed interest in communal living. "Dropping out" was a popular idiom for disengagement from the seemingly pathologically impersonal and overly rationalistic structures of mass society.

Orrin Klapp's (1969) *The Collective Search for Identity* offered a quick study of the intellectual and popular forces fueling, what for countless thousands of the young and a few not so young people, was something of a social movement. Charles Reich (1970), in *The Greening of America*, was attempted to analyze what had happened to consciousness in America during the preceding decades, during the decades of growth of mass society and the corporate state. His "consciousness III" group were the young who were making evident a new energy and enthusiasm. Reich proposed that consciousness III would triumph. Yet, a critic of Reich stated that Reich's book ignored some harsh realities. Consciousness III was a reaction to mass society and corporatism, but it lacked ties to the real world of live communities (Marin, 1970).

> Reich fails to explore the critical contradictions within this consciousness—without much effort, one can list so many problems he ignores: (1) The extreme terror and isolation inherent in it. (2) The repressive reaction to it and the increasing repression or destruction of "new" persons. (3) The fact that liberated persons are part of a monied class still living off stolen land, labor and time. (4) The inability of those with new consciousness to find any viable way to express it in politics. (5) The existence of a growing, revolutionary and almost "traditional" violence among those with consciousness III. (6) The simultaneously unliberated condition of every minority group. (7) The fact that no new consciousness is ever as pure as Reich makes it, but a tangle of present and past, all too often a disguise for older kinds of transcendence, withdrawal, passivity or alienation. (p. 3)

The new consciousness also was anomic and thus would have problems surviving and connecting to real (versus contrived) traditions.

Post-eclipse-of-community works emerged. Roszak's (1969) *Making of a Counter Culture*, a popular book on the "new generation" of the 1960s, tried to force deep thinking about technocratic achievements. His basic question was, Which will work better for humankind, a better person or a better machine? His descriptions of a questioning generation were at times outrageous but not unrealistic. He mentioned the gurus of the new generation, among them Paul Goodman with his ethos of small community and participatory democracy. In *Person/Planet*, Roszak (1978) addressed the epidemic of bureaucracy that had invaded all American institutions. Roszak pointed out and mourned that the family was the only social institution that had escaped bureaucratization; the family had lost its community ties and community spirit and had turned inward. Roszak also recognized that the communitarianism of the 1970s regrettably had been born out of dissent. Unlike the kibbutzniks who had built communities with the approval of the culture and the nation, many of the communities of the 1960s and 1970s had gone against the culture, resulting in the collapse of some of them.

Other researchers analyzed the products of the period of renewed interest in community, locality, and localism. Carrying neither the political nor romantic idiom of Roszak and Reich, Suttles's (1972) findings were within the more traditional parameters of social science scholarship. His work corrected the textbook images of inner-city slums as areas emphasizing disorganization, mass society, and anomie. Suttles (1972) introduced the concepts of *defended neighborhood*, the local ties that emerge when a local area is threatened by external change, and *contrived community*, a "conscious community" (Hunter, 1978) that emerges when groups develop assertive ways of articulating a shared belief system. Both communities have essentially local ties. During the 1970s, many groups that organized to respond to conflicts with developers became contrived communities in which the members found ways to articulate their ideological positions, for example, their commitment to urban living in racially integrated neighborhoods or commitment to the survival of small-scale arrangements in nonmetropolitan environments.

Studies that emerged presented a more realistic examination of the eclipse-of-community thesis. Local identity had not been entirely abandoned in decision making.

> The most influential studies of rural town social organization have popularized the generalization that increasing ties with the larger society have decreased ties within the community, with a resulting decline in the ability of the local community to determine its own affairs. While there is little question that mass society has made its presence known in small towns across the country, there is considerable reason to doubt that such presence constitutes a juggernaut for communities. . . . To overcome the illogic of the mass-society-as-demiurge thesis, comparative studies must be promoted that will consider vertical integration as a variable capable of causing a variety of possible social organizational consequences. (Richards, 1978, pp. 573–574)

Mass society had not succeeded in erasing local attachments, although it may have softened them, given them new areas to manifest themselves, and perhaps delineated or narrowed their influence more to the area of personal interaction and helping networks among local residents.

HUMAN SERVICES EDUCATION, THE SERVICE DELIVERY MODE, AND LOCALISM

Human services organizations and professional training of human services workers experienced significant growth during the period of the eclipse-of-community perspective. Believing that locality and localism were of small import in day-to-day life, human services personnel and agencies were shaped to serve individuals who had been identified through the tools of the demographer (numbers and demographic characteristics) rather than the tools of the cultural anthropologist, humanist, or even journalist, who would have been more concerned with the cultural fabric of the communities. However, human services organizations did not necessarily ignore community variables completely. On the contrary, students and practitioners referred to locality and territorial attachments, but merely as referents that explained the settings where clients lived. Community and local ties generally were seen as obstacles and not assets to service. Emphases centered on the delivery of service and, thus, on the development of comprehensive bureaucratic organizations that could administer and accomplish that delivery.

President Johnson's Great Society era was the heyday for the delivery perspective. This is not necessarily a criticism of war-on-poverty efforts but a commentary on its prevailing human services ethos. "Delivery system," a euphemism for bureaucracy, entered the jargon of academics and agency workers. Many social and community workers with benevolent intentions aspired to a desk on the third floor of the city hall or courthouse, equipped with a telephone, a computer printout of known problem areas, and a federal pamphlet outlining guidelines for service. Unfortunately, as soon as a structure for service to clients was in place, mayors or boards of commissioners announced decisively to the press that problems were being met head on. Typical of bureaucracies is the ambiguity that exists when only a structure for service has been created but the assumption is that service actually is being provided (Edelman, 1977).

Truly participatory community development and organization generally remained outside the orthodoxy of service delivery, which was carried out by professionals in vertically organized delivery systems. The community and the commonwealth were part and parcel of the public language of politicians and human services influentials. Although mental health clinics were now community-based, care, for the most part, was provided by professionals who used fairly standardized practices. In practice, social or psychological problems were not dealt with by capitalizing on the unique elements of indigenous local social structure and cultural norms. Rather, individuals with problems were named clients and "serviced" on an individual basis. The service provider, usually an energetic professional or functionary of the bureaucracy, often "serviced" the client with individual "interventions" that relied on introspection and explored primarily psychological dimensions, often foreign to the client and disconnected from local resources, networks, or realities. Often those interventions did not make use of other community agents; for example, beauticians, bartenders, and clergy always had been used as part of the helping network of communities, but their potential now often was ignored.

In ethnic communities, important caretakers also were ignored. Hispanic and Latino communities, for example, often were undervalued by professionals (Badillo Ghali, 1977; Delgado, 1977; Martinez, 1977). In exploring factors that led to the alarming rate of placement of Native American children, Byler (1977), the director of the American Association of American Indian Affairs, observed that

> in judging the fitness of a particular family, many social workers, ignorant of Indian cultural values and social norms, make decisions that are totally inappropriate in the context of Indian family life, so that they frequently discover neglect or abandonment when none exists. (p. 1)

Probably the best example of caring in the broad context of community is the collective responsibility assumed by Native American communities for their members. However, natural, informal caretakers in the context of community cultures only were rediscovered by the formal system during the 1980s. The human services interventions of the eclipse-of-community era were not only likely to be foreign to the community but often were disdainful of it. The human services worker, although describing himself or herself with a consumer-oriented metaphor—"service provider"—behaved in a Messianic fashion toward the local community. Thus, the locals were made to devalue their own local wisdom and information.

In a novel about agricultural workers in Cumbria, England, Melvin Bragg (1969) described the way in which a hired hand felt about his own experiential or locality-based wisdom:

> In the district he was known for his consistency in all things and his pride lay in keeping that record. Within that tiny locality he was erudite but this knowledge, though different not in kind but only in the material it drew on from that of educated men, he considered as "knowing nothing" whenever faced by a fact or remark outside his experience. (p. 14)

The outside expert in the service delivery mode often caused locals to feel they knew nothing even though they had been solving problems for centuries. Some human services workers attempted to scale down and adapt delivery systems in ways that did not ignore local culture, customs, and lore. Some mental health practitioners went out of their way to recognize the influence of local culture and mores on the definitions of mental illness and mental health (Mazer, 1976; Segal, 1973). But the interventions generally continued to rely on knowledge brought into the community. Practitioners feared that the local community would cause harm to their clients. As a result, a new specialty in social work, now known as rural social work, was built on the premise of locality-specific or locality-relevant services (Ginsberg, 1976; Martinez-Brawley, 1981; Mermelstein & Sundet, 1978). This specialty, partly a social movement, partly a professional focus, called for a new form of localism. Social workers taking a more "radical" approach deliberately encouraged local collective resourcefulness and power to solve problems and overcome excesses of power and privilege as they impinged on disadvantaged individuals and their collective predicament. Because these "radical" strategies often encouraged conflict, they were (and still are) not always popular with the larger society, nor were they readily embraced by rank and file workers and local public figures.

The decades of the 1970s and 1980s brought forth a wholly different mood in relation to local matters. Localism became the fashionable key word for agencies to use to combat the financial crunch that was being experienced by the social services. Conservative leaders for whom localism was a way of diverting funds from social services, rather than taking a philosophic stance on how best to care for people, gave the word a new ring, but unfortunately a negative one among human services practitioners. Now, localism was not only invested with the traditional negative meaning of lack of sophistication, but added the dimension of ultraconservatism. Social services providers feared that making use of the broad resources of a local community would simply mean fewer governmental funds. The dubious intellectual and political tradition of localism was becoming more complicated. Although the term was beginning to be one social workers and other caregivers could not ignore, it still was not one they could relish.

Richard Margolis (1981), a journalist advocate of the identity-giving aspects of localism but not of its abuses, tried to clarify the matter in a 1981 article:

> The left's recent romance with localism is understandable and even laudable, given bureaucratic processes and the failure of many public agencies to accomplish much in the face of private power. But there is localism and localism. And there is ample evidence about the fate of social change programs entrusted to the care of the local elites—especially when the local elite was the original obstacle. (p. 33)

Margolis put his finger on the dilemma. The new problem with localism was separating its folk-oriented, antibureaucratic, and locality rooted positive elements from its political components. Decentralization and locality-based efforts in the social services, which had become extremely popular in Britain after 1968, crossed the Atlantic. Roger Hadley and Morag McGrath (1980) in *Going Local* captured the concerns of British social workers:

> Many of the ideas underlying the present organization and management of the [local authority welfare] services are outdated and inappropriate. [This book] questions the emphasis placed on bureaucratic and professional conceptions of service delivery and the centralized, hierarchic organizations that have been created to apply them. (p. 1)

Smaller units operating within the local context and respecting the rich traditions and resources of local communities were the most effective and efficient way of caring for people. Although localism had a complicated history, locality and territoriality still were essential elements that could facilitate caring for those in need (see, for example, "Creativity in Government" on pp. 175–176 and "Keeping the Land" on pp. 195–197).

However, positive and lasting returns on programs of human development and renewal that were rooted in the local informal and institutional fabric of day-to-day life were likely to be a long-term proposition.

Thus, this strategy was unpopular with administrators and politicians faced with defending budgets and budgetary requests with proof of progress on a year-to-year basis. Despite support of a community orientation, the accent on service delivery and client count made for more bookkeeping and was more readily adapted to the rhetoric of effort. As Fabricant (1985) suggested, "The drive to increase the productivity of social workers in large public-sector agencies has contributed to the erosion of certain craft elements of practice" (p. 389). In earlier decades, the tasks of the social worker were "to be based not on one model of practice but rather on the different circumstances of individuals and communities. This commitment to differential diagnoses paralleled the industrial artisans' desire to comprehend fully the various component parts of their work" (p. 389). Today, "the functions of social work are becoming increasingly repetitive and mechanistic and opportunities to exercise judgement . . . are becoming limited" (p. 389). A premium is being placed on getting quantitatively more from fewer resources, and aspects of the social worker's role that do not fit this efficiency drive are becoming suspect.

Because of the rise of demographic data collection, processing, and its popular access through the media, the public is relatively well-informed on the extent of human pathology. Under such conditions, there is likely to be little patience with slow processes of structural development and reform, especially at the level of day-to-day life. All things considered, the eclipse-of-community perspective provided an "academically certified" rationale for a human services bureaucracy designed to deal with clients, not as participants and residents in a local setting, but as victims of ills who need individual attention. Despite renewed emphasis on localism and locality in recent community research, the established human services bureaucracy remains operationally and professionally attached to the eclipse-of-community perspective.

> It is within this [the formal bureaucratic context] that income maintenance centers have replaced social workers with clerks and that child welfare functions are reorganized primarily into policing and accountability services. Relatedly, quality service is redefined as quality control. This new form of quality emphasizes "getting the statistics in on time" and "moving cases through the process within a time limited schemata." (Fabricant, 1985, p. 393)

Unfortunately, many of the current models of social services provision have more in common with the industrial or assembly line ethos than with the ethos of fostering nonanomic communities in which caring relationships among people will flourish.

REDISCOVERING LOCALITY AND LOCALISM

Budgetary deficits, widespread economic recession, and increasing popular as well as political disillusionment with service delivery appears to be forcing human services professionals to reassess established bureaucratic modes of service delivery and its management, albeit not always in fruitful directions. A major obstacle to development and experimentation with alternative approaches is that the present cohort of professional human services leadership for the most part has been schooled in the eclipse-of-community perspective. Another obstacle is that political influentials have borrowed from industrial practices heavily imbued in Taylorist principles. The emphases of Taylorist structures was on "more limited encounters with citizens, narrow definitions of roles and routinized function" (Fabricant, 1985, p. 392). The result of Taylorist practices both in industry and human services has been a decline in the quality of products and services, respectively. Many social agencies have shifted from long-term, preventive, and broader community-based activities that focused on the enhancement of communal interactions to short-term, crisis-oriented, and cheaper practice models.

To cope productively with social problems in the context of reduced resources it is necessary to reeducate midcareer professionals—those who now occupy strategic positions as supervisors, administrators, and senior workers in social agencies—using findings other than eclipse-of-community research. Educators must try to reach midcareer professionals with the new ways of conceptualizing community and locality.

Community studies have documented the importance of locality and collective sense of place in the maintenance of order and well-being. Josiah Royce (1908), an idealist philosopher, saw in *province* and *provincialism* safeguards against "the levelling tendencies of recent civilization" and rise of "the mob spirit" (p. 54):

> A province shall mean any one part of a national domain, which is geographically and socially sufficiently unified to have a true consciousness of customs, and to possess a sense of its distinction from other parts of the country. . . . Provincialism [is] first, the tendency of such province to possess its own customs and ideals; secondly, the totality of these customs and ideals themselves; and thirdly, the love and pride which leads the inhabitants of a province to cherish as their own these traditions, beliefs, and aspirations. (p. 55)

Royce warned against the danger of a false provincialism manifesting itself in narrow sectionalism—such as the one implied in "My Dear, You Really Must Come to the Thanatopsis This Afternoon" (pp. 113–116). He also warned against making local, unique values the ideal, because other people's unique values are also ideal for them. Royce did not see conflict between nation and province. The province provided the essential human scale where the goals and ideals of a nation could be realized:

> I should say today that our national unities have grown so vast, our forces of social consolidation have become as paramount, the resulting problems, conflicts, evils, have been so intensified, that we must flee in the pursuit of the ideal to a new realm. It is the realm of the province. There we must flee. I mean, not in the sense of a cowardly and permanent retirement, but in the sense of a search for renewed strength, for a social inspiration, for the salvation of the individual from the overwhelming forces of consolidation. The nation by itself, apart from the influence of the province, is in danger of becoming an incomprehensible monster, in whose presence the individual loses his right, his self-consciousness, and his dignity. (Royce, 1908, p. 93)

Royce intuitively understood and appreciated the problem of scale. For millions of people, the world, the nation, and the city are too big as referents for ordering and giving meaning to the daily round of life. In multiethnic nations such as the United States, people are advised to be aware of the negative consequences of sectionalism and bigotry; yet, they must avoid unwittingly rationalizing the eclipse of community as a desirable policy without appreciating the unanticipated consequences of collective and individual rootlessness.

Pluralism and heterogeneity are healthy as long as various groups can share in a broader or national vision rooted in the smaller realities of the day-to-day activities within more local or provincial boundaries. *Pride of place* gives greater meaning to people's daily experiences and energizes citizens to participate fully in the communities they know and appreciate. The current movement to declare English as the official language of the United States, for example, is rooted in artificial nationalism. Healthy provincial or local cultures can coexist and lend strength to the larger nation. People can feel strong loyalties to family, locality, ethnic group, their profession, and the nation all at the same time.

Ross's (1989) comments in a recent article on the demise of the melting pot model could be made in relation to provincial, local, or territorial attachments:

> My own initial questioning of the melting pot model came not in New York, where I grew up, but as a young field researcher in East Africa in the 1960s, where I was repeatedly told: "Don't mess with ethnicity and tribes; nations are being built." The melting pot model and modernization theory, so prominent at the time, predicted that ethnicity, religion, and other primordial identifications were carry-overs from the past that would, given time, decline in importance. But I saw example after example and turned up systematic data which indicated that Kenyans were not abandoning ethnic identities at all. In fact, the patterns that I found were the opposite of what I had been told to expect. Ethnicity was socially and politically strongest among the better educated individuals, those most attached to city life, those who held better paying jobs. . . .

> Many American researchers were coming up with similar results. For example, a prominent study in the late 1960s looking at the rise in support for the idea of black power, which was controversial at the time, found support the greatest among younger, educated blacks, exactly the ones whom the melting pot model predicted would show evidence of declining ethnic loyalty.
>
> I believe that early social science theories erred because they underrated the role of group processes in shaping an individual's identity and self-esteem. The focus on individual, but not collective sources of identity is one reason both social scientific and popular images of ethnicity clung to such conceptions as the melting pot, even in the absence of evidence to support them. (p. 1)

Similarly, social science theories underrated the identity-giving aspect of locality and community attachments, be they ethnic, geographic, or both. Government bureaucracy, civic organization, and goodwill and welfare agencies regardless of their sensitivity and compassion cannot substitute for the nurturing and identity-enhancing aspect of the rich social mosaic of day-to-day association interlacing landscapes of familiarity.

In his research in an inner-city neighborhood in Chicago, Suttles (1972) emphasized how attachment to locale gave individuals not only identity but a real sense of security. Suttles described how the sentiments and loyalties of primary relationship formed the basis for the social order of the inner-city neighborhoods he researched. The student of modern small towns will observe the same phenomenon. Primary ties and local sentiments give real direction, albeit not always positive, to the daily activities of most people. For example, "It's a New Day in State Center, but What Will Life Be Like at Dusk?" (pp. 130–136) and "Lack of Teamwork Hinders State Center's Fight to Survive" (pp. 137–141) clearly illustrate how the familiar rhythms of the locale are the focus of the efforts of town's citizens and leaders alike. Welch's (1987) column on local government ("Go Ahead, Run" on pp. 203–204) is a call to leadership in the local context. Campoamor's (1989) report on one woman's efforts to save the *churro* sheep in Los Ojos, New Mexico, from extinction, also shows how local efforts strengthen past culture and promote present well-being (see "Keeping the Land" on pp. 195–197). People live their day-to-day existences within the intimate confines of the province. Misguided intellectuals and literary critics too often have undervalued works with a provincial, local, or regional emphasis. Yet, the most universal of all human experiences happen "at home," where one's deepest emotions are revealed.

Contemporary literary critics, reevaluating the work of women from a feminist perspective, are attempting to redefine the "regional novel," because the problem of devaluing the region or province has existed in many fields, and cuts across racial and ethnic lines. Writing about Harriet Arnow, a Kentucky novelist, Hobbs (1985) stated,

> Writing about hill people from her native state of Kentucky, she is alternatively called a "woman" or a "regional" writer. While it is generally conceded that the former tag is pejorative, few have considered the assumptions behind the term "regional." It is, I suspect, employed as condescendingly as the qualifier "woman"; a "regionalist" can be "good" but only in a limited sphere. (p. 83)

Yet, the life of a region or locality is generally used as the medium to express basic and universal concerns. It is a healthy pride and appreciation of locality that allows people to be universal in their concerns. This point is beautifully illustrated in an essay by Alice Walker (1983), who wrote about Zora Neale Hurston, a black anthropologist, novelist, and folklorist who lived between 1901 and 1960:

> Zora was interested in Africa, Haiti, Jamaica, and for a little racial diversity (Indians)—Honduras. She also had a confidence in herself as an individual that few people (anyone?), black or white, understood. This was because Zora grew up in a community of black people who had enormous respect for themselves and for their ability to govern themselves. Her own father had written Eatonville [Florida] town laws. This community affirmed her right to exist, and loved her as an extension of itself. (pp. 85–86)

Hurston returned to Eatonville to do her work:

> I didn't go back there so that the home folks could make admiration over me because I had been up North to college and come back with a diploma and a Chevrolet. I knew they were not going to pay either one of these items too much mind. I was just Lucy Hurston's daughter, Zora, and even if I had—to use one of our down-home expressions—had a Kaiser baby . . . I'd still be just Zora to the neighbors. If I had exalted myself to impress the town, somebody would have sent me word in a match-box that I had been up North there and had rubbed the hair off of my head against some college wall, and then come back there with a lot of form and fashion and outside show to the world. But they'd stand flat-footed and tell me that they didn't have me, neither my sham-polish, to study 'bout. And that would have been that. I hurried back to Eatonville because I knew that the town was full of material and that I could get it without hurt, harm or danger. (Hurston, 1935b)

The rhythms of everyday life are local but also universal. Pearson (1985a) observed how local speculation provides a great deal of entertainment and is the subject matter of people's interaction, the fabric of the daily rounds of experience. The observations are local; their significance is universal. He observed the speculation surrounding an upstanding, albeit eccentric, citizen of his small North Carolina town:

> Apparently, Miss Pettigrew had not taken up a pen for some considerable years when she set about making out invitations to her July the fourth party of 1970, and even Momma was somehow distressed by Miss Pettigrew's penmanship. She had hopes for something a little more graceful and proper and for a time she seemed inclined to hold with Mrs. Estele Singletary and Mrs. Treva Jane Boyd McKinney, of the block and mortar McKinneys, who insisted that Aunt Willa had filled out and addressed the

> invitations and so was responsible for the scrawl. But all of the available evidence, including testimony by several esteemed witnesses, indicated that Aunt Willa had never learned to write and could not read either. So eventually, Momma had to bring herself to accept the fact that there were just some things about Miss Pettigrew that were not utterly elegant, and when she had grown accustomed to the idea, Momma decided that penmanship was certainly an expendable item. (p. 324)

Fiction is rich in descriptions of local culture and ties. Works that describe what people were thinking and feeling about locale include Hurston's (1935b) *Mules and Men*, Arnow's (1949) *Hunter's Horn*, Giardina's (1987) *Storming Heaven*, Pearson's (1985a) *A Short History of a Small Place* and his *Off for the Sweet Hereafter* (1987), and Nichols's (1974) *The Milagro Beanfield War*.

COMMUNICATING IN THE LOCAL SETTING

Many authors have discussed the "high" or "low" values that are ascribed to various forms of communication. Unfortunately, in the formal setting of government, educational, or other institutions, "we learn to ascribe a high degree of formality and rationality to the utterances of educated people, especially if they express themselves in the conventional speech of the upper middle class, and to derogate the conventional speech of the working class and the poor as imprecise, sloppy and impoverished" (Edelman, 1977, p. 114). In addition to having been acculturated to the language of academic institutions, human services providers are also acculturated to the language of bureaucracy. The language of bureaucracy is rigid and fragmented; calls attention to roles, skills, and competencies; and serves to control people's performances. The language of bureaucracy is not rich in description and storytelling, but is immersed in categories and codes that shortchange the human elements of the interaction. A distance exists between the local language of people with a high investment in their everyday creative activities (such as farming, painting, baking, building, selling, or rearing children) and the language of the bureaucrat who is being judged by his or her identification with the norms of a complex organization. It is not surprising that human services professionals and locals often fail to communicate.

In *Beyond Culture*, Hall (1981) advanced a perspective on communication and intergroup relations which, if diligently studied and translated into practice, could contribute to human services workers' increased competence in working with people in the context of their immediate community—that is, a theory that engenders respect for localistic differences. Hall differentiated between *high-* and *low-*context linguistic style:

> A high-context communication or message is one in which most information is either in the physical context or internalized in the person, while very little is in the coded, explicit, transmitted part of the message. A low-context communication is just the opposite, i.e., the mass of the information is vested in the explicit code. (p. 91)

The following example illustrates high-context communication. A client in a "basic needs" program, who needed to have a grocery order filled, would tell the student who worked in the program that his former social worker always took his order to X rather than Y food bank. It was only after many months that the student discovered that X bank was much more generous in its responses (cans were larger and frozen items were more appealing). The client never explicitly mentioned to the student the disadvantages of Y food bank, even though the student would have been responsive.

High-context people are likely to be locals; low-context people are likely to be cosmopolitans (Hall, 1981):

> One of the reasons most bureaucrats are so difficult to deal with is that they write for each other and are insensitive to the contexting needs of the public. The written regulations are usually highly technical on the one hand, while providing little information on the other. That is, they are a mixture of different codes or else there is incongruity between the code and the people to whom it is addressed. Modern management methods, for which management consultants are highly responsible, are less successful that they should be, because in an attempt to make everything explicit (low contexting again) they frequently fail in their recommendations to take into account what people already know. This is a common fault of the consultant, because few consultants take the time (and few clients will pay for the time) to become completely contexted in the many complexities of the business. (p. 93)

Low-context younger professionals face many problems in working with high-context clients in hills and valleys as well as inner-city neighborhoods. One may assume the clients are nonverbal (not low-context). However, the issue lies not so much in the client's inability to communicate. Rather, it lies in the human services workers' underdeveloped skill in receiving high-context messages that combine body and verbal language in an idiom shaped and colored by the immediate sociocultural environment with unstated references to common experiences and events that constitute the cultural bases of interaction. Pearson's (1985a) narrative is an excellent example of a high-context explanation of the reasons Momma was surprised by Miss Pettigrew's poor penmanship.

High-context people are event centered. When asked a question, rather than provide specific answers, high-context people tell stories (see, for example, "Talk at the Gas Station" on pp. 151–154). In a study of farm families (Martinez-Brawley & Blundall, 1989), the interviewer asked a farmer about the personal characteristics he would like to see in a human services worker. With much gesticulation and relish, the farmer began telling about a father and son team of photographers who many years ago had visited the area and photographed his farm. The farmer pointed out how the young photographer, the son (evidently low-context), was unable to get the farmer to buy the photograph while the older photographer, the father (high-context), got the farmer to buy two copies. The summarizing statement was that the older photographer had been "a peach of a guy!" There the story ended and the interviewers were left to surmise that the qualities of that "peach of a guy" the farmer had found so irresistible were the ones he would want to see in a human services worker who visited the farm.

Low-context, information-centered interviewers looking for specific answers may become impatient with high-context respondents. Their impatience, despite attempts to cover it, is readily apparent to high-context people who are skilled at reading nonverbal signs. Lack of information, a problem for low-context professionals, results not because information is absent but rather because the interviewer lacks skill in entering the high-context linguistic world of the respondents and joining in the story. Their knowledge is not grounded in the eventful lives of real people, often as a result of their education. People are cataloged and described in the certified low-context language of academic studies or agency practice. Furthermore, when someone happens to reveal evidence of more intimate knowledge and insight, he or she is likely to append disclaimers to the more personal anecdotes told. The classroom is not a high-context environment. Therefore it is difficult to introduce cultural analysis of localism and its rich high-context language in ways that elicit serious student response. Instructors, especially those who have spent significant time in practice or in field research, may share with students experience with high-context clients and informants. They may show films that deal with localism and high-context communication and illustrate the richness of locality. However, these films often are treated as data and examined in the low-context idiom of the classroom rather than in their full richness.

Students can be introduced to the "real world" of human services work in the provincial or local context through internships and field experience in small communities. However, the agencies to which students are assigned often are staffed by professionals who view negatively the more informal ways in which the small community functions. Even in small community agencies, students often have little opportunity to work outside bureaucratic parameters. For example, one student, in analyzing her small-town agency experience, wrote:

> Once this summer, I was asked by "Jane" (the student's supervisor) to take a woman to the grocery story. I was curious about the woman because Jane did not like her at all, so I was glad to do it. After I brought the woman back, she invited me in. Although

I should have gone back to the office and worked on records, I decided to go in. I figured out that the woman not only wanted to talk to someone but probably also felt it was polite to invite me in after I had done her a favor. In talking to her, I found out a little more about her life (I stayed on two hours!) and although her case was closed after that, I was glad that I had visited with this woman.

There were many times when I spent hours at someone's house talking to them. I knew this would have been considered inefficient, but I felt people trusted me much more after I had put time finding out about their lives beyond our worker/client relationship.

Extended residence in a small community along with the watchful instruction of an instructor sympathetic to the community might be an effective means for learning the intricate details of microcommunity structure and its system of communication. A group practicum conducted in the community has the added advantage of letting students see collectively the work of agencies at close range as well as the real life of the community. Thus, students have the opportunity to learn how clients relate and attempt to adapt to life between two cultures: the little community of daily contact and the scheduled contact with agency personnel. Removed from the low-context setting of a university campus, the class faces collective practical problems of sufficient magnitude to guarantee major behavior changes and intellectual and linguistic reorientation. Working together on joint projects will enable high- and low-context people to discover ways of understanding each other's culture. For example, in one class, future social workers were asked to immerse themselves in a joint undertaking with a community group. During a community experience, a class organized an award presentation for a group of 200 senior citizens from the small towns of a relatively rural county. Students told of how the various day-to-day problem solving occurred. They told of a widow who needed a ride but never asked for one; instead, she recounted how life was different when her husband was alive and her daughter lived nearby. Students also told of many elderly people who brought crafts to display during a luncheon event. The elderly people, who were eager to sell them, mentioned how their friends and neighbors often sought their useful items. Little communication occurred that was not couched in the high-context stories of the seniors.

To overcome problems formally trained and certified human services professionals face in working productively with their clients, these professionals should engage in intercultural experiences. Hall (1981) makes a case for intercultural experiences as a way to bridge the gap between low-context and high-context individuals. Used properly, intercultural experiences can be a tremendous eye opener, providing a view of one's self seldom seen under normal conditions at home. Intercultural experiences, if controlled and directed, can help people learn about the ways in which the cultural context affects one's behavior in space—for example, elevators or other close places; in time—for example, people's sense of punctuality; in relation to sharing—for instance, communal meals and sleeping quarters. Intercultural experiences are a magnificent way of becoming cognizant of "culture" (one's own and that of others) as a dimension controlling daily patterns of interaction. Culture orders personalities that, in turn, have a profound effect on the ways people look at things, behave politically, make decisions, order priorities, organize their lives, and think (Hall, 1981). Students often must be reminded that intercultural experiences do not always require travel to distant lands. Sufficient cultural variation exists within the bounds of a city, county, or state to observe and participate in microcultural systems often excitingly divergent from one's own. The differences of the provinces and the uniqueness of various localities are nearby.

Smaller cities, towns, villages, and the rural hinterland have attracted people from major metropolitan centers. A strong motivating factor pulling people toward small settings for residence and work is the lure of scaled-down civic and municipal infrastructure and the hope of a less hectic lifestyle closer to nature. For many people who do not choose to leave the city, renewed effort to revive urban space into more supportive and satisfying neighborhoods is increasingly commonplace. People in the city and countryside are experimenting with ways to recover and maintain a scaled-down and, at the same time, enlivened and enriched lifestyle. Sense of place is an important factor promoted in these efforts. The significance of place and the need for roots appear to be increasingly appreciated as contributing factors to civic order and personal stability. The significance of place and cultural roots has motivated important and creative business ventures that help keep alive the locality.

Empty and near-empty public treasuries make local volunteer assistance and mutual aid less avocational and recreational and more central to day-to-day life. These times of economic trial will reaffirm that the good life, regardless of one's station, is life together in settings where one knows and is known as a named person with definite community status and purpose. A renewed sense of social responsibility and interdependency and a corresponding decline in the pursuit of individualism and self-sufficiency have occurred.

THE PROFESSIONAL'S PREDICAMENT

Warren's (1966) vertical–horizontal paradigm is widely used to describe the relationship between local communities and the wider society.

What is missing from the Warren analysis is a more thorough investigation of the professional worker's complex and often bewildering work setting in the community. Workers daily face translating vertically generated policies and programs into specific action programs geared to the municipal, civic, and overall sociocultural style of the community. Professional workers burdened with this responsibility need to be, out of sheer necessity, informed, "worldly" locals. They must think globally or nationally, but act locally in appropriate ways.

These contradictory forces, especially for younger workers, are likely to be major sources of job anxiety and personal discontent. Workers in the vertical system rarely "see" clients or work with locals on a continuing basis. Vertical incumbents "see" social problems the way they were presented in low-context language. They formulate policies and administrative regulations for people in the abstract—for theoretical, not real, communities. The horizontally placed worker sees people in all their concrete manifestations embedded in the local high-context sociocultural milieu. Because the responsibility for program adaptation and integration falls on the shoulders of the horizontally situated (that is, local or county) worker, that worker needs to reconceptualize the local context in a more positive manner if he or she is to survive. Vertical incumbents (or officials in the central offices of bureaucracies) speak somewhat cavalierly about the need to adapt and the great opportunity local workers have to be imaginative and innovative in shaping centralistic programs (be they federal or state) to meet local needs. However, they seldom provide local workers with helpful perspectives on making these adjustments.

Because new workers in human services bureaucracies often begin work in the local community, the local community should become a major focus in courses of study so that new workers will be able to translate centralistic tendencies to local contexts. However, this has not been the case. Educators often teach community to prospective professionals as if they were immediately to hold upper echelon staff positions in state capitals or in the nation's capital. Professionals should know the big picture; unfortunately, career advance often means moving from the horizontal to the vertical system. Nonetheless, the local community is the locus of program payoff and it is here that the new worker begins.

What then is required for a human services worker to be successful and to survive in the local context? First, the local worker must shed preconceived notions of "good" and "bad" communities. Community in and of itself is a positive force for those individuals who find in it support for their daily existence. There are no ideal communities comprising only supportive people, or open-minded people, or generous people, or benevolent people. Real communities will exhibit positive as well as negative characteristics. It is how workers use those attributes that matters.

Second, the local worker must realize that, in community, he or she is working where real-life encounters occur. In community, helping is not an abstract activity reduced to systematic entries in books where not even the names of those helped appear. Helping in the local context is making sense of the tortuous lives of those who live close to the worker. Helping in community is using the resources of neighbors to lend a hand to other neighbors. If the small-town worker is uncomfortable with this personal and intimate way of relating, and seeks more bureaucratic encounters, he or she will be uncomfortable and dissatisfied and will not become a positive force in the helping networks of the community.

Third, the worker must be aware that local attachments translate into relationships not with abstract people but with real individuals—people with names, faces, and unique idiosyncrasies. Those unique individuals in turn will relate in the same fashion to the worker. Small community relationships are personal. Local attachments will not only reduce anonymity but also curtail freedom. The worker will not be an anonymous face but a known member of the group and people will be interested in his or her activities, thoughts, and feelings. For individuals not used to this degree of personalism, the "gossip lines" may curtail freedom in painful ways. Only those workers who are willing to exchange anomie for a measure of scrutiny find the local community satisfying.

Fourth, the worker in local settings must be prepared to change his or her way of understanding and learning about the world. Local information will be provided in high-context language. The story, the anecdote, the bit of news all will convey important information whose meaning the worker must decipher. Listening to a lengthy anecdote told by a local person will not be a waste of time but rather a way of discovering the locality's ethos. The worker must recognize that local attachments are alive because people live their daily existences within the boundaries of locale. Attachment to locale should be viewed neither as an exclusively positive nor as an exclusively negative force or a psychological burden. Both healthy and unhealthy local attachments arise because people seldom can feel significant in influencing the events of the larger society, but they can feel significant in affecting the events of the immediate locale. Even those locals who are cognizant of the interrelatedness and interdependence of the world usually only can act locally. A positive way of counteracting negative localism when it arises is to encourage and facilitate actions that, although local, highlight the global aspects of human existence.

PART 2
THE COMMUNITY IN FICTION AND THE PRESS

❧

5

SMALL-TOWN USA: TRADITION AND CHANGE

In 1976, in reaction to the bad publicity the small town had received throughout the 1950s and 1960s and in anticipation of its revival, Benjamin Stein (1976) wrote an amusing essay entitled, "Whatever Happened to Small-Town America?" Stein, in his introduction, recounted that

> Jim Rockford, private detective in NBC-TV's popular "The Rockford Files," is in trouble. He is driving along in rural northern California on routine detective business, when his car suddenly hits a big bump and is incapacitated. Rockford, who is used to life in Los Angeles, is frantic. There he is, in the middle of nowhere, without any means of getting out; no taxicabs, no rental cares, no buses, no limousine service, nothing.
>
> Then salvation comes, in the form of a tow truck operator who just happens to be passing by. He offers to tow Rockford into the nearest town for repairs. . . . But while he is having lunch and waiting for the car to be fixed, Rockford learns that the repairs which he thought would be minor, are going to cost over $1,500. . . .
>
> Naturally, the car can't be fixed until the next day. So Rockford is consigned to the local motel, where he soon finds himself in the arms of a seemingly confused but seductive teenybopper. Suddenly someone bursts in and takes a compromising photograph; then while Rockford is still holding the supposedly shaken girl, a deputy sheriff comes roaring up, gun drawn, and threatens him. The deputy turns out to the be girl's fiancé, and he suspects that Rockford has been messing with his girl. . . .
>
> This characterization of the smâll town as evil and threatening to innocent city dwellers is now a staple of contemporary American mass culture. But the small town wasn't always seen that way. Over a relatively brief time, cultural attitudes toward small towns have changed virtually 180 degrees, from the old view of the small town as the bastion of everything good about America to the current view of the small town as everything frightening and corrupt about America. The change has been so complete that when we see a vestige of the old view appear, we are startled. (pp. 17–18)

To understand Stein's position, it is important to review the actual changes in the vision of small-town America. This literary review begins at the turn of the century with Booth Tarkington, a novelist who saw the small town as epitomizing the best qualities of human coexistence. By contrasting Tarkington's early vision with that of more contemporary American authors (such as Lewis, Davis, and Sayers), the reader will get a sense of the evolution of the layperson's perceptions of Gemeinschaft through the years, yet maintain a focus on the continued importance of the small town in American society.

A ROMANTIC VISION

Booth Tarkington's (1900a) *The Gentleman from Indiana* was first published in 1899; it depicted the small town as the place where moral principles, in the long run, triumphed, where community spirit not only existed but prevailed, and where people were able to create close genuine and lasting relationships. Plattville, Indiana, was a microcosm of society. As such, there was good and evil in the town. What was distinctive about Tarkington's depiction of the small community, unlike Sinclair Lewis's depiction (see pp. 113–116), is that with Tarkington, good and integrity prevailed in the end without need for extreme compromise. Those virtues, however, coincided with business interests of the town, a matter that gave the book a great deal of popularity among middle-class readers at the time. As Lingeman (1980) commented,

> Plattville, Booth Tarkington's seat of small-town folksiness in *The Gentleman from Indiana*, has a promoter drilling for oil—a former bunco artist who was reformed by the noble hero. This now-honest wildcatter does indeed strike oil, among the many happy endings in which the book abounds; and Plattville seems on the verge of moving to some vaguely defined higher plateau of prosperity without, of course, losing any of its deeply ingrained folksiness. Whether Tarkington's novel had any basis in fact is beside the point; its author, as an accomplished sensor of the popular mind, knew that his middle-class audience needed to believe in the happy ending of wealth from striking oil. (p. 339)

The Gentleman from Indiana is the story of John Harkless, a newspaper editor, and his involvement in the small town of Plattville. Harkless chose to return to Indiana after some years spent in the big cities of the East. "I always had a dim sort of feeling that the people out in these parts knew more, had more *sense* and were less artificial, I mean—and were kinder, and tried less to be somebody else, than almost any other people anywhere" (Tarkington, 1900a, p. 182). Harkless had returned to Plattville in search of Gemeinschaft. He did not accuse city folk of cruelty or disloyalty, but he did not feel that the city was *his* community. He needed a personal community. So, Harkless had, by chance, stumbled on *The Herald* and bought it. The novel's plot revolves around Harkless's crusade against the rowdiness and vice of the nearby shantytown at Six-Cross Roads and around his involvement in local politics. He is deeply committed to cleaner political activity and to elimination of the less desirable element of Plattville, the "hooded Whitecaps." Harkless' adventures against the hooded Whitecaps "anticipated the organized violence of the Ku Klux Klan in Indiana two decades later" (Goist, 1977, p. 16). In this sense, *The Gentleman from Indiana* is fiction to be viewed as social and historical prediction.

At one point in the novel, John Harkless is nearly beaten to death by hooded Whitecaps, but after a long convalescence he recovers and showing the strength of his community ties, he returns to Plattville. During his absence, he had been nominated for Congress amidst great jubilation. Unlike Carol Kennicott who, in Lewis's (1920b) *Main Street*, "reluctantly acquiesced to a town whose values she [could] only partially share" (Goist, 1977, p. 29), John Harkless realized his ambitions and ideals "within the context of the homey, middle class qualities of small town" Plattville (Goist, 1977, p. 17).

Although a sense of the romantic and ideal pervades Tarkington's writing—the town is gathered together to welcome its "hero"—anyone who has participated in a recent small-town welcoming parade will recognize the pervasive communal elements of small-town culture, elements that, although often ignored by social work practitioners, must be understood and appreciated. The following excerpt illustrates these elements.

THE GREAT HARKLESS COMES HOME

The Harkless Club of Carlow wheeled into Main Street, two hundred strong, with their banners and transparencies. Lige Willetts rode at their head, and behind him strode young William Todd and Parker and Ross Schofield and Homer Tibbs and Hartley Bowlder, and even Bud Tipworthy held a place in the ranks through his connection with the "Herald." They were all singing.

And, behind them, Helen saw the flag-covered barouche and her father, and beside him sat John Harkless with his head bared.

She glanced at Briscoe; he was standing on the front seat with Minnie beside him, and both were singing. Meredith had climbed upon the back seat and was nervously fumbling at a cigarette.

"Sing Tom!" the girl cried to him excitedly.

"I should be ashamed not to," he answered; and dropped the cigarette and began to sing "John Brown's Body" with all his strength. With that she seized his hand, sprang up beside him, and over the swelling chorus her full soprano rose, lifted with all the power in her.

The barouche rolled into the Square, and, as it passed, Harkless turned, and bent a sudden gaze upon the group in the buckboard; but the western sun was in his eyes, and he only caught a glimpse of a vague, bright shape and a dazzle of gold, and he was borne along and out of view, down the singing street.

Glory! Glory! Hallelujah!
Glory! Glory! Hallelujah!
Glory! Glory! Hallelujah!
As we go marching on!

The barouche stopped in front of the courthouse, and he passed up a lane they made for him to the steps. When he turned to them to speak, they began to cheer again, and he had to wait for them to quiet down.

"We can't hear him from over here," said Briscoe, "we're too far off. Mr. Meredith, suppose you take the ladies closer in, and I'll stay with the horses. You want to hear his speech."

"He is a great man, isn't he?" Meredith said to Helen, gravely, as he handed her out of the buckboard. "I've been trying to realize for the last few minutes, that he is the same old fellow I've been treating so familiarly all day long."

"Yes, he is a great man," she answered. "This is only the beginning."

"That's true," said Briscoe, who had overheard her. "He'll go pretty far. A man that people know is steady and strong and level-headed can get what ever he wants, because a public man can get anything, if people know he's safe and honest and they can rely on him for *sense*. It sounds like a simple matter; but only three or four public men in the country have convinced us that they are like that. Hurry along, young people."

Crossing the street, they met Miss Tipps; she was wiping her streaming eyes with the back of her left hand and still mechanically waving her handkerchief with her right. "Isn't it beautiful?" she said, not ceasing to flutter, unconsciously, the little square of cambric. "There was such a throng that I grew faint and had to come away. I don't mind your seeing me crying. Pretty near everybody cried when he walked up to the steps and we saw that he was lame."

Standing on the outskirts of the crowd, they could hear the mellow ring of Harkless's voice, but only fragments of the speech, for it was rather halting, and was not altogether clear in either rhetoric or delivery, and Mr. Bence could have been a good deal longer in saying what he had to say, and a thousands times more oratorical. Nevertheless, there was not a man or woman present who did not declare that it was the greatest speech ever heard in Plattville; and they really thought so—to such lengths are loyalty and friendship sometimes carried in Carlow and Amo and Gaines.

He looked down upon the attentive, earnest faces and into the kindly eyes of the Hoosier country people, and, as he spoke, the thought kept recurring to him that this was the place he had dreaded to come back to; that these were the people he had wished to leave—these, who gave him everything they had to give—and this made it difficult to keep his tones steady and his throat clear.

Helen stood so far from the steps (nor could she be induced to penetrate further, though they would have made way for her) that only fragments reached her, but what she heard she remembered:

"I have come home. . . . Ordinarily a man needs to fall sick by the wayside or to be set upon by thieves, in order to realize that nine-tenths of the world is Samaritan, and the other tenth only too busy or too ignorant to be. Down here he realizes it with no necessity of illness or wounds to bring it out; and if he does get hurt, you send him to Congress. . . . There will be no other in Washington so proud of what he stands for as I shall be. To represent you is to stand for realities—fearlessness, honor, kindness. . . . We are people who take what comes to us, and it comes bountifully; we are rich—oh, we are all Americans here!

This is the place for a man who likes to live where people are kind to each other, and where they have the old-fashioned way of saying "Home." Other places, they don't seem to get so much into it as we do. And to come home as I have to-day. . . . I have come home. . . ."

Every one meant to shake hands with him, and, when the speech was over, those nearest swooped upon him, cheering and waving, and grasping at his hand. Then a line was formed, and they began to defile by him, as he stood on the steps, and one by one they came up, and gave him hearty greetings, and passed on through the court-house and out at the south door. (pp. 366–370) ❧

SOURCE: Tarkington, B. (1900b). The great Harkless comes home. In *The gentleman from Indiana* (pp. 346–384). New York: Grosset and Dunlap.

AN AMBIVALENT VISION OF MAIN STREET

Even at the turn of the century, people had different perceptions of community. Although Tarkington offered a positive view of the cohesive Gemeinschaft, where citizens realize their ideals and where life of the soul and of the body are nurtured, there is a counterpart. During the 1920s and 1930s, a host of American writers rebelled against the constrictions of Gemeinschaft as represented by the small towns and villages across America. Few of those writers surpassed Sinclair Lewis (1920b), whose *Main Street* epitomized the struggle of a young intellectual city woman against the suffocating forces of small town.

However, through various cultural waves, the rebellion against small-town provincialism of the 1920s changed again in the 1930s, a testimony of the wax and wane of rural and small-town values in the culture at large. Lingeman (1980) commented on this phenomenon:

> The sociologist Carl Withers recalled that in the twenties, the impact of *Main Street* caused small-town boys attending urban colleges to feel ashamed of their background and become objects of pity to their urban classmates. But in the thirties this attitude changed; small town boys were regarded as "true Americans," exemplifying the rural traditions that had suddenly become so attractive (at a distance) to the students from the city. (p. 394)

What characterizes Lewis's fiction is its endurance. Although the story takes place between 1912 and 1920, when Carol Milford, a young city college graduate, marries Willi Kennicott, a provincial doctor, and arrives to settle in Gopher Prairie, Minnesota (population 3,000), Carol Kennicott's plight has been reenacted during the 1980s in many provincial towns. The limiting and often suffocating social environment that Carol perceives in relation to her personal life in Gopher Prairie often has been encountered by professional workers who take jobs in small communities, unaware that just as community nourishes one's soul, community also limits one's horizons.

Community is tightly bound to *culture*, the traditions, institutions, people, and places that mold the life of a particular locale, region, or nation. It is unrealistic to expect that a given group of people who have been contented with a way of life for decades or even centuries would readily welcome innovations, even if potentially more satisfying. Human nature clings to the known. Generalist social workers must learn that just as the inevitable process of physical growth represents a threat to the integrity of the child or young adult's ego, so the often inevitable striving for change and development within communities represent a pull of forces, a painful struggle for survival.

The merit of good fiction is that it is enduring and transcends time. Another element of Carol's struggle in Gopher Prairie that is contemporary is the ambivalence that characterizes her search for community. On the one hand, Carol is searching for the simplicity and equality of a former time; on the other, she is fascinated by the intellectual excitement and liberal views of a new age. As Goist (1977) pointed out, Carol's "yearning for community is clearly not merely a local matter. Though many of her efforts are misdirected, Carol's hope is that what she can accomplish in Gopher Prairie be linked to a worldwide struggle for freedom and comraderie among all peoples" (p. 28). Carol Kennicott wants to strengthen the vertical ties, which can weaken the horizontal ones. In Carol's mind, individuals who actively search for the satisfactions of community are looking for higher universal values, hoping to find them all embodied in a single communal entity, and of course, that is what Carol cannot find:

> I believe all of us want the same things—we're all together, the industrial workers and the women and the farmers and the Negro race and the Asiatic colonies, and even a few of the Respectables. . . . We want our Utopia now and we are going to try our hands at it. (Lewis, 1920b, pp. 201–202)

In the book, Carol rebels against the small town, and for a time, Washington offers her a momentary sense of community. She finds her own people, and is gratified by intellectual stimulation. Yet, in the end, Carol returns to Gopher Prairie. The city had offered her a community of interests; the town offers her stability, which, after her fling with excitement, she can more readily tolerate. As Goist (1977) commented,

> The town . . . stands for a community of stable familiarity. Carol [chooses the town] . . . essentially, not because she loves the town, or even likes it much, but because it is a familiar environment to deal with. She has decided she can maintain a critical stance without waging war with the town as she had done previously. (p. 29)

Carol's episode probably is rewritten in the life script of millions of contemporary small-town residents. Social workers functioning in the context of small-town communities probably will come in contact with many Carol Kennicotts whose invaluable help and wisdom can be activated to make life better in small towns and villages. Human services practitioners may easily identify with Carol Kennicott because they recognize that all individuals are ambivalent about the virtues of their communities and that they will rebel against and, yet, adopt its mores, all at the same time.

The following excerpt provides a lively description of an episode that leads to Carol's improvising—or perhaps formulating—a theory of social change for the Gemeinschaft. When confronted with the presumptuousness of the local cultural club discussing all of the English poets at once, Carol wonders whether to erupt and confront the members of the Thanatopsis Club with their ignorance and lack of sophistication or whether to introduce, in moderate or incremental fashion, her point of view.

MY DEAR, YOU REALLY MUST COME TO THE THANATOPSIS THIS AFTERNOON

She had often been invited to the weekly meetings of the Thanatopsis, the women's study club, but she had put it off. The Thanatopsis was, Vida Sherwin promised, "such a cozy group, and yet it puts you in touch with all the intellectual thoughts that are going on everywhere."

Early in March Mrs. Westlake, wife of the veteran physician, marched into Carol's living-room like an amiable old pussy and suggested, "My dear, you really must come to the Thanatopsis this afternoon. Mrs. Dawson is going to be leader and the poor soul is frightened to death. She wanted me to get you to come. She says she's sure you will brighten up the meeting with your knowledge of books and writings. (English poetry is our topic today.) So shoo! Put on your coat!"

"English poetry? Really? I'd love to go. I didn't realize you were reading poetry."

"Oh, we're not so slow!"

Mrs. Luke Dawson, wife of the richest man in town, gaped at them piteously when they appeared. Her expensive frock of beaver-colored satin with rows, plasters, and pendants of solemn brown beads was intended for a woman twice her size. She stood wringing her hands in front of nineteen folding chairs, in her front parlor with its faded photograph of Minnehaha Falls in 1890, its "colored enlargement" of Mr. Dawson, its bulbous lamp painted with sepia cows and mountains and standing on a mortuary marble column.

She creaked, "O Mrs. Kennicott, I'm in such a fix. I'm supposed to lead the discussion, and I wondered would you come and help?"

"What poet do you take up today?" demanded Carol, in her library tone of "What book do you wish to take out?"

"Why, the English ones."

"Not all of them?"

"W-why yes. We're learning all of European Literature this year. The club gets such a nice magazine, *Culture Hints*, and we follow its programs. Last year our subject was Men and Women of the Bible, and next year we'll probably take up Furnishings and China. My, it does make a body hustle to keep up with all these new culture subjects, but it is improving. So will you help us with the discussion today?"

On her way over Carol had decided to use the Thanatopsis as the tool with which to liberalize the town. She had immediately conceived enormous enthusiasm; she had chanted, "These are the real people. When the housewives, who bear the burdens, are interested in poetry, it means something. I'll work with them—for them—anything!"

Her enthusiasm had become watery even before thirteen women resolutely removed their overshoes, sat down meatily, ate peppermints, dusted their fingers, folded their hands, composed their lower thoughts, and invited the naked muse of poetry to deliver her most improving message. They had greeted Carol affectionately, and she tried to be a daughter to them. But she felt insecure. Her chair was out in the open, exposed to their gaze, and it was a hard-slatted, quivery, slippery church-parlor chair, likely to collapse publicly and without warning. It was impossible to sit on it without folding the hands and listening piously.

She wanted to kick the chair and run. It would make a magnificent clatter.

She saw that Vida Sherwin was watching her. She pinched her wrist, as though she were a noisy child in church, and when she was decent and cramped again, she listened.

Mrs. Dawson opened the meeting by sighing, "I'm sure I'm glad to see you all here today, and I understand that the ladies have prepared a number of very interesting papers, this is such an interesting subject, the poets, they have been an inspiration for higher thought, in fact wasn't it Reverend Banlick who said that some of the poets have been as much an inspiration as a good many of the ministers, and so we shall be glad to hear——"

The poor lady smiled neuralgically, panted with fright, scrabbled about the small oak table to find her eye-glasses, and continued, "We will first have the pleasure of hearing Mrs. Jenson on the subject 'Shakespeare and Milton.' "

Mrs. Ole Jenson said that Shakespeare was born in 1564 and died 1616. He lived in London, England, and in Stratford-on-Avon, which many American tourists loved to visit, a lovely town with many curios and old houses well worth examination. Many people believed that Shakespeare was the greatest playwright who ever lived, also a fine poet. Not much was known about his life, but after all that did not really make so much difference, because they loved to read his numerous plays, several of the best known of which she would now criticize.

Perhaps the best known of his plays was "The Merchant of Venice," having a beautiful love story and a fine appreciation of a woman's brains, which a woman's club, even those who did not care to commit themselves on the question of suffrage, ought to appreciate. (Laughter.) Mrs. Jenson was sure that she, for one, would love to be like Portia. The play was about a Jew named Shylock, and he didn't want his daughter to marry a Venice gentleman named Antonio——

Mrs. Leonard Warren, a slender, gray, nervous woman, president of the Thanatopsis and wife of the Congregational pastor, reported the birth and death dates of Byron, Scott, Moore, Burns; and wound up:

"Burns was quite a poor boy and he did not enjoy the advantages we enjoy today, except for the advantages of the fine old Scotch kirk where he heard the Word of God preached more fearlessly than even in the finest big brick churches in the big and so-called advanced cities of today, but he did not have our educational advantages and Latin and the other treasures of the mind so richly strewn before the, alas, too offtimes inattentive feet of our youth who do not always sufficiently appreciate the privileges freely granted to every American boy rich or poor. Burns had to work hard and was sometimes led by evil companionship into low habits. But it is morally instructive to know that he was a good student and educated himself, in striking contrast to the loose ways and so-called aristocratic society-life of Lord Byron, on which I have just spoken. And certainly though the lords and earls of his day may have looked down upon Burns as a humble person, many of us have greatly enjoyed his pieces about the mouse and other rustic subjects, with their message of humble beauty—I am so sorry I have not got the time to quote some of them."

Mrs. George Edwin Mott gave ten minutes to Tennyson and Browning.

Mrs. Nat Hicks, a wry-faced, curiously sweet woman, so awed by her betters that Carol wanted to kiss her, completed the day's grim task by a paper on "Other Poets." The other poets worthy of consideration were Coleridge, Wordsworth, Shelley, Gray, Mrs. Hemans, and Kipling.

Miss Ella Stowbody obliged with a recital of "The Recessional" and extracts from "Lalla Rookh." By request, she gave "An Old Sweetheart of Mine" as encore.

Gopher Prairie had finished the poets. It was ready for the next week's labor: English Fiction and Essays.

Mrs. Dawson besought, "Now we will have a discussion of the papers, and I am sure we shall all enjoy hearing from one who we hope to have as a new member, Mrs. Kennicott, who with her splendid literary training and all should be able to give us many pointers and—many helpful pointers."

Carol had warned herself not to be so "beastly supercilious." She had insisted that in the belated quest of these work-stained women was an aspiration which ought to stir her tears. "But they're so self-satisfied. They think they're doing Burns a favor. They don't believe they have a 'belated quest.' They're sure that they have culture salted and hung up." It was out of this stupor of doubt that Mrs. Dawson's summons roused her. She was in a panic. How could she speak without hurting them?

Mrs. Champ Perry leaned over to stroke her hand and whisper, "You look tired, dearie. Don't you talk unless you want to."

Affection flooded Carol; she was on her feet, searching for words and courtesies:

"The only thing in the way of suggestion—I know you are following a definite program, but I do wish that now you've had such a splendid introduction, instead of going on with some other subject next year you could return and take up the poets more in detail. Especially actual quotations—even though their lives are so interesting and, as Mrs. Warren said, so morally instructive. And perhaps there are several poets not mentioned today whom it might be worth while considering—Keats, for instance, and Matthew Arnold and Rossetti and Swinburne. Swinburne would be such a— well, that is, such a contrast to life as we all enjoy it in our beautiful Middle-west——"

She saw that Mrs. Leonard Warren was not with her. She captured her by innocently continuing:

"Unless perhaps Swinburne tends to be, uh, more outspoken than you, than we really like. What do you think, Mrs. Warren?"

The pastor's wife decided, "Why, you've caught my very thoughts, Mrs. Kennicott. Of course I have never *read* Swinburne, but years ago, when he was in vogue, I remember Mr. Warren saying that Swinburne (or was it Oscar Wilde? but anyway:) he said that though many so-called intellectual people posed and pretended to find beauty in Swinburne, there can never be genuine beauty without the message from the heart. But at the same time I do think you have an excellent idea, and though we have talked about Furnishings and China as the probable subject for next year, I believe that it would be nice if the program committee would try to work in another day entirely devoted to English poetry! In fact, Madame Chairman, I so move you."

When Mrs. Dawson's coffee and angel's-food had helped them to recover from the depression caused by thoughts of Shakesepare's death they all told Carol that it was a pleasure to have her with them. The membership committee retired to the sitting-room for three minutes and elected her a member.

And she stopped being patronizing.

She wanted to be one of them. They were so loyal and kind. It was they who would carry out her aspiration. Her campaign against village sloth was actually begun! On what specific reform should she first loose her army? During the gossip after the meeting Mrs. George Edwin Mott remarked that the city hall seemed inadequate for the splendid modern Gopher Prairie. Mrs. Nat Hicks timidly wished that the young people could have free dances there—the lodge dances were so exclusive. The city hall. That was it! Carol hurried home.

She had not realized that Gopher Prairie was a city. From Kennicott she discovered that it was legally organized with a mayor and city-council and wards. She was delighted by the simplicity of voting one's self a metropolis. Why not?

She was a proud and patriotic citizen, all evening. (pp. 124–128) ❧

SOURCE: Lewis, S. (1920a). Chapter 9. In *Main street* (pp. 131–143). New York: Harcourt, Brace. Note that the title of this excerpt does not appear in the original version.

THE SOUTHERN BLACK TOWN

In the essay "The Black Writer and the Southern Experience" (1983), Alice Walker discussed the sense of community reflected in the reminiscences of southern black Americans. She recounted a story told by her mother of an episode that occurred during the depression when the family lived in a small Georgia town. Walker (1983) narrated how the family, who were sharecroppers, had to submit vouchers signed by local officials to collect flour (an item difficult to obtain), which was distributed for the government by the Red Cross:

> One day, [when] my mother was to go into town for flour she received a large box of clothes from one of my aunts who was living in the North. The clothes were in good condition, though well worn, and my mother needed a dress, so she immediately put

> on one of those from the box and wore it into town. When she reached the distribution center and presented her voucher she was confronted by a white woman who looked her up and down with marked anger and envy.
>
> "What'd you come up here for?" the woman asked.
>
> "For some flour," said my mother, presenting her voucher.
>
> "Humph," said the woman, looking at her more closely and with unconcealed fury. "Anybody dressed up as good as you don't need to come here begging for food." (pp. 15–16)

Walker said her mother refuted the accusation of begging by stressing that the government was giving away flour to those who needed it and that she needed it, but to no avail. Walker described the white woman's anger and her mother's humiliation as she and her children walked back into the street with no flour. The point of the story was not to stress the humiliation or lack of "community-ness" reflected in the white woman's behavior, but rather to highlight the communal feelings of other black citizens who responded to the family's predicament:

> "What did you and Daddy do for flour that winter?" I asked my mother.
>
> "Well," she said, "Aunt Mandy Aikens lived down the road from us and she got plenty of flour. We had a good stand of corn so we had plenty of meal. Aunt Mandy would swap me a bucket of flour for a bucket of meal. We got by all right."
>
> Then, she added thoughtfully, "And that old woman that turned me off so short got down so bad in the end that she was walking on two sticks." And I knew she was thinking, though she never said it: Here I am today, my eight children healthy and grown and three of them in college and me with hardly a sick day for years. Ain't Jesus wonderful. (Walker, 1983, p. 16)

Walker stressed how this story reveals the strength of people. People who when humiliated by the larger society used religion and the closer, more meaningful ties with the ethnic group as an antidote against bitterness. Walker commented that when she listened to her mother tell the story, the white woman's vindictiveness was less important than her Aunt Mandy's generosity or the group's sense of community.

Perhaps no southern writer better conveys the sense of richness, cohesiveness, culture, and spirit of the small southern black town than Zora Neale Hurston, a black novelist and anthropologist. Her (1935b) book, *Mules and Men*, a collection of stories gathered by Hurston in her native community of Eatonville, Florida, is a mirror in which life in the small black southern town of the 1930s is reflected. Hurston was a strong and controversial writer whose works captured the strength of her small town. However, her work has remained little known.

In her essay "Looking for Zora" (1983), Walker suggested that Hurston's rich prose came from her rich experiences in Eatonville, Florida. "Not many black people in America come from a self-contained, all-black community where loyalty and unity are taken for granted. A place where black pride is nothing new" (Walker, 1983, p. 100).

The following excerpt is Zora Neale Hurston's description of her arrival in her native town of Eatonville, as she embarks on an expedition to collect black folklore among those she knew and loved in a Florida county town of the 1930s.

ARRIVING IN EATONVILLE, FLORIDA

As I cross the Maitland-Eatonville township line I could see a group on the store porch. I was delighted. The town had not changed. Same love of talk and song. So I drove on down there before I stopped. Yes, there was George Thomas, Calvin Daniels, Jack and Charlie Jones, Gene Brazzle, B. Moseley and "Seaboard." Deep in a game of Florida-flip. All of those who were not actually playing were giving advice—"bet straightening" they call it.

"Hello, boys," I hailed them as I went into neutral.

They looked up from the game and for a moment it looked as if they had forgotten me. Then B. Mosley said, "Well, if it ain't Zora Hurston!" Then everybody crowded around the car to help greet me.

"You gointer say awhile, Zora?"

"Yep. Several months."

"Where you gointer stay, Zora?"

"With Mett and Ellis, I reckon."

"Mett" was Mrs. Armetta Jones, a intimate friend of mine since childhood and Ellis was her husband. Their house stands under the huge camphor tree on the front street.

"Hello, heart-string," Mayor Hiram Lester yelled as he hurried up the street. "We heard all about you up North. You back home for good, I hope."

"Nope, Ah come to collect some old stories and tales and Ah know y'all know a plenty of 'em and that's why Ah headed straight for home."

"What you mean, Zora, them big old lies we tell when we're jus' sittin' around here on the store porch doin' nothin'?" asked B. Moseley.

"Yeah, those same ones about Ole Massa, and colored folks in heaven, and—oh y'all know the kind I mean."

"Aw shucks," exclaimed George Thomas doubtfully. "Zora, don't you come here and tell de biggest lie first thing. Who you reckon want to read all them old-time tales about Brer Rabbit and Brer Bear?"

"Plenty of people, George. They are a lot more valuable than you might think. We want to set them down before it's too late."

"Too late for what?"

"Before everybody forgets all of 'em."

"No danger of that. That's all some people is good for—set 'round and lie and murder groceries."

"Ah know one right now," Calvin Daniels announced cheerfully. "It's a tale 'bout John and de frog."

"Wait till she get out her car, Calvin. Let her get settled at Mett's and cook a pan of ginger bread then we'll all go down and tell lies and eat ginger bread. Dat's de way to do. She's tired now from all dat drivin'."

"All right, boys," I agreed. "But Ah'll be rested by night. Be lookin' for everybody."

So I unloaded the car and crowded it into Ellis' garage and got settled. Armetta made me lie down and rest while she cooked a big pan of ginger bread for the company we expected. (pp. 23–24) ❧

SOURCE: Hurston, Z. N. (1935a). [Chapter 1]. In *Mules and men* (pp. 23–24). Philadelphia: J. B. Lippincott. Excerpt from *Mules and Men* by Zora Neale Hurston. Copyright 1935 by Zora Neale Hurston, renewed © 1963 by John C. Hurston. Reprinted by permission of Harper & Row, Publishers, Inc.

Note that the title of this excerpt does not appear in the original version.

A Contemporary View of the Industrial Small Town

Arensberg (1955) wrote that the mill towns or factory cities born in Britain spread "like any other cultural ware" throughout the United States and reached their peak around 1925 (p. 1144). After that, although no longer spreading with vigor, they continued to exist and leave their marks in the social structure of many communities. Arensberg writes about the mill town's use of space:

> This use of space is telltale. Far from being merely chaotic and lawless, the "unplanned" form the early industrial cities of American took was a new and distinctive (if unlovely) community form. The new use of space gives us the typical banded and strategied zonal ordering. . . .
>
> This use of space bands and zones the middle-class dwellings and the middle-class shops in the middle and crams the mills and the warehouses and the industrial warrens of factory workers and immigrant hands in the narrow blighted bottoms which once were the marketplaces and the crossroads of the older towns. It creates a new assemblage center in the railroad station and the "downtown center" about it and a new pattern of withdrawal whereby the same railroad or the avenues—pushing out the "Main Line"—put the better off and higher occupations of the common factors on which all depend in progressively farther removed residential blocks. It makes visible in external display these graded and successive zones of better or worse neighborhoods and mirrors perfectly an open-class system's scalar stratification of incomes, of power, and of prestige in the zonal successions one sees moving inward from withdrawn garden suburb to blighted tenement district. (p. 1158)

Arensberg's stratified "mill or industrial town" is made contemporary in Peter Davis's (1982b) description of Hamilton, Ohio, where "the West and East sides never liked each other, blacks and whites have been uneasy for over a century, rich and poor have been estranged since the town's first industrialist. . . ." (p. 17).

In Peter Davis's (1982b) *Hometown*, he provided shrewd, yet poetic descriptions of the spirit, "the sentiment" of a midsized industrial community. Unlike the early 20th century writers, Davis did not sing only about the beauty and supportive networks of Gemeinschaft; he was not a romantic but a realist who recognized that small and midsized communities were plagued by problems. He recognized that however cohesive, these communities were divisive; that however nourishing of an individual's social needs, they also could be punishing.

The following excerpt by Davis is a statement of the permanency of the mill or industrial town as a form of American community, the permanency of its problems, and the permanency of many of its patterned solutions. In Hamilton, the Ohio community described by Davis, there is stability in change. Just as communities did in the past, Hamilton often finds elements of cohesiveness or common cause in its own fragmentation—a sad but true state of reality. Does that mean that it lacks any socially redeeming qualities? No. It simply means that Hamilton is far from perfect. It simply means that, apparently, perfectly harmonious communities such as those bucolic places described by turn-of-the-century romantics are not attainable in the contemporary industrial world.

Hometown is seen as a microcosm of society. Although Davis did not deny the interrelationship of the town to the world, he emphasized the self-sufficiency of the many social networks of its inhabitants. The inhabitants of Hamilton play many roles and act through many social institutions. If horizontal ties are strong, if a sense of "we-ness," usefulness, and satisfaction is achieved, it is done precisely through those various roles and tasks, internal to the community itself rather than through any associations with the outside world. For Davis, Gemeinschaft, imperfect as it might be, is alive and struggling through all people.

GETTING THERE

I went to Hamilton not so much looking for as assuming change. The prevalence of change is a given in America. Yet what I found was an astonishing, striking, virtually genetic resemblance between Hamilton's past and its present. The desire to sell, build, expand, advertise, migrate, win, get more for the children—all of this has been in Hamilton for over one hundred fifty years. Dazzled by the vividness and clutter of technology, Hamiltonians themselves remark on how much has changed in the town. Buildings are replaced, everything runs by computer, people are ciphers. Sidewalks are no longer safe, everyone gets mad at his neighbor too easily, public officials are dishonest, kids leave town if they get an education. Yet each of these complaints echoes one in the nineteenth century. The bootlegging city marshal of the 1870s is mirrored in the sheriff who in the 1970s was convicted of embezzlement, conflict of interest, and income tax evasion. The rapid pace of change disturbed those Hamiltonians of the 1890s who longed for "the gentler days gone by" when families stayed together, indeed for their own youth: "The maypole surrounded by a bevy of girls dressed in every color of the rainbow, a beautiful sight that reminded many a heart, whose youthful throb had become chilled, of the merry times of long ago." New buildings were condemned for shoddy workmanship; fighting in the streets made evening walks perilous.

As for technology, Hamiltonians proudly and somewhat fearfully recorded the "radical changes" that had made the 1890s different from the early nineteenth century—the railroad, telegraph, telephone, electric light, microphone. These made them feel they lived in a time the world had never known, and of course they were right. But so had their own grandparents been right when they declared that canals, steamboats, and daguerreotypes had changed the world forever.

When the town celebrated its 1891 centennial, Hamilton High School had a history of twenty-nine years. Only thirty-six percent of its graduates still lived in Hamilton, compared with forty-four percent of the class of 1950 who were in town three decades later. Comparisons can be misleading when life expectancy, methods of record-keeping, and population size are as different as they are between nineteenth- and twentieth-century Hamilton. Yet it seems clear that despite hometown nostalgia for a stabler past, Hamilton's young were at least as unlikely to remain nestlings one hundred years ago as they are today. Hamiltonians who look back longingly are those, obviously, who still live there. *Their* parents did stay. But not all their aunts and uncles did. The point is not that Hamiltonians are wrong to think their children footloose; the point is only that they always were. America was not where you started but where you started over. In Europe the frontier was a border where you had to stop; in America the frontier was a horizon stretching as far as the imagination. We move a lot, one fifth of us changing homes every year, and always have.

Blinded by speed, inventions, new means of transportation, we focus on change to the exclusion of permanence. What generation since the founding of the Republic had not thought itself living in transition, had not longed for the time when children obeyed, a dollar was worth a dollar, the boss knew all his workers by their first names? It is hard to escape the conclusion that permanence, continuity, relative fixity are paid insufficient attention in a society that, even when fearful of it, reveres and generally profits from change. In thrall to the gospel of change, we overlook what is continuous; one of the most enduring features of the American landscape is change itself.

What changes far less than is suspected by most social researchers and commentators, it seems to me after six years of observing Hamilton, is the nature of family relationships. When the novelist William Dean Howells was growing up in Hamilton in the 1840s, he noticed that "Between the young and the old there is a vast gulf, seldom if ever bridged. The old can look backward over it, but they cannot cross it, any more than the young, who can see no thither side." More than a century later, "generation gap" was coined and pushed as an insight into a current phenomenon. Howells himself did not present his recollection as anything new; he was simply paying attention to his own childhood, making observations as applicable to the 1980s as they were to the 1840s. Howells also found Hamilton's class structure oppressive, even as a boy, criticizing "social cruelties which are the modern expression of the savage spirit otherwise repressed by civilization." The continuities are not necessarily reassuring, but they are still continuities. The novelist Fannie Hurst, a child in Hamilton sixty years after Howells, was equally aware of the generation gap and of social distinctions that would have circumscribed her, as a Jew, had she stayed in her hometown all her life. Yet neither was alienated, both enjoyed their Hamilton childhoods. "I am treating myself to a debauch of nostalgia," Fannie Hurst said when she returned to Hamilton after several decades. Howells, too, loved Hamilton. "The home of my happiest years," he wrote, "what an incomparable town for a boy to be a boy in." Though a New Englander for half a century, the writer never tried out a new pen without inscribing on the nearest piece of paper:

William Dean Howells
Hamilton, Ohio

As for Hamilton's being split into factions, the West and East Sides never liked each other, blacks and whites have been uneasy for over a century, rich and poor have been estranged since the town's first industrialist, John Woods, refused to give his employees a five-cent-a-day raise in 1836. Hamilton's mayor, Frank Witt, worried about the city's divisions in the late 1970s. Just forty, he was a three-term mayor already and had an eye that fixed itself well beyond Hamilton. Both his friends and enemies expected higher office for him; God only knew where he would go from here. "Remember this and you'll know Hamilton," Mayor Witt said as a January afternoon darkened outside his flag-decked, municipally correct office in the City Building. "We are a deeply fragmented community. We're *nice* to each other so much of the time we get the idea that's all there is. But since the problems and misunderstandings remain pretty consistent year after year, I have to assume we don't actually like each other as much as we claim to. Maybe nice is what you have to be or you'd be swinging at each other all the time. Still, if you don't recognize your divisions, it's going to be pretty hard to heal them." The bright, ambitious young mayor—shrewd, handsome, supple—was perfectly in tune with his predecessors who, in the 1890s, were already mourning the loss of a sense of community in Hamilton.

The town's past and present seem to contain each other the way an orange contains a seed that is itself the beginning of a new orange. Change is, as always, everywhere. To deny it is to baffle the sounds of our time. Yet there is a correspondence between nineteenth- and twentieth-century Hamilton, an essence in what happened there over one hundred years ago leading very certainly, on direct course, to what the town is today. In the world around Hamilton, there is a sense in which the nineteenth century—from Darwin to Verne to Marx to Edison to Einstein to Freud—can even be said to have *dreamed* the twentieth. It is not a simple *plus ça change*. Much does change; even more remains. Hamilton's identity is composed of elements that evolve and accrue gradually, incrementally, yielding to the latest patents and annual trends only the way the Grand Canyon does to wind. (pp. 14–18) ❧

SOURCE: Davis, P. (1982a). Getting there. In *Hometown: A contemporary American chronicle* (pp. 9–20). New York: Simon & Schuster.

THE SMALL-TOWN REVIVAL

Thornton Wilder (1938) wrote *Our Town* not only to offer pictures of life in a New Hampshire village, but also to attempt to convey the significance of the daily routines of the people in the village. Wilder reflected on life in small towns as it once was and as it was changing. Wilder's characters were fond of and concerned about the small town and criticized the gentrification of the village. Dr. Gibbs, one of the play's protagonists, commented about the villagers as they were seen by the old-timers: "They're all getting citified, that's the trouble with them. They haven't got nothing to burgle and everybody knows it" (p. 50). Dr. Gibbs also recognized that "some people ain't made for small town life" (p. 49) and was distressed by his inability to predict where it would all end.

The following exhibit picks up where Wilder left off in *Our Town* and illustrates the direction in which change has taken the sleepy New Hampshire village. In 1981, following the population shifts that were occurring in the United States, two reporters visited Peterborough, the town where Wilder reputedly wrote much of the play. What they found in 1981 was described in their report. Yet, Peterborough was getting citified; development was strong and much bureaucratization had occurred in the town's ways. Change was no longer necessarily a welcome or spontaneous process but had to be controlled by a "planning board." However, many people were still charmed by small-town life and many things had remained the same. The exhibit illustrates the many ways in which life has changed in small-town America and how an old-fashioned slow pace is still prevalent and desirable in many places.

OUR TOWN IN 1981

The people of Peterborough, N.H., think of "Our Town" as their town. Peterborough is set in the same beautiful southern New Hampshire valley as Grover's Corners, protected by Mount Monadnock and lush with mountain laurel. And Wilder wrote large parts of "Our Town" at the MacDowell Colony for artists in Peterborough. As in Grover's Corners, the pace is slow, the wants are small and the people generally follow Wilder's small-town dictum to "do all we can to help those that can't help themselves and those that can we leave alone." But while Peterborough celebrates its claim to fame with *Our Town Realty* and *Our Town Landscaping*, its problems in the 1980s are a time and a world away from Wilder's classic play about small-town life. If Grover's Corners evoked the way things were at the turn of the century, Peterborough represents the way things are today.

Newcomers: From a sleepy village of middle-class folk, Peterborough has grown into a town with a population of 4,897—up 32 per cent since 1970. Unlike Grover's Corners, where the earliest tombstones in the town cemetery carried the same names as families who still lived in town, Peterborough has become a village of newcomers. The old textile mills have been replaced by mail-order firms, the subject of condominium conversions is a new town preoccupation and beyond Main Street are shopping malls, single-family subdivisions and a new industrial park where 1,500 Peterborough citizens work for the town's largest employer, New Hampshire Ball Bearing. When old-timers meet for coffee at Nonie's Bake Shop, however, the feeling is as it always was. "People are searching for peace and quiet," says town clerk Stella Sumner. "They want closeness, a sense of belonging."

The influx of people has forced the town to grapple with the question of growth. Partly due to the persistence of newcomers, Peterborough adopted zoning laws in 1970. Now, says Paul C. Cummings, Jr., 67, publisher of *The Peterborough Transcript*, one of two town newspapers, "no board has more life-and-death power in town than the planning board." As a result, Peterborough has no flashing neon signs, no McDonald's and it retains the look and mood of a Grover's Corners. But Peterborough's slow-growth policies have a less fortunate consequence: most housing is too costly for those who hold jobs in the area.

"Indifferent": The townsfolk are still predominantly Protestant and Republican, with the rest, as Wilder wrote of Grover's Corners, "indifferent." Despite a steady turnover of policemen, crime is not a problem. Most thefts are attributed to out-of-staters, murders and muggings are unheard of and the town drunk cleans out the town septic tanks. The biggest problem for many newcomers is simply adapting to Peterborough's old-fashioned ways. Explains Jere Morris, a Peterborough native: "In a small town you cannot always speak your mind."

And yet, as Wilder wrote, "In our town we like to know the facts about everybody." To update that tradition, *The Peterborough Transcript* now lists births to unwed mothers along with marriages and deaths—while the town's annual report includes those who fail to pay their taxes. "That makes it a best seller," says Cummings. The town's cultural life has kept up with the times and includes a chamber-music festival and summer stock by the Peterborough Players. But the real attractions to life in Peterborough are less tangible. "It's nice to not be honked at, to really mean it when you say hello," says Debby Fuller, an expatriate from Cleveland. "It's old—but I feel like I've come home." (p. 28) ❧

SOURCE: Morganthauw, T., et al. "Our town" in 1981. *Newsweek*, p. 28. From NEWSWEEK, July 6, 1981.

An even more recent update of life in small towns across America had a similar tone to that of "Our Town." The following exhibit (Cook, 1989) is an article on Lisbon, North Dakota, in 1989. Even after the devastating effects of the agricultural crisis, reporter Cook still concludes that Lisbon is a great place to grow up.

LISBON

Lisbon is still the pretty little Sheyenne River Valley town I recall from half a century ago. The population has barely grown, to 2,200, and it remains, as everyone says, "a great place to raise kids." Few lock their doors when they leave home or take the keys from the ignition or the rifles from the racks when they park their pickups. Chief Harlan Wilke, head of the town's two-man police force, has to think a bit to recall the last serious crime. "In 1986, someone broke into the Coast-to-Coast store," he finally says. Hardworking descendants of Norwegian immigrant homesteaders sometimes still exclaim "uff-da!" ("my goodness!") and celebrate their heritage with church suppers of pungent lutefisk, cod tenderized with lye. ("I've been around it for 11 years, and I haven't managed to get it down yet," confesses Lutheran pastor John Wolenzien, who is of German ancestry.) The long, dark winters when temperatures plunge to below zero for days on end haven't changed, either. "That's what keeps out the riff-raff," boasts a local company's brochure.

Like every little town in the agricultural Great Plains, Lisbon is swimming against a cruel tide. Advanced mechanization has dramatically reduced the region's farm population. While the fertile soil yields more wheat, corn, barley, soybeans, sunflowers and beans than ever before, it doesn't take many people to grow the crops these days, so there are fewer farmers shopping on Main Street. J.C. Penney's, for years the biggest store in town, closed its doors a year ago, shocking merchants who depended on its size to draw shoppers. "The present trend of declining population, fewer job opportunities and an overall shrinking economic base . . . is not a temporary situation," North Dakota civic leaders stated bluntly in a newspaper supplement distributed statewide this fall. "Our population is aging, and our small towns are shrinking away."

Factory jobs on the prairie. Lisbon, though, is far luckier than most. Fifteen miles south in the village of Gwinner, the Melroe Company, a division of Clark Equipment, builds Bobcats, the world's most popular skid-steer loaders. An operator can use a maneuverable Bobcat to move debris at construction sites, muck out barns or, as the Soviets soon will do, clean out grainship holds. Bobcat sales this years will top $385 million, up from just $28 million in 1981, and local employment is climbing apace. Out of 685 Melroe workers (50 more will be hired by Christmas), 182 live in Lisbon, providing industrial-scale wages in a community where the most expensive house costs $85,000. Without his job making Bobcat wheel rims, says welder David Edland, "I'd be working in Minneapolis." More to the point, says implement dealer David Meyer, "if it wasn't for Melroe, there wouldn't be much of a Lisbon."

Because of Melroe, a new wave of optimism ripples along Lisbon's Main Street. Ross Cole is expanding the hardware store founded by his great-grandfather 110 years ago, though he promises not to rip up the wonderfully creaky, oiled hardwood floors when he remodels the original section. The John Deere dealer last month opened a Chevrolet-Pontiac-Buick garage, replacing the failing franchise that Morris Saxerud closed two years ago. Saxerud says he wasn't much of a car dealer, but his 11-man business assembling Bobcat fuel tanks and instrument panels is growing so fast that he just broke ground for a new factory.

The first recruit by the town's economic-development commission, Nancy Sanders of Minneapolis, last month launched Million Dollar Baby in a former lumberyard spiffed up by the town. Her first 10 employes are now stitching expensive little girls' party frocks for sale through elegant big-city stores.

Sanders regularly zips back to Minneapolis, where her husband still works, and she just bought a house and enrolled her son and daughter in elementary school, which she terms "wonderful." But not all newcomers are enthusiastic about the homogeneity dictated by agriculture, harsh weather and rural isolation. Bill Hanson, Melroe plant manager and Lisbon resident, says that recruiting professionals like computer programers often poses difficulties. "The employee gets all wrapped up in his work," he says, "but the one at home goes nuts." Melroe, consequently, tries to hire outsiders whose families have had some rural experience.

Yet Lisbon's remoteness also helps it survive. "We're about an hour from everybody," says Sean Kelly, publisher of the *Ransom County Gazette*, the weekly newspaper. Fargo, the nearest metropolitan area, is 70 miles away, so most do their basic shopping locally. As a result, says Mayor Roger Hamre cautiously, "I really feel the town will remain as a small-business area."

But that won't provide enough jobs to keep the kids. "The ones who go off to college don't come back," says Lisbon High Principal Wayne Levang. "A lot of people think of North Dakota as an exporter of grain products," he adds. "We're also exporting well-educated youths." Take senior Theresa Lyons, homecoming queen and student-council president, who hopes for a career in broadcasting. "You've got to get out," she says, "if you're going to be big."

Ambitious young entrepreneurs, however, can find local opportunities. Everyone laughed five years ago when Terry Loomis proposed to start a *radio station* in such a little town. But "hit kicking" KQLX, with snappy country music, broadcasts of high-school games, agricultural news and slick local ads, is a big regional success. David Meyer, 37, started Ransom County Implement in 1977 with three employes. He weathered the rough farm years of the early 1980s and now has the largest farm-implement dealership in the region, with more than $10 million in sales, 50 people on the payroll and a toll-free 800 number.

The implements Meyer sells have transformed agriculture, enabling a few farmer-businessman-mechanics to survive droughts and low prices to work farms that get bigger, on average, every year. "The land my son and I farm used to be five complete farms with families on them," says Carsten Fugl. Fugl, 62, still lives with his wife in the farmhouse he grew up in 20 miles from Lisbon, though the two-story house now has satellite TV and a business-band radio linking the modern kitchen with a small fleet of trucks, tractors and combines.

Going it alone. Like many of the area's big commercial farmers, Fugl, his son Allan and daughter-in-law Jodi employ no hired help. They till 2,500 acres (some leased) and raise 200 pigs a year with the aid of a yardful of enormous, expensive machines. There is, for instance, an air-conditioned, stereo-equipped IH 1460 combine (new price: $100,000) that rolls across a cornfield like a giant insect in a Japanese horror movie, devouring six rows at a time, 4 acres an hour. There's a huge, four-wheel-drive Versatile tractor, also air-conditioned, also costing $100,000 or more new, that pulls a 30-foot-wide chisel plow. Jodi, 26, says it's her "home for half the summer." When Carsten retires, Allan will take over, as Carsten did from his father, virtually the only way a young person can enter such a high-stakes business.

Off hours, Jodi bowls and Allan plays softball. But there are other, less common entertainments around Lisbon. Blackjack has been legal in North Dakota for over a decade as are "tip jars" from which you can, for a price, draw slips of paper that pay off for lucky numbers. By law, gambling has to be sponsored by a charitable organization. The tables at the Eagles Club have poured $1 million into the community, funding a new swimming pool, hospital equipment and, says Chief Wilke, the new red light and radar guns on his cruiser. "I'm all for that gambling," he says. "It brings a lot of money into the community."

I know. The ageless blackjack dealer at the Stake-Out Supper Club, Jan Aardahl, brought in $10 of mine for the American Legion charities in no time.

"Where are you from?" she inquired pleasantly as she shuffled. "Actually, I'm from here, a long time ago," I replied. "My father was the Ransom County agricultural agent during the 1930s." "Your name's Cook!" she exclaimed, her jaw dropping. "My sister was your baby-sitter when you were an infant." (pp. 64–65). ❧

SOURCE: Cook, W. J. (1989, December 18). Lisbon. *U.S. News & World Report*, pp. 64–65.

THE CONTEMPORARY VILLAGE

The small-town revival is not just an American phenomenon. The village has always played a salient role in English imagery and literature. During the 18th and 19th centuries, English villages were the object of much idealization and praise by poets and novelists, many of whom wrote about country life with an eye more to poetic concerns than to report or reflect on the realities of village life (Darley, 1978). Painters produced pastoral scenes and village images, which remained very popular into the beginning of the 20th century.

Toward the end of the 19th century, however, as industrialization spread throughout the more agricultural counties and as realism became prevalent in the literature, many believed that people's fascination with the bucolic village would end. Surprisingly enough, country life continued to be an intriguing topic in 20th century literature, probably because it was still the ideal of many people in real life. From a contemporary perspective, the village continued to hold its centrality in English life, particularly in southern England. Even today, the quaint or picturesque village intrigues English and non-English people alike, and, although writers and journalists might be more realistic about its merits and demerits today than they ever were before, village nostalgia continues to be a force in determining people's settlement choices.

The following commentary (May, 1979) reflects the polarities that often characterize village life today. The commentator, a British economic analyst, comments on the contradictions that plague the contemporary English village. This commentary should be particularly useful to social work practitioners who often are dismayed with the shortsightedness of laypeople who do not see the uglier side of much current prosperity, a comment that is equally applicable in the United States and the United Kingdom. This commentary clearly illustrates that hardship in many of the more prosperous regions is not easy to see because it is disguised by facades of contentment. Although John Allan May intended his comments to be applicable to the affluent, suburban English village, they also are applicable to many small, prosperous rural towns in the United States. Small towns near growth areas in New England, California, or the Southeast often hide poverty behind facades of contentment.

VILLAGE LIFE—IN CRISIS OR CLOVER?

As someone who has experienced and analyzed a dozen or more economic crises over the past nearly 50 years—I got my first job in the Great Slump before the second world war; fought in the war; covered the regeneration of wartorn Europe for this newspaper and wrote about umpteen crises and evaluations in the years thereafter—a stroll around the village where I live is a great help in putting present problems in perspective.

I pass the Men's Club. It used to be the Working Men's Club. Subscriptions were kept to the barest minimum, thanks to the fact that the club was financed by two wealthy gentlemen who lived in big houses, side by side, on the hilltop. Now it is not even truly a Men's Club, let alone a "Working Men's" club. Women now also belong. The club finances itself and indeed has a financial surplus. And the major problem is that the car park is far too small to hold the automobiles of the members.

Not far away is the village free school. In its case, there is not enough room for the cars of the mothers, even in the street, as they drive their children to school in the mornings. In saying that the street is blocked from 8:30 a.m. to 8:50 I am scarcely exaggerating.

And the Sports Club? What troubles we had raising not only teams but also money for equipment. In the cricket team our star performers were the two head gardeners from the "big houses" on the hill, supported by the village bobby, the young doctor and the driver of the local bus. Our lopsided wooden clubhouse was built with our own fair hands, under the supervision of a carpenter who had recently done a term of imprisonment as a confidence trickster.

Now there are two smart cricket teams, lawn bowls, archery, hockey, and squash courts and a modern Pavilion which is about to be enlarged. Half our old football field has become a car park.

I walk round roads that in my early days were fields for cattle and where now the fine houses of moderately well-to-do people sit back contentedly within well-tended gardens.

A friend I played football with 35 years ago has a large inflation-proofed pension from a multinational company and in addition an exceptionally well-paid job in the industrial consultancy field, a yacht, a new car every year and vacations wherever he likes in the world. Recently he and his family returned from a month in the Bahamas.

At the golf club my Winter League partner who returned from the Royal Air Force in 1946 to earn a wage of £5 (then $20) a week as a printer in Fleet Street these days comes home with about £150 ($300) a week after tax.

Now I know as I walk round the village that behind the drawn curtains there are some tales of hardship. Even one very wealthy neighbor has money troubles because he is educating three children privately and pays tax on his top slice of income at 75 percent, so that there's truly not much money left at the end of each month.

And I know another friend who was suddenly made redundant at the age of 55, was without a job for seven months, and now has had to accept a position at only half his former salary.

Yes, and there are others trying desperately to live decently on fixed incomes or on pensions from private companies that have not increased along with inflation (100 percent over 5 years). No one would pretend that for all of the villagers times are easy.

And yet.

And yet, I remember too once when I was about 15 a little ragged girl of 13 rang the bell of our duplex and asked, "Ma says 'ave yer got any stale bread?"

Wage-earners' wives queued at the bakery shops on Saturday mornings in those days for stale loaves. And if they missed out they asked around among friends. Or their employers.

Yes, so while I stroll around the village and I see the cars choking the street in front of the free village school and outside what was the Working Men's Club, and I hear about holidays in the Bahamas or Spain or Greece, although I know there are hardships behind the closed evening curtains I also see the latest economic crisis in a less desperate perspective. (p. 23) ❧

SOURCE: May, J. A. (1979, February 21). Village life—In crisis or clover? *The Christian Science Monitor*, p. 23. Reprinted by permission from *The Christian Science Monitor*.

A DAY IN THE LIFE OF SMALL-TOWN AMERICA

The rebirth of small towns reported by the 1980 census (*Statistical Abstract of the United States: 1980*, 1981) was not an even phenomenon across the United States. Although small towns surrounding metropolitan areas grew and prospered, other small towns across the heartland were struggling for survival. The young were leaving and the old were staying behind. The energy crisis, the farm crisis, and other economic problems exacerbated the struggles of those small communities. Midwestern farming towns, Appalachian coal mining towns, or Texan oil towns all struggled with the ghosts of depopulation and depression. The cadences of life in the small towns that were the heart of the nation were being disturbed by economic realities. How were those communities going to survive? Would they survive?

In a series of articles written for *The Des Moines Register*, Ken Fuson (1988a, b) documented the struggle of one small town in the center of Iowa. Fuson captured the changing rhythms of the town across four seasons. Two of those articles highlight separate but equally tearing dilemmas. In his opening article for the series, "It's a New Day in State Center, but What Will Life Be Like at Dusk?" Fuson (1988a) described the daily patterns of a heartland town. State Center, Iowa, is the small town featured in Fuson's article. Yet, as he suggested, the communication patterns, the pulling interests, the anxieties, the concerns articulated in relation to State Center were not unique to that town. They represented a composite of the daily lives of thousands of American small towns.

Although there is hopelessness in Fuson's article, there is also hope in the probability of change. Fuson showed, among other issues, how the town's parochialism and resentment of outsiders caused it to miss economic opportunities. Apparently, as the reporter was told, a cadre of local residents were concerned with the possibility of people different from themselves, particularly ethnic and racial minorities, coming to live in the town. "Years ago," recalled a local citizen, "the town spurned advances by Maytag and Fisher Controls to build plants in State Center."[1] That was the hopelessness. The hopeful signs are that the town's residents today are beginning to recognize that, in hurting others, they hurt themselves. "Today," commented Fuson, "State Center pays for that attitude. Only five new homes have been built since 1979. Last year's retail sales were the lowest in 11 years."

IT'S A NEW DAY IN STATE CENTER, BUT WHAT WILL LIFE BE LIKE AT DUSK?

As the first light of a fresh spring dawn brushes the new water tower and the old grain elevator, a small town stirs to life.

"I'm gonna die!" a boy groans at the high school, where track team members sprint in the morning chill, thick puffs of frosty air trailing them.

Nearby, Leland Weuve, 74, heads for the Trojan Inn, where men with calloused hands, seed corn caps and bibbed overalls cram into wooden booths for a cup of coffee before they leave for the fields.

Along Main Street, at the elementary school, buses return from the six towns that feed the West Marshall School District. Alison Clark, a third-grader, hops from the Melbourne bus, ready for her spelling test.

Down the street, Olaf Klomsten sweeps the Main Street Tap. The regulars—Ralph Moody, Duwane Miller, Ubbe Rops and the rest—will straggle in soon for another day of playing cards, drinking beer and cursing friends.

Here comes Ralph Moody now, in his rusty green pickup truck with the cracked window (he hit a pheasant). Like most of the town, Moody, 65, rises before the sun, a habit acquired during 20 years of owning the garbage business. These days, he's

---

[1]The quotes here and at the end of this paragraph have been deleted from the accompanying exhibit.

either buying rounds at the Main Street Tap, feeding the 300 sheep he bought "just for something to do," or introducing his town to strangers.

. . . . .

"I love this town," Ralph Moody says. "I'll die here."

He swings past the funeral home on Main Street and looks at the sign above the door. If the red light is shining, somebody has died during the night.

The light is dark.

Spring beckons in State Center.

Struggling for a place

This cool morning, with skies the color of a swimming pool and clouds as plump as pastries, finds State Center neither thriving nor dying. It is, as its name and location suggest, somewhere in the middle, one of 832 towns in Iowa with fewer than 2,500 people that are struggling to find their place in a new era in rural America.

A year in an Iowa farm town is no different from a year in a Texas oil town or a West Virginia coal town or any other small town where economic forces have assaulted a way of life. It's the daily battle of proud people who believe they have a tradition worth protecting and a community worth saving—but don't know where to begin.

The backbone of the country, the rural towns were called, first as outposts for Western expansion, then as collection centers for the nation's food, always as custodians of the most cherished American values: hard work, fair play, respect for the land, service to the church. Places worth keeping. Home.

Then it changed.

. . . . .

Today, grain prices and land values are rising, thanks to government farm payments. Mike Eckhardt, Erik's father, says the tax returns he prepared in April for area farmers were some of the healthiest in years.

Yet apprehension reigns, scars still tender from the farm crisis. State Center has lost 10 percent of its population since 1980. Selling a home takes an average of six months. School enrollment will decline by 30 students next fall. One of four people in town is a senior citizen.

Those are only numbers.

They don't tell how the State Center Garden Club was forced to cancel its flower show because members are too old to lug the heavy displays.

They don't tell how Kristin Robinson, graduating senior, star athlete and homecoming queen, got so sick she couldn't eat when her parents lost their farm two years ago.

And they don't tell how Nelda Grade waits for customers to visit her year-old crafts store, Aunt Jane's Attic. When she and her partner held an open house, three people came.

No longer master of its own universe, the town is wrapped in a straitjacket of confusion and indecision. "To be honest with you, I don't think we have any planning for the future in this community," says Mayor Larry Bohnsack, 39.

. . . . .

Heart of the heartland

From a distance, State Center's new water tower stands as a beacon of progress, the most visible symbol of the town.

The old tower was shaped like the Tin Man's head; the new tower, built last year, looks like a bloated egg plopped atop a giant golf tee, gleaming white, as slick as porcelain.

But somebody goofed. The logo on the tower—a rose surrounded by the words *State Center, Rose Capital of Iowa*—is too small to read from the highway. No matter. Few people happen upon State Center by accident.

Boxed in on all sides by some of the world's richest farmland, the town sits along U.S. Highway 30 between Ames and Marshalltown, 45 miles from Des Moines, 30 miles from the nearest interstate highway and 13 miles from the nearest McDonald's. If Iowa were a dart board, State Center would be the bull's-eye.

The town is small enough that no presidential candidates campaigned here last winter, but large enough that residents can rent R-rated movies from the Gutekunst Library (although the most popular rental is "Grease").

State Center has produced few notable sons or daughters in its 121-year history. Oh, Debbie Sue (Weuve) Rohrer was crowned Miss Iowa in 1975. Larry Poling, a city councilman, portrayed Nikita Khrushchev in "Miles From Home," the movie filmed in Iowa. And Bob and Dennis Baker smashed the state record for average soybean yield last year. But that's about it.

"I wouldn't call it a progressive town, but it's not as dead-set against new ideas as some small towns," says the Rev. Ken Stuber of the First United Presbyterian Church.

When he arrived three years ago, Stuber's sermons tackled sensitive issues: foreign policy, racism, gossip.

"I had some people very upset with me," he says. "I've learned to be more diplomatic."

Word travels fast. When Roger Evans, the high school guidance counselor, rented an apartment one night, the first person he saw at school the next morning asked him about it. Melissa Billman, 12, says she enjoys small-town living, "because you get to hear stuff you're not supposed to know."

Ask the people in State Center to describe their town and they haul out the familiar traits: safe, clean, friendly. Sure, petty jealousies exist, but there's an understanding, as in any family, that what you hear stays here. As more people and businesses leave, small towns grasp even tighter to their image of pastoral wholesomeness. It's their one drawing card.

Moderation is king. Don't make too much money, or get into too much trouble, or act too different, and everything will be just fine. Evans says the first boy who wore an earring to school nearly had it yanked from his head by another student.

"The problem is our kids aren't tolerant of differences," he says. "There isn't a good appreciation of people who look different or dress different or think differently."

State Center is white, mostly Republican and of predominantly German heritage, the telephone book filled with Henzes, Hillemans and Riemenschneiders.

The railroad gave birth to the town—even now, some 50 times a day, freight trains rumble through without stopping—but farming supplies the lifeblood. When President Reagan needed to mend relations with farmers in 1982, he chose the Dee Brothers farm outside State Center. He said he particularly enjoyed the homemade peach ice cream.

There are six churches, one for every 200 people, but you still can find a dice game at night if you know where to look and promise not to tell.

. . . . .

Many of the fire department members belong to other civic groups. As small towns lose population, and those who remain get older, the demands pile on the people who are left.

Margaret Hemphill, 65, a librarian, watched the seniors leave town when her late husband was the school superintendent. Most of them, she knew, were gone for good.

Earlier this month, her son, Jim, 27, who had been living at home while he worked at a Marshalltown television station, left for a magazine job in San Diego.

"You know how mothers are," Hemphill says. "I went in and cleaned up his room and cried the whole time."

For every Jim Hemphill who leaves, a Jim Maish must pick up the slack or watch the town slide.

Maish, 63, who owns a plumbing and heating business, belongs to the Lions Club, the Commerce Club, the Methodist Church board, the Marshall County Conservation Board and helps his wife, Dorothy, with the Welcome Wagon. He also prepared the lemon chicken dish for the church's mother-daughter banquet this spring.

"You think about a laid back, rural community and it isn't like that at all," Maish says. "You're stressed and pulled in so many different directions, trying to do the right thing.

"There's a feeling that everybody has to take their turn."

Reinforcements are needed. Boyd Van Metre, the real estate agent, says enough vacant housing exists for 20 families.

But where would they work?

Main Street

In April, the City Council postponed Roger Yeager's request to put a billboard along the highway, lamented drag racing on Main Street and approved a new toilet for the City Hall restroom.

Then Mayor Larry Bohnsack dropped a bombshell. He had talked with a businessman who expressed interest in building a manufacturing plant in town, he said. Maybe 40 jobs. He declined to say more.

Like most in Iowa, the town is separate for new business. When the Des Moines City Council rejected a loan for a condom factory, Irma Henze, 50, who owns a clothing store, and other business leaders joked that State Center should offer a site. It was just as well they didn't. The last thing a town whose school nickname is the Trojans needs is a condom factory.

. . . . .

"We have many business opportunities that we turned down for what we considered to be strong economic reasons," [Jim] Jorgensen [President of Central State Bank] says. "If that's a deterrent to economic development, I guess I have to look at our business first. It's more important to this town to keep the bank open."

. . . . .

Only the Commerce Club, representing the town's 41 businesses, shows signs of life.

At the April club meeting, members discussed whether to build a float for the summer's Rose Festival parade. The vote was three yes, with 13 abstaining.

Nothing stretches the limits of town and business cooperation more than the event for which State Center is best known, if it is know at all: the Rose Festival.

Thirty years of roses

Bill Haesemeyer was hot.

"It's not supposed to look like this," he says, pointing to the dandelions and brown stems that littered the beds in the town's rose garden.

"This one's dead. That one's dead. This one. This one. Over here. Here. Here."

Haesemeyer, 74, the bank owner, played a major role 30 years ago in State Center's coronation as the Rose Capital of Iowa.

This June, as it does every summer, the town will be the host to about 10,000 people for the three-day festival.

The trouble is, the people who started the event want the young adults to take over. The young adults say they're busy—and they're still bitter.

Years ago, a swimming pool was planned for the area where the rose garden now sits. "We still want a swimming pool," says Deb Horn, 35.

A handful of volunteers keep the Rose Festival afloat, with the responsibility for cleaning the garden and planting fresh roses passed like a virus among the City Council, the Jaycees and the Rose Board.

. . . . .

Future of State Center

The largest buildings on Main Street are occupied by Goodman Milling and the schools, appropriate given the importance of agriculture and education. But Don Goodman, elevator owner and school board president, knows which comes first.

"The school's what keeps this town," he says.

In that case, the future of State Center gathered on an April afternoon to color ducks, sing about eensy-weensy spiders and practice standing in line for recess.

Kindergarten round-up was a success. A total of 69 children attended, more than Superintendent Jerry Nichols had expected.

Nichols, 54, who watches enrollment trends as closely as Goodman monitors grain prices, has seen the number of West Marshall students decrease from 1,300 in 1969 to the 780 expected for next fall.

The impact is seen in everything from the high school chapter of the Fellowship of Christian Athletes, which has three members, to sporting events. West Marshall will compete in a new sports conference next fall with small schools.

Nichols worries that if Iowa legislators force school districts to maintain a minimum enrollment of, say, 1,000 students, State Center could lose its high school.

"Ultimately, we're probably going to have to restructure," he says.

Right now, Tyler Dose, a freckle-faced tow-headed 5-year-old, only cares about the duck he's coloring during kindergarten round-up.

"I know what color their feets are supposed to be," he says. "Orange. Because that's what color the baby chicks' feets are."

Upstairs, the 17 students in Dolores Horn's third-grade class also are discussing birds. Alison Clark, a pixie-faced 8-year-old, says her brother saw an owl holding a snake. Gross, the kids say.

The class protects Alison. In March, her father, Dan Clark of rural Melbourne, was killed in a truck accident near Tama.

Horn, a teacher for 31 years, took doughnuts and a plant to the house. Several students brought presents for Alison.

"The whole class was real sweet," Horn says. "They still are. Everything she does, they pull for her."

In music class, when Alison misread the song Old Dan Tucker as Old Dan Trucker and began to cry, several students hugged her.

And sometimes, Horn will find a note at the bottom of Alison's spelling test, such as, "I hope my Dad is all right."

"I'm sure he is, honey," Horn writes back.

The tie that binds

West Marshall High School enjoyed a productive spring. Gita Nason's trumpet-playing won an outstanding performance award at the state solo and ensemble contest. The mixed chorus received a top rating at state. And both performances of "The Music Man"—whose cast included townsfolk to supplement the students—received standing ovations.

But sports is the tie that binds the school district.

One the west side of the elementary school, Brian Winkler and his eighth-grade friends shoot baskets far into the night, their silhouettes outlined on the pavement.

Winkler, 14, who was born with cerebral palsy but stars on the basketball team, jumps and dangles from the chain net.

"We're talkin' serious hang time now," he says.

Winkler's father, Ken, has coached the football team to the state playoffs the past four years. This spring, the boys' track team won four first-place trophies and set several school records.

Wade Baker was a member of the relay team that broke one of those records. But the 17-year-old junior is best known as one of two boys who broke into the high school two years ago, causing about $50,000 in damage and outraging the town and students.

Baker returned to school last fall after spending 11 months in a Fort Dodge boys home. "I noticed some of the teachers looked at me like, 'Oh, boy, he's back.' But I think it had mostly been forgotten or forgiven," he says.

With brown hair, braces and a winning smile, Baker says he's trying to behave better, but trouble seems to find him. If it finds him too often, he risks violating his probation.

He and his classmates minded their manners prom night, the boys sharp in their black and gray tuxedos, the girls elegant in their satin strapless gowns and puffy bubble dresses.

At the dance, Principal John Dotson, 31, stood sentry in the door, with the slightly uncomfortable look of a man whose sole goal in life was to last until dawn without hearing from the county sheriff.

For the 89 seniors, the last of the large West Marshall classes, prom represented the final rite of high school before graduation ceremonies this afternoon. College or trade schools await most of their graduates. Few will find jobs in State Center.

"They have to leave," Don Goodman says. "There's nothing for them here."

Cards, beer, friends

The Main Street Tap is a dank, dark sanctuary, a place to belch, scratch and solve the world's problems, but mostly a place to play cards and drink a few beers. Or a lot.

"Drink, Vince?" Ralph Moody asks.

No answer.

"Drink, Vince?" Moody asks louder.

"Why, sure."

"Need a draw, Kenny?" Moody asks.

He does.

There's Moody, 65, war veteran, former boxer and baseball catcher, who started the town's garbage business 20 years ago with three customers and sold it last fall.

There's Ernie Westphal, 78 and ornery, who played billiards there when he was a kid, dropping the pool cue through a hole in the floor when his father walked in .

There's Duwane Miller, 53, who everyone calls Cooter, a retired Navy veteran. He has blood and kidney problems, but that doesn't stop him from drinking shots of brandy, which he orders with a glass of water, or smoking Chesterfield cigarettes, which he places atop a package of Vicks cough drops.

"This used to be quite a town, by God," Westphal says. "We had four implement dealers at one time, and two or three car dealers and three or four grocery stores. There were two movie houses in town. We used to sneak into the Princess Theater. You could always tell when the train was coming through because the screen would shake."

All day long, the regulars sit in front of the only window in the bar and play Queens, an incomprehensible card game in which diamonds are trump, tens beat kings and queens are better than everything. The men keep score by trading kernels of corn and cuss worse than prison inmates. The constant dealing of cards has worn a white cross in the table top.

"It could be a pretty good town if people wanted to change it," Miller says. "But they don't want to change it. They want it to be like it was 25 years ago.

"This town has to change in order to get disparity—whatever they call that word, disparity, diversity. Improve, improve, improve."

Later, at night, after a full day of cards and beer, Ralph Moody leans close, showing pale blue eyes, flushed cheeks and hair parted almost in the middle, the style in old movies.

"I'm proud of State Center," he says. "This is a good little town. I'm so satisfied here."

When the bar closes, Moody swings past the funeral home for one last look above the door.

The light is still dark.

State Center has survived another day. (pp. 1A–8A) ❧

SOURCE: Fuson, K. (1988, May 22). It's a new day in State Center, but what will life be like at dusk? *The Des Moines Register*, pp. 1A–8A. Reprinted by permission, *The Des Moines Register*.

The second article, "Lack of Teamwork Hinders State Center's Fight to Survive" (Fuson, 1988b), focuses on the issues that surround economic development in small towns. State Center has placed its hopes on economic development. However, development is not by itself a panacea—it brings alienation and loss of accommodation to needs, evidenced by the fact that the 95-year-old man who drives a lawn mower because he cannot get a license will no longer be able to park his "vehicle" on the street. The town's council, in its efforts to attract development, is going to enforce a great many "clean-up" ordinances. According to the reporter, there are other areas of dissent. Value tensions are obvious. The people are worried about their town, but teamwork is not easy to achieve. Yet, the outside observer can clearly see that the continued existence of value and priority conflicts within the town is an indication that there is still plenty of life left.

LACK OF TEAMWORK HINDERS STATE CENTER'S FIGHT TO SURVIVE

The question strikes with the punch of a linebacker—at any time, in any situation—whenever Coach Ken Winkler wants to jolt his football team.

"WINNERS OR LOSERS?" he shouts.

"WINNERS!" the 53 players thunder.

From the football field to the cornfield, from City Hall to the pool hall, this is a fall in which the question of winning or losing dominates in State Center. Whether it be touchdowns or harvests, business growth or civic development, the season consists of keeping score and cutting losses.

. . . . .

Hail to the chief

Pass the word: Gov. Terry Branstad is coming to State Center.

"It's a campaign gimmick, that 's all it is," says Boyd Van Metre, a real estate agent.

"I'm starting to feel used," adds Irma Henze, a clothing store owner.

Despite the reaction, the town basks in the attention. People act honored to receive an embossed invitation (and miffed if they don't; a minister is inadvertently omitted from the mailing list).

If he lived in State Center, Branstad might understand the surliness. The town has endured a dry, depressing summer. Temperatures danced around 100 the first two weeks of August.

For farmers, watching crops is like seeing a friend die. Corn appears spindly, as yellow as bad teeth, the ears dropping toward the ground. Goners.

Humor helps. The hardware store advertises rain gauges for 50 cents ("$2 if it rains") and Kelly and Nina Biensen hold a "drought party" in the middle of a 3-acre plot that died early.

Grain prices improve, but it's relative. Don Goodman, co-owner of Goodman Milling, a grain elevator, flips through mice-chewed sales receipts. On Sept. 15, 1947, his father paid $2.44 for a bushel of corn. The price was $2.45 in September 1988.

Such is the state of State Center when the governor comes to promote community development. Warmly received by 180 people at the golf clubhouse, Branstad appears relaxed, even funny, like the class president who returns home to help out. But his message is stern.

"It's your home, it's your future and it's up to you to decide what happens," he says.

One of the speakers, Harlan Quick, a social studies teacher, provides a history lesson.

"Iowa and State Center, we believed, were islands of stability in a world of change—stable economy, stable population and stable values. The recession has changed this."

Quick announces formation of the State Center Economic Development Corp., another attempt to spur the local economy. Ideas include restoring Main Street and building a wedding chapel in the Rose Garden (State Center calls itself the Rose Capital of Iowa). Mayor Larry Bohnsack suggests luring tourists with a huge wooden rose proclaiming the town the center of Iowa, if not the nation.

Branstad invites comments about industry.

Silence.

He asks if anyone wants to start a business.

People seem too scared to talk.

"You can leave it to somebody else," the governor says, "and chances are it isn't going to happen, and then you can bitch and complain and say it's all the state's fault, or the federal government's, or somebody else's fault.

"But it isn't. It's your fault."

How many people, he asks, would invest $25 in a town fund? Almost everyone raises their hands. Whew! He finally hit the right button.

Residents leave excited. Relaxing in the clubhouse, Bohnsack talks of the council's clean-up ordinance as a way to build momentum. Stricter enforcement of the ordinance will require property owners to get rid of junk cars, weeds, old tires, anything that detracts from the town.

"It's a start," the mayor says.

It also will cause all hell to break loose, but first things first. It's game time.

. . . . . .

Cleaning up is hard to do

Word ricochets through town: Police Chief Glen Mast, acting on orders from the City Council, is running around with a three-page list, warning 54 residents and property owners to comply with the city's clean-up and parking ordinances.

Terry Collier, who owns a body shop, is told to get rid of his junk cars. Jim Guffey, whose business makes wooden toy parts, must remove bags of sawdust. And John Starn, the owner of Starn Welding, learns he can no longer leave farm equipment on Main Street overnight.

You can chart the seasons by the equipment at Starn's shop—planters in spring, balers in summer, combines in fall and manure loaders in winter. Starn says he has to store them on the street.

"Looks like their economic development is going to put me out of business," he says.

But Starn, 50, a city council member for 13 years, voted for the ordinances three times.

Friends filter in, each one angry. Former Mayor Roger Yeager, who owns a antique shop, says, "I think this is the dirtiest thing this town has ever done."

Sparks fly from the rumor mill. Somebody hears that banker Bill Haesemeyer received a ticket for burning leaves (not true). Somebody else hears that Glynn Nolta, 95, who drives a John Deere riding lawn mower because he can't get a driver's license, is told he can't park on the street (ditto).

At Road Hog's Bar—renamed when Butch Horn, owner of the Steak Center restaurant, bought the Main Street Tap—the regulars say the council has generated the most talk since a young woman gave birth 10 years ago in the bathroom of the Wood Duck, a now-closed bar, or since friends hired a go-go dancer for Ernie Wesphal's birthday.

Tension builds. One night, "just to test them," Starn parks a six-row stalk chopper on the town's major north-south road, blocking one lane of traffic. The cop makes him move it.

Sixty-five people sign petitions calling for the resignation of Mayor Bohnsack and Councilman Sandy Wise.

The arguments turn personal. Bohnsack and Wise hold good jobs at Risher Controls International Inc. in Marshalltown. Many of the angry residents work with their hands.

"If you make your living out of town, stay out of town," Yeager says. "Don't come telling me what to do." Starn says he wants the cop to give the mayor a ticket for his barking dog.

Other residents, including Commerce Club members, agree with the clean-up.

Not Jim Guffey. Come to the council meeting, he says. "I'm going to wear my clown suit."

The meeting draws 60 residents. Two Marshall County deputies stand guard. Duwane "Cooter" Miller, a bar regular, talks first. This is his 54th birthday, but he has promised to remain sober for the meeting.

"You're moving too fast for these people," he tells the council. "This isn't Ames. This is a small town. . . "

BANG!

Rich Goodman accidently knocks over a folding chair. Everybody in the room jumps, then laughs, like after a scary moment in a horror movie.

Bohnsack also defuses the tension. All the council wants to do, he says, is to enforce ordinances that have been long ignored, to bring in people and businesses, to save the high school. But he agrees that using a policeman to spread the word was a mistake.

"If that's part of the reason you're all here tonight, I guess I should apologize for that, and I think the council should, too," Bohnsack says.

From the back of the room: "It'll never happen."

Bohnsack: "What will never happen?"

"An apology," bellows Bruce Sautter, 32, a city employee.

The economic development group, Bohnsack continues, should mediate complaints. His face red, he calls for compromise.

"All we're doing is pissing everybody off," he says. "You've pissed me off. I've pissed you off. The council has pissed you guys off, and you've pissed the council off. . .

"I think basically we need to put our heads together and quit being so damn bullheaded and stubborn."

But it's not going to be easy. As soon as the mayor finishes, Terry Collier lambastes Councilman Wise for smiling while Miller was talking.

"If you were sitting there smarting at me outside, you wouldn't be smarting for long," Collier yells.

And halfway through the meeting, after Bohnsack asks him to quit interrupting, Sautter saunters to the council table, slams his hand on the table and says:

"Mayor Bohnsack, you remember this. I'm done. I quit. I've got a better job somewhere else. Up your nose. Good night, Irene."

Sautter returns to work the next day. He says he may have drunk too much before the meeting.

Compromise wins; both sides agree to work together. Guffey, minus the clown outfit ("I couldn't find it"), presents the petitions, "only because we want you guys to know we're upset."

The clean-up goes on hold, but State Center has other problems. The Trojan Inn, a cafe, is for sale. Unless the bank restructures their loan, the newspaper owners will close their doors (co-owner Roxanne Goecke lands a part-time job for extra money). Dave Karsjen and Nile Hall are frustrated because the council won't approve their plans for a carwash.

"I'll tell you what," Bohnsack says, explaining why few people want to serve on the council, "this goddamned job isn't gratifying whatsoever."

. . . . .

Past, future, present

His doe-wide eyes locked in wonder, 10-month-old Ryan Steichen gently touches the chin of his great-great grandmother.

"He's looking right at you," Karleen Steichen says. "He's smiling and listening to you."

Young Ryan and his mother join dozens of relatives who gather at the State Center Manor to celebrate the 100th birthday of Mary "Abbie" Bracy. Blind and in a wheelchair, she claps nervously as relatives and friends sing Happy Birthday.

Between 1970 and 1980, the number of people 65 and older increased 14 percent in Marshall County. In State Center, where a fourth of the population is older than 65, two apartment complexes and the manor serve the elderly.

That demographic fact is one reason Superintendent Jerry Nichols is taking a more active role in economic development.

"If you lose your high school, your community shuts down," he said at a city council meeting. "So help me, that's exactly what will happen."

Nichols pegs enrollment this fall at 781, down 26, despite the arrival of a family of 12, whose nine school-age children will mean an additional $24,300 in state aid.

But West Marshall loses a student when Ken and Betsy Buck decide for religious reasons to teach their daughter at home, even though Betsy Buck substitute teaches and her husband is a member of the school board.

On the first day of school, dew-soaked grass wets brand-new tennis shoes as Tyler Dose, 5, and the 70 members of the Class of 2001 begin kindergarten.

In Donna Deardorff's classroom, Tyler begins by reciting the Pledge of Allegiance and coloring. "It's harder in preschool," he says.

Later in the week, after learning that he won't be spending the day with his father, a tearful boy in Tyler's class raises his hand and asks, "Mrs. Deardorff, can I have Fridays off?"

To keep kindergarten classes full, Nichols says, the town needs more young couples to live in the area and raise families.

Al and Karri Eckhart are such a couple. Al, 28, farms 500 acres. Karri, 21, works at the Bridal Connections. For their August wedding, the couple bought everything they could from local businesses—the tuxedos and dresses, the photographs, the food for their party.

More than 400 people attend their reception. As a horse and buggy take the newlyweds from the church, kids give chase, tossing birdseed and mauve streamers.

"Isn't it nice to see a couple of State Center kids stay in State Center?" Irma Henze says, a tinge of wistfulness in her voice.

. . . . .

Early harvest

Combines roll a month early. After a year of drought, spider mites, grasshoppers and aflatoxin, a corn mold, it's as if the farmers hope to purge the crop from memory. Yields are sliced in half.

Many farmers have insurance; others will qualify for federal assistance.

"I don't like it," Alvin "Lou" Edwards, 74, a retired farmer, tells Ralph Moody, 65, in the bar. "I never went to the government in my whole life. Am I right or wrong, Ralph?"

"You're right."

"Too many people don't pay their debt. Am I right or wrong, Ralph?"

"You're right."

While George Bush and Michael Dukakis unveil plans to help rural America, few in State Center are listening. Campaign signs are as rare as good yields.

"I think there's a feeling that it doesn't matter who's in there," says Jim Jorgensen, president of the Central State Bank.

No, people here rely on each other. When Kevin Blood, 33, who runs one of the area's largest farms, is thrown from a horse and breaks his neck, his family receives more offers of help than they can use.

And there's always football.

On a frigid night, West Marshall plays Ogden. If the Trojans win, they'll have a good chance at a fifth straight playoff berth.

Ogden scores the first 32 points. Good night, Irene.

"There's no joy in Mudville," Inne Taylor, the newspaper co-owner, says afterward.

All is not lost. The newspaper owners get their restructured loan. The economic development group plots strategy. Ken Winkler reminds the players they still have two more games.

WINNERS OR LOSERS?

As ever in State Center, and particularly in the fall of 1988, the answer proves elusive. (pp. 1A–4A) ❧

SOURCE: Fuson, K. (1988b, October 16). Lack of teamwork hinders State Center's fight to survive. *The Des Moines Register*, pp. 1A–4A. Reprinted by permission, *The Des Moines Register*.

CRISIS IN THE VILLAGE

The resiliency of small-town and village inhabitants when faced with a crisis has been a popular topic of novelists and journalists. Mutual help, supportive networks and a positive sense of community have often helped small-town people respond to great demands.

Many small towns and villages in the U.S. heartland recently have had to face the tragic results of a slumping farm economy. During 1985 and 1986, the national media reported on farm foreclosures, farmers' suicides, and crumbling small towns. As small farmers struggled against the continuing economic crisis, small towns were losing people and, thus, losing businesses and services. Journalists from the heartland states reported on the demise of villages. For example, *The Des Moines Register* ("Iowa's Small Towns," 1987) described the situation in Early, a small Iowa town of 670 people:

> "It's like 15 years of decline in one year," said Mayor Frank Scott, who has seen his town's business district wither during the 1980s until it has more vacant storefronts than active businesses.
>
> "What's happening in Early, population 670, is happening to hundreds of Iowa's small cities and towns. A combination of federal and state cutbacks and a dismal farm economy are eating away at the foundations of those communities. Some face extinction.
>
> "It's sickening. The other night I did cry. I try not to let this bother me, but when you look and see what a wonderful town it was, you can't help it," said Jerry Irwin, a county worker who.was born in Early.
>
> Signs of it are almost everywhere. In the Farmers Co-op Elevator at Rockwell is a hand-lettered sign with a dollar bill taped to the window that says "Rich Ermer's last dollar."
>
> Left by area farmer Ermer, the bill is part joke, said manager Terry VanAhn, and part serious message. It reminds visitors that farmers are having it tough—and so are towns like Rockwell that depend on them.
>
> "There used to be some positive things going on in town, people looking on the bright side of things. But you can't even get that anymore," VanAhn said.
>
> "The towns are dying," said the Rev. William Olmsted, pastor of Greenfield's United Methodist Church. "People that you depend on for leadership, for financial support, psychological support, being present to help contribute creative ideas just aren't there anymore." (p. 1B)

Like the revival of small towns reported in the 1980 census (*Statistical Abstract of the United States: 1980*, 1981), the crisis phenomenon is not distributed evenly across America. Not all midwestern towns were or are dying. Some, because of proximity to larger cities, or food industry centers, or malls, are still surviving, but the problem of erosion of the fighting spirit that once characterized small towns still exists. Worried town officials described the situation to reporters:

> Larry Kauzlarich, superintendent of the Rockwell-Swaledale School District, said enrollment has fallen 40 percent, from 598 students to 387 students, in the past decade, and much of the decline has been linked to the exodus of young families.
>
> "There is apprehension as to what the future holds," he said. "But our schools continue to get excellent support from the parents. We're seeing more people watch their money. The school continues to be a focal point."
>
> At Rockwell's grain elevator, manager VanAhn said that small-town life as he remembers appears to be changing.
>
> "Small towns used to buckle down together," he said. "You don't see as much of that as you used to. I like the quietness and the schools and the friendliness. Now you see that I-have-to-bust-my-rear-to-make-it-attitude." ("Iowa's Small Towns," 1987, p. 6B)

However, positive reports showed the collective spirit of economically depressed communities. Under an attention-getting but meaningful headline, *The Cedar Rapids Gazette* in "We Won't Roll Over and Die: Hawkeye Is a Small Town Fighting Back" (Wiley, 1986) reported on the resiliency of the hard-pressed citizens of Hawkeye, a small Iowa village in the depressed heartland. The resiliency of the people who are trying to prevent the demise of a Pacific Northwest town in Oregon is illustrated in exhibits in chapter 6.

WE WON'T ROLL OVER AND DIE: HAWKEYE IS A SMALL TOWN FIGHTING BACK

The disastrous October 1983 fire at the Hawkeye Community Center may have been the best thing that could have happened to the town.

From the ashes of the old hall of Main Street rose a new, expanded hall in time for a New Year's Eve dance.

It was a proud moment for this Fayette County community of 512 people and it taught them a lesson.

"We discovered something about ourselves," says Mayor Glen Boie. "The community is willing to work together for various things. There was a lot of volunteer effort put into both the old and the new building."

Last summer, the volunteering continued when many people worked to improve Hauth Memorial Park.

The fruits of these labors and the enthusiasm that brought them about not only make Hawkeye a better place to live, but they may ensure the town's survival.

In late February, a town meeting attended by 75 people focused on "How to make Hawkeye a community of the future." Since then, a Hawkeye Betterment Committee has formed to bring business to the town and improve it for those who already live there.

It's an issue faced by every community in Iowa, "a state of small towns."

"We've got 966 towns in Iowa and over 600 are 1,000 population or less," says John Schaffner, director of community resources for the Iowa Development Commission.

During the depths of the farm economic crisis, naysayers predicted the effects would spell the death of many small towns.

But, while many communities have lost businesses, some are fighting back for forming economic development committees and arming themselves with plans for change. Like Hawkeye, these towns refuse to roll over and die.

"We figure that unless we work at it, Hawkeye isn't going to remain this way," says Mel Ellason, manager of Hawkeye Cooperative and chairman of the Hawkeye Betterment Committee. "They say that 50 percent of the towns aren't going to survive and I'd just as soon be in that other 50 percent that's going to survive."

Sixty-three Iowa communities sent representatives last week to a three-day workshop at Iowa State University on "The Future of the Iowa Community."

Participants were given historical background and advice about how to attract jobs.

Statistics from the recent past aren't rosy.

From 1979–86, Iowa lost 1,250 of 4,171 automotive service stations; 328 of 1,866 grocery stores; 214 of 1,131 automobile dealers; and 208 of 1,821 major appliance dealers, according to figures released by Ken Stone, professor of economics at ISU.

School consolidation in some communities has taken away another long-held source of jobs and community recognition.

On the positive side, home-based craft shops and beauty parlors have shown tremendous growth, Stone says.

The decline on Main Street has finally forced some people to wake up and realize what has happened, says Stone, who has conducted retail trade analyses for more than 300 Iowa towns.

"I would suggest there are more opportunities (for small towns) than they may realize, especially in the service industries—like auto repair, doctor and dentist offices," says Stone. "If you can keep people coming in for medical services, groceries and hardware, it's crucial in keeping people there."

Stone suggests that towns may want to form regional cooperatives in pooling talent, money and buildings to attract business. "Osceola actually sent a business to another town in the area because it didn't have the right facility," Stone says. "If you can attract the business in the area, people can continue to live in the smaller town and commute. Then maybe in time we can see the reopening of businesses."

Small towns can and do attract industry, according to officials of the Iowa Development Commission.

Eddyville, pop. 1,116, landed a $100 million Cargill corn processing plant in 1964.

Grafton, pop. 253, pursued and wooed a small furniture assembly plant and 14 jobs.

"There are success stories," says the IDC's Schaffner. "But first, towns need to determine what marketable assets they can work with. I do think there's a future for small communities if they can find what their niche is."

River towns can develop tourism business, Schaffner suggests. Interstate towns are valuable sites for warehouses.

The Iowa State Extension Service or the Iowa Development Commission will work with communities to help inventory assets and market them. But local community leadership is essential for success.

"(Towns) need a sparkplug to muster enthusiasm," says Schaffner. "With that absent it is very difficult to do anything."

Many businesses do prefer to locate in small towns because of a high quality of life, productive work force and advanced literacy of Iowans, according to Schaffner.

Residents themselves still believe a small town is a good place to live, according to a survey by Vernon Ryan, ISU associate professor of sociology and anthropology.

Polls of five towns with fewer than 7,500 residents in 1980 and 1985 showed that while people no longer believed the economic outlook was bright and that the community was not as capable of planning or solving its problems, residents showed an increase in pride, willingness to help others and belief in local leadership.

It appears that Hawkeye's got leadership, community spirit and momentum. Leaders have inventoried the town and have found it a good place, but not perfect.

There are few jobs in Hawkeye. The largest employers are the co-op and the elementary school. Most out-of-town jobs are in the Fayette County seat, West Union, about eight miles away.

Hawkeye's population has declined by fewer than 80 people in the past 20 years. The community boasts a good library, its own telephone company, good water and sewer facilities and low housing costs.

Taxes are low and "we don't have any bonded indebtedness," says Mayor Bole. "And we probably have some of the best cooks in the state."

There's still a grocery store, service station and part-time offices of two out-of-town doctors and dentist.

Residents are proud of their name—a real eye-catcher in the Hawkeye state and smack dab in the middle of the University of Iowa Hawkeye fan zone.

The community would like to attract a small pharmacy, a welding shop, and a variety store.

"We felt as we looked at our town, we were not in as bad a shape as others, but we want to maintain what we already have," says Don Bole, president of the Hawkeye Businessmen's Association.

To that end, he is organizing "scoop the loop" sessions in which "we are going to tour the town with other than rose-colored glasses." Fix-up projects and cleanup of ditches are goals.

The "loop" in Hawkeye is only a few blocks long but that doesn't mean there isn't room for improvement, says Don Bole. "There are lots of things that don't take money that we can do immediately."

Their goals are modest but far-sighted. "We want to make Hawkeye a better place to live and make sure it's here in 25 years," says Glen Bole. "We are determined to go forward." (pp. 15A, 16A) ❧

SOURCE: Wiley, D. (1986, March 30). We won't roll over and die. *The Cedar Rapids Gazette*, p. 15A, 16A. Reprinted courtesy of *The Cedar Rapids, Iowa, Gazette*.

OLD-TIMERS AND NEWCOMERS IN THE TOWN

A characteristically persistent rivalry in small towns that the current growth phenomenon has exacerbated is the rivalry between old-timers and newcomers. Small communities are, at the same time, supportive and rejecting of newcomers. Neighborly pleasantry does not always mean acceptance, and in many places, people are "newcomers" for a long time. Most small towns in the 1980s were in a quandary: development often meant the only way to survive the exigencies of the 20th century, yet the influx of outsiders that comes with development often meant the town's loss of identity. The situation is exemplified by the dilemmas of many small towns. Crested Butte, Colorado, a silver boom town whose historic buildings are protected, is experiencing unprecedented growth because of its privileged mountain location, attractive to skiers and people who enjoy fishing.

> Pro-development residents say Crested Butte could become "the next Aspen"—which is precisely what the town's preservationist majority aims to prevent. People from large cities like Crested Butte for its quaintness and want it to say that way, says Ann Vitti, who owns a ski-togs shop in fast-growing Mt. Crested Butte and favors the pace there. Nothing's going to stay small and quaint anymore, I'm afraid. Preservationists like Gil Hersch, who publishes a weekly newspaper in Crested Butte, prize their town's easy tempo and ready access to the outdoors. I work 25 or 30 hours a week and spend the rest of my time in the back country, Hersch says.
>
> The preservationists are meanwhile fighting on a wholly separate front as well—a rear-guard action against a huge molybdenum mine on nearby Mount Emmons, the picturesque peak that forms a backdrop for the town. The project, now under state review wants to attract mine workers into Gunnison County, a prospect that Crested Butte views with dismay. There's a lot of elitism in Crested Butte, and I think there's an underlying bias against industry, says Joseph Blumberg, a spokesman for the mining company. They remember what they left, and they don't want Crested Butte to look like Newark. (Morganthauw et al., 1981, p. 37)

However, for the starkness of its choices, Crested Butte could be any of many American small towns: its future is at stake but its residents are divided between ideals and survival. For example, 25 years ago, many small Florida towns were homogeneous hamlets struggling for survival. Today, those residents who lived there treasuring peace and tranquility can barely protect themselves from the intrusions of buildings and people.

In a recent article, Levine (1988) reported on a survey of the stress of a number of metropolitan areas. State College, Pennsylvania, the hub of a countywide recent Standard Metropolitan Statistical Area (SMSA) but still very much a small town, was identified as the "least stressful city to live in." A local columnist (former newspaper editor and current editor of philatelic magazines) published a tongue-in-cheek column on the newfound fame of the town that he rightly called the "wet-behind-the-ears newcomer to the world of SMSA's." The columnist bemoaned the changes that have occurred in this once small college community as a result of growth. Regardless of whether the town is seen by others as low stress, the columnist regarded growth in itself as stressful and offered insightful comments with descriptions that tailor to the memories of insiders, but are, nevertheless, symbolic:

> I am an expert on stress, having held one of the most stressful jobs (executive editor of this newspaper) and one of the least stressful (editor to the nation's stamp collectors) in our low-stress city. The former task cost me my hair. The latter, inexplicably, has given me an ulcer. Actually, I can't blame the latter ailment on my employment. I think it results from the changes taking place in our community, which may be the least stressful of cities but which is a city nonetheless.
> For low stress you should have been here when:
> • There were no one-way streets.
> • There were three traffic lights.
> • The only organized activity between Memorial Day and Labor Day was the Alpha Fire Company parade and carnival. . . .
> • No one locked their doors.
> • You could get a hand-brewed Coke at Hoy Brother's General Merchandise for six cents.
> • There was no way to get from here to New York City.
> • There was no scheduled air service.
> • There was no fast food, only the tasty slow variety served up by the Penn Hi-Boy, J & L Barbecue and Fred's Restaurant.
> • Stores had wooden floors.
> • There were only two malls, both of them on campus and both of them elm-lined.
> • Teen-agers hung out at PeRo's on West Nittany Avenue and at Prexy's pool hall in Boalsburg.
> • Stress was something in an engineering textbook. (Welch, 1988, p. B4)

Newcomers have been difficult to resist but even more difficult to welcome. Many old-timers leave as newcomers enter a town because the character of the towns they know changes with the arrival of new people and the security the familiar landscape provided fades with those changes. Yet, without newcomers, many towns would die. The dilemma of keeping small towns alive without changing their character entirely is one that preoccupies citizens and government officials. The following editorial, "Towns—Coming and Going" (1987), addresses this issue.

TOWNS—COMING AND GOING

For growing numbers of American young people, small towns are great places to visit—but they wouldn't want to live there. A recent National League of Cities survey confirms anew that older citizens make up a growing share of the population in cities of under 50,000.

Mayors of such cities complain they are hard pressed to attract enough industry and jobs to keep young people from leaving; city officials say they feel the pinch in both the tax base and a rising demand for social services.

Along with cheerleading, complaining about the dearth of funds to support city services is part of any top local official's job these days; like a pitch for fund raising from a college president, we expect to hear it.

And it is true that many small cities face tough economic challenges, especially stemming from recent farm foreclosures and small-business closings. Some small towns have lost schools and post offices.

Yet if small towns were all thumping economic success stories, they wouldn't be small towns anymore. The very absence of the much-discussed urban race to compete and achieve remains a part of their charm. Most city-dwellers feel better just knowing that small towns are there, a permanent ideal in the American psyche. When city life becomes too much, an unhurried walk down a quiet bowered street of a small town where residents still have time to talk with their neighbors can do wonders. Even if residents sometimes know more than they should about each other and get a little too nosy, anyone who grew up in a small town knows the at-home, accepted feeling that can come from knowing everyone around by name and being known.

Indeed, these small clusters of population that dot the American map are far from being on the way out. The 1980 census showed that in the '70s, more people moved away from cities and suburbs than to them. Towns of fewer than 2,500 experienced a strong spurt of growth. The majority of officials queried in the League of Cities survey described their local economies as either unchanged or improving.

Small towns are an important part of America's landscape and heritage. The nation would be poorer without them. In this mobile age it is understandable that any young person growing up in a small town may want to broaden his experience with city living for a while—whether or not enticing local jobs are available.

For large numbers of others, small towns are just where they want to be. As the ring of suburbs around major cities continues to expand, many in once-isolated small towns now find they can live in the country and work in the city. Aside from a sometimes rigorous commute, they can enjoy the best of both worlds. (p. 15) ❧

SOURCE: Towns—coming and going [Editorial]. (1987, August 17). *The Christian Science Monitor*, p. 15. Reprinted by permission from the Editorial Page of *The Christian Science Monitor*.

One of the acid tests of newcomers in small towns is their ability to find places whose location is supposed to be common knowledge for everyone in town. This acid test applies also to social workers who often are newcomers and need to navigate small towns based on directions received from their clients. New social workers often are seen fumbling and searching in vain for nonexistent landmarks. Perhaps, the problem is not so much the directions received but the different frames of reference used by older people or by old-timers compared with the frames of reference used by social workers, who usually are not only younger but also newcomers. The article by Bill Welch (1986), "Your View of Town May Depend on Your Age," provides useful clues to this problem. Perhaps social workers—like other newcomers—should first identify a common navigation map with those who provide directions, before launching out to find small-town hideouts.

YOUR VIEW OF TOWN MAY DEPEND ON YOUR AGE

We all navigate by "mental maps," visualizing where we are, want to go, have been. Your age will determine many of the landmarks on your mental map.

This sort of generational geography no doubt occurs in most communities, but I especially notice it in State College, which has been undergoing rapid change for the last quarter of a century.

If my 17-year-old daughter were to give you directions on how to walk from the Pugh Street parking garage to the Fraser Street parking garage two blocks away, it might go something like this:

"Go up Calder Way, past Rapid Transit and Harvard Square, make a left at the Fraser Street Mini-Mall, and you'll see it."

If her father were to give the same directions, they'd sound like this:

"Go up Calder alley, past Metzger's and the Nittany Theatre, make a left at the CDT building and go up to the old Scurotino market. You can't miss it." Or, if I was talking to a fellow survivor of the Sixties, I might mention Peoples Nation, which briefly flowered in the Metzger's space. The name came from scraping the appropriate letters off the Peoples National Bank sign on the window, the only reminder that the bank had occupied the space for a short time. Peoples Nation was a sort of voo-doo version of "Hair," an indoor Arts Festival with lots of incense, black lights, cigarette papers and underground comics. It soon withered and we radicals went back to buying New Directions paperbacks at Nittany News.

An earlier generation than mine might use the Pastime Theatre and the borough power station as landmarks. (Both stood on the south side of the 100 block of Wester Calder Way.)

And for the generation that still remembers, the early years of this century, when a long automobile ride was one from the corner of College and Atherton all the way out to Buckhout Street—a trip Ethel Wahl once told me she made shortly after coming to town in 1907—the presence of parking garages must seem fantastic.

Generational geography has a corollary in our town's hidden geography: those place names that everyone, of a certain age knows, but that are not written down anywhere, that go unproclaimed by signs. Here are a few; long-time residents will have many more to offer:

Catholic Hill: The steep hill on South Fraser Street south of the Fairmount Avenue intersection. The name comes from Our Lady of Victory Catholic Church which once stood at that intersection. The hill long was considered the most challenging street for winter sledding, although College Heights kids liked Ski Hill, a more gradual, unpaved slope that ran down to the Bellefonte Central Railroad tracks, below Sunset Park.

Mudville: More properly known as Lytle's Addition, this area today is bounded by South Atherton Street, Westerly Parkway, South Allen Street and West Hamilton Avenue. ("Addition" meant that the area had been annexed to the borough.) Nadine Kofman's home town.

The College Township Island: This was a small piece of land belonging to College Township that, thanks to several "additions" to State College Borough, became completely cut off from the township. The "island" was located around the 700 block of South Atherton Street, about where the Pizza Hut now stands. The island ultimately was annexed to the borough, sometime in the 1960s.

Windcrest: This was a trailer park that sprang up immediately after World War II to provide housing for returning student veterans and their families. Located on the slope now occupied by Penn State's South Halls, along East College Avenue, Windcrest had more mud than Mudville.

. . . . .

While we're on the subject of geography, here's a quick quiz to test your State College knowledge:

Where is the highest point of land in the borough?

Want some clues? All right, it's not Catholic Hill.

How about College Heights, Ridge Avenue, Hillcrest Avenue?

The borough's high point is near the Nittany Lion Inn, at the corner of West Park Avenue and North Atherton Street.

That no doubt explains what [*sic*] that intersection is so often piled high with traffic. . . . (p. B4) ❧

SOURCE: Welch, B. (1986, October 4). Your view of town may depend on your age. *Centre Daily Times*, p. B4. Originally published in the *Centre Daily Times*.

HOW NEWS TRAVELS: SMALL-TOWN INFORMATION

Lack of anonymity, informal patterns of communication, accurate and inaccurate information that is shared by community members, conjecture about small events, and attention paid to small details from which stories grow, are all part of small-town living. For example, Ginsberg (1981) told the following story to a meeting of mental health providers:

> As I was at the pharmacy association meeting in White Sulphur Springs, West Virginia, recently, I went running down the main street . . . kind of anonymously. I ran into this little gift shop, and started looking at things. The owner came out, and asked where I was from; do you know so and so, and suddenly we discovered that his best friend's father was an employee of mine, and that he went to school with another friend of mine from Morgantown. All this in about half an hour. I ran back to White Sulphur Springs and somebody yelled at me and it was an old friend from Charleston who a colleague of mine had fired, in another department of state government so we commiserated about that for half an hour and then I finally got back to the hotel. That is just the way you live in rural communities; you don't walk around anonymously on the streets of most small towns. (p. 94)

Communication flows in and out of a variety of centers in small towns as this example illustrates. However, even inaccurate information, sometimes innocently given, can take hold in small communities, as illustrated in the following excerpt, "A Pretty Girl," the prelude to a novel by Valerie Sayers (1987a). At the same time, this excerpt also shows how communities often provide explanations for the information that circulates.

A PRETTY GIRL

She walked down River Street every afternoon to buy the paper and her father's cigarettes. She was a pretty girl, tall and rangy, with slender hips and long graceful hands. But there was a vacant look in her gray eyes, a friendly, absent dreaminess, and her father's friends watched her with an awkward concern. There had been so much talk about sending her up to the state hospital when she was younger.

She had never been sent—it was only a rumor, only something her father had discussed with a handful of men—and no one had actually seen her do anything that could really be called crazy. She had jumped out of her aunt's car one night, and she would forget she'd been spoken to while she was buying her father's things at the drugstore; but she was only a teenager, and girls in Due East always got wild at that age. (p. 1) ❧

SOURCE: Sayers, V. (1987a). A pretty girl. In *Due east* (p. 1). New York: Doubleday. Excerpt from *Due East* by Valerie Sayers,

Small-towners often are preoccupied with events that would pass unnoticed in larger environments, as is illustrated in "Talk at the Gas Station," part of a chapter in the novel *A Short History of a Small Place* by T. R. Pearson (1985b), a contemporary writer. The protagonist, a young boy, in a small southern town, captures the dialogue that follows the exit of an out-of-town car from the local gas station. The dialogue is partly entertainment for the participants and partly serious business. In the novel, the out-of-towners are coming to visit a maiden lady who has recently committed suicide. Pearson's novel is about family and life and madness in Neely, a small speck on the map in North Carolina.

TALK AT THE GAS STATION

Mr. Russell Newberry told me and Daddy he believed it was a Louisiana tag, but he'd hardly closed his mouth good when Mr. L. T. Chamblee and Mr. Raford Britt's eldest boy, Coley, said it was not any such thing. Mr. Chamblee recollected the outline of a palmetto tree behind the numbers and so insisted it was a South Carolina plate, while Coley Britt, who could not recall any specific vegetation, said he's been reading ever since he was nine and guessed he ought to know the words West Virginia when he saw them. Along about then Mr. Covington came out through one of the service bay doors wiping his hands on a rag, and before he could even tell me and Daddy how do you do, Mr. Newberry and Mr. Chamblee and Coley Britt were all over him wanting to know was it Louisiana or was it South Carolina and especially was it West Virginia since Coley Britt had fairly much put his education on the line. But Mr. Covington just looked at the three of them as he finished wiping his hands and then stuck the rag partway into his back pocket and said, "What?"

"Where was it they come from?" Mr. Chamblee asked him.

"Who?" Mr. Covington said.

"That man and his wife," Coley Britt told him. "Just where was it they come from?"

"Up that way," Mr. Covington said and flung his arm in a direction the road didn't go exactly.

"What sort of plates did they have, Bill?" Mr. Newberry wanted to know.

"Jump got his gas for him," Mr. Covington said. "I didn't ever see the plates."

So while Mr. L. T. Chamblee set in to bellowing for Jump to come out from wherever it was he's gotten off to, Coley Britt told Mr. Newberry, "West Virginia's up that way."

And Mr. Newberry told him back, "So's Alaska."

"Well they couldn't have driven down from Alaska in a Pontiac," Coley Britt said.

And Mr. Chamblee broke off his bellowing right in the middle of it and told Coley Britt, "Hadn't no Pontiac been in here all day. It was a Chevrolet as big as life."

"For God sakes, L. T.," Coley shot back at him, "that thing was a Bonneville pure and plain."

"Tell him Russell," Mr. Chamblee said, "tell him what it was."

But Mr. Newberry said he didn't know one car from another and all he could recollect for certain, aside from the license plate, was the color, which he remembered as a dull green all over.

And Mr. Chamblee conceded that it did look a little green to him at first also. "But it turned out to be blue," he said, "turned out to be a blue Caprice Classic."

Then Daddy asked Coley Britt if, in his estimation, a man could drive a blue Chevrolet Caprice Classic down from Alaska, and Coley looked at Daddy out from the side of his face like maybe he was sizing him up for a tire-iron necktie. "How about from Michigan?" Daddy said, and Coley spat twice on the asphalt and appeared to be formulating some sort of germane threat when Jump Garrison, who was actually Coolidge Garrison but got called Jump, came out from around the far side of the station where he'd been hosing down Mr. Covington's rest rooms so as to keep them as clean as all the signboards said they were. Jump was what Daddy called a blue-gummed negro which meant he was about the color of the bottom of a full hole. He had been with Mr. Covington for going on seven years and so had become somewhat attached to the gas pumping business and especially to the gas pumper's uniform which he kept all pleated and creased like a tuxedo and which was no end of pride to him except maybe for the shirt since it did not say "Jump" in the little white oval over the pocket and did not say "Coolidge" either but said "Bill" instead, even after seven years.

He came round the corner mopping himself with a brick-colored rag, which he carefully folded and slipped into his back pocket once he was done with it, and even before he could manage a full stop and clasp his hands behind his back so as to stand fairly much at ease Mr. Covington asked him, "Jump, you remember a blue Chevrolet coming through here today?"

"A Caprice Classic," Mr. Chamblee added.

And Jump licked the inside of his bottom lip. "No sir," he said.

"You remember a green Pontiac," Mr. Covington asked him.

"No sir."

"How about a blue Pontiac or a green Chevrolet?"

"No sir," Jump said.

"They was a man and a woman," Mr. Chamblee told him. "They won't from around here."

"Yes sir," Jump said. "I remember. Them two come through in a green Buick with a black vinyl top."

"For Chrissakes, a Buick?" Coley Britt said and laughed and then he said it again and laughed again and then he made a most mean and vicious remark against negrodom in general which Jump Garrison accepted with the blandest of expressions like maybe Coley had merely speculated on the weather.

"I give him fourteen dollars and fifty cents worth a Good Gulf," Jump said, mostly to Mr. Covington, "and then I checked his oil, which was awright, then he come out around the front a the car and asked me to put some water in his battery. He told me he paid nearly ninety-seven dollars for that battery and he wanted to keep it slam full up with water. He said a man had to be willing to pay for quality, he said he was lucky he could afford to. But the battery didn't need any water so I put some in the radiator instead and checked the belts and wiped the duster off before I closed the hood up. Then his wife decided she had to go right away and couldn't wait for me to get the key so she took it off the wall herself and he give me a twenty and followed me into the station, but before I could take out for the gas he got himself some nabs and got his wife some peanuts and come away from the drink box with two Brownies but he opened the first one up before he shook it so I let him put it back and get another one and I only took out for the two Brownies along with the nabs and the peanuts and the fourteen dollars and fifty cents worth a Good Gulf. Then me and him went on back outside and presently his wife come round the corner and give me the key. Then him and her both want to know where they can find Miss Pettigrew. And I say to him, "What Pettigrew?" And he says back to me, 'Miss Myra Angelique Pettigrew.' A course I didn't know what to tell him, so I figured I'd fetch Mr. Covington and let him do it for me, but I looked up here into the service bay and seen him in the grease pit under a Torino so I guessed I'd have to do it for myself and as I figured it there wasn't any way to go about it but head on so I said to him, 'I'm awful sorry, Mister, but Miss Pettrigrew's dead. Died yesterday.' And along about midway through the sorrowful news him and his wife both turned up their Brownies, then she ate one a his nabs and he ate some a her peanuts. 'I know that,' he says to me. 'Where is she?' Well, then I tell him I suppose she's at Mr. Commander Tuttle's and he wants to know where that is to so I get him out alongside the road and show him how to hit the boulevard and tell him where to cut back past the square and he thanked me and seemed considerably gracious so I went ahead and asked him flat out if he was some sort of Pettigrew relation. And he finished off his Brownie, handed me the bottle and said, 'You're looking at the heir, buddy.' Then his wife handed me her bottle too and him and her got back in the Buick and damned if he didn't light out in exactly the wrong direction." (pp. 251–254) ❧

SOURCE: Pearson, T. R. (1985b). *Mayor*. In *A short history of a small place* (pp. 251–303). New York: Ballantine Books. Reprinted courtesy of the author.

Note that the title of this excerpt does not appear in the original version.

In a recent book about information centers, Oldenburg (1989) reviewed hundreds of such centers in cities and small-town America. Local cafes, churches, firehalls, and soda fountains are not only information centers but also places that play a role in relieving the stresses small-town people often experience. In many ways, these local centers provide informal therapy and support. Although some observers, commenting on the strength being gathered by national food chains and fast-service restaurants, predict the demise of these local operations, other observers believe they will continue to thrive. In a recent article in *The Wall Street Journal*, reporter Richards (1985) wrote from Napoleon, North Dakota:

> While experts say that the small town populations and traditions are on the wane, the tradition of the cafe coffee table seems to be gathering steam. North Dakota officials, for example, recently suggested that agents of the agricultural extension service head for the local cafe when they want to spread the latest crop information. In Fredonia, N.D., local officials raised nearly $80,000 in federal and state cash this year to build their own cafe. And last year, when their local cafe burnt to the ground, residents of Kanawa, Iowa, pitched in and rebuilt it themselves. Where else were we going to get together in the morning? says Kanawa town clerk, Lois Abbas. (p. 1)

In "Alpharetta Cafe Stands Test of Time: Alpha Soda Hub of Activity, Symbol of Small-Town Values," Scroggins (1988) showed the role that Alpha Soda, a small shop in Alpharetta, Georgia, has played throughout the decades. Despite the changes undergone by small-town shops across the United States, centers like the Alpharetta cafe have retained their character and their value for those who want to take the pulse of small communities.

ALPHARETTA CAFE STANDS TEST OF TIME: ALPHA SODA HUB OF ACTIVITY, SYMBOL OF SMALL-TOWN VALUES

In 1931, when falling cotton prices threatened Milton County with bankruptcy, Alpharetta's leading citizens met at Alpha Soda to negotiate the county's merger with Fulton County.

Last month, 57 years later, Alpharetta's leading citizens gathered again at Alpha Soda to discuss the mayor's proposal to secede from Fulton County.

Since the day Louie Jones opened the soda fountain at the back of his patent medicine store in 1920, Alpha Soda has been Alpharetta's favorite gathering place.

As the hub of social and political life, and one of the last original drugstore/ restaurants in the Atlanta area, Alpha Soda has endured through Alpharetta's changes from a frontier outpost to bustling suburb.

When Billy Hunter's father moved his family to Alpharetta in 1932, Main Street was a dirt road. In those days, the future councilman and his parents stood in line with other Alpharettans to pay 15 cents for a shower at the barber shop. But if paved streets and indoor plumbing have made life easier, Hunter says, Alpha Soda has preserved the rural Georgia atmosphere that makes it worth living in Alpharetta.

Over the past 68 years, the cafe behind Alpha Drugs on Main Street has changed locations three times. Joyce and Harry Thigpen, its current owners, can't remember how many times it has changed hands. Except for a few mementos on the walls, Alpha Soda's modern furnishing give little hint of the role it has played in Alpharetta's history.

To its patrons, however, the sunny restaurant with the soda fountain and the checkered tablecloths embodies the small-town values—as wholesome as its chicken-fried steak and mashed potatoes—Alpharetta is struggling to maintain in the face of rapid urban growth.

"I think by having a good family place where everybody meets, like Alpha Soda, people can see that, even with the fast pace of development, we're maintaining our homespun atmosphere," says Alpharetta Mayor Jimmy Phillips. Phillips has been eating Alpha Soda's chili cheeseburgers since he was in grammar school.

Old-timers say they see a lot of new faces at Alpha Soda these days. According to the Atlanta Regional Commission, Alpharetta's population has more than tripled since 1970, from 2,455 to 9,389.

"It used to be you knew everybody there," said Hunter. "Now you see more people you don't know. But it's still the place you can go and see somebody who'll say, 'Hey, did you know Mr. Grizzle fell down on the ice and broke his arm?' "

Every weekday morning newcomers and regulars can still watch 10 mostly retired men observe one of Alpharetta's time-honored traditions. Between 10:30 and 11 a.m., the men sit down at a table set aside for the daily meeting of The Coffee Club. Drinking from mugs the Thigpens had imprinted with their names, the friends pass the morning swapping stories about golf and grandchildren and talking local business and politics.

"Most of us are Alpharetta Lions Club members and we've been going to church together and meeting at the coffee shop for 20 years," said Pearce Thompson, a member of the club.

Charlie Phillips regularly stops by Alpha Soda in the mornings for a breakfast of Streak O'Lean and hash browns, but the 74-year-old funeral director says work keeps him too busy to stay as long as he would like. Guy and Audrey Griffiths, the young co-pastors of Alpharetta's new Presbyterian church, prefer to meet at the cafe to discuss their ministry over soup and a plate of fresh vegetables.

Except for Fridays in the fall, Alpha Soda is closed at night. On those afternoons, cheerleaders at Milton High School and their mothers come in to festoon the restaurant with red fight banners. Then around 5 p.m., the strapping Milton eagles crowd inside to feast on hamburgers and milkshakes before the big game.

And while some days there may be more transplants than natives dining at Alpha Soda, many of them say they have developed the same loyalty as born-and-bred Alpharettans.

Shari Polluck, a reporter for the bi-weekly Alpharetta Review who moved to Alpharetta from Wisconsin in 1973, is a self-described "former Yankee for'ner."

Yet it was Ms. Polluck, rather than a native, who wrote "Ode to Alpha Soda," a poem that regulars say sums up their feelings about the coffee shop:

It's not the polish, the glitz and veneer, that appeals to us townfolk year after year

It's that Southern comfort, that sense of home, that brings us back from wherever we roam. (p. 1) ❧

SOURCE: Scroggins, D. (1988, January 26). Alpharetta cafe stands test of time: Alpha Soda hub of activity, symbol of small-town values. *The Atlanta Constitution*, p. C1. Reprinted courtesy of *The Atlanta Journal-Constitution*, © 1988.

In "If It's 9 a.m., It's Time for the Lakeview Sagehens," reporter Juillerat (1987) captured the activity at an Oregon coffee shop, where locals meet to "solve the problems of the world." The informal relationships developed among decision makers and influentials in the town are evident. The traditional structure of an all-male coffee group also is apparent.

IF IT'S 9 A.M., IT'S TIME FOR THE LAKEVIEW SAGEHENS

The waitress looked at the clock—it was 8:45 a.m.—slurped down her coffee and stood up.

"I've got to get up and get ready for those coffee guys."

Minutes later she and a second Indian Village waitress paraded their way to the long table in the dining room, each carrying a tray filled with fresh coffee and hot water.

By 8:59 the first of the coffee guys walked in the door. Within a few minutes the table was ringed with 14 men. Just as they do five days a week, the Lakeview Chapter of the Oregon Sagehen Protective Association had come to meet, but not necessarily come to order.

"You've got to have tough skin because sooner or later you're in the barrel," explained Vic Lasater of the Sagehens, the nearly two dozen Lakeview businessmen who meet like clockwork from 9 to 9:30 a.m. weekdays.

"Everything, everything under the sun. Politics, sports, off-color jokes—and some of them not even funny," confessed Lasater of the banter that mixes into a dozen conversations during the gatherings.

This particular day the jabber ranged from Mike Ditka to ways of raising money to George Burns to digs at the U.S. Postal Service to Jack Brazeal's new measuring tape, which came complete with a flashlight for making measurements in the dark.

"That's where you find out everything you know in this world," explained Lasater, probably the longest-term Sagehen. Lasater, who owns the nearby Lasater's

Jewelry, has been wandering over to "coffee gang" sessions since setting up shop in 1941.

"If I miss a sale, too bad," he says of the half-hour of missed work.

Lakeview Postmaster Orval Layton, another long-time coffee club member, says he and Lasater have persisted while "the rest of them died of an overdose of coffee."

Lasater remembers meetings at the upstairs rooms at the former Lakeview Elks Lodge, where morning conversationalists gobbled up for coffee and homemade rolls that cost 5 cents each "so it wasn't expensive to get stuck" with the bill.

Over the years Lasater, 69, recalls coffee groups meeting at the News and Sweets, a store offering newspapers and drinks, and Van's Cafe. The Indian Village has been the gathering spot since about 1963.

In those earlier years the klatch used to see more visiting politicians. Lasater remembers slurping coffee with then-Oregon Secretary of State Mark Hatfield and the then-young Rep. Al Ullman.

There are different versions of how long the Sagehens name has been used, but the membership form lists 1981. There's also some disagreement about where the Sagehen name comes from, but most think it has to do with saving the once-prolific gamebird.

Through the years, Lasater recalls a traditionally strong representation from various school offices, a pattern that continues. This particular morning Fred Archer, Lakeview School District No. 7 superintendent, was absent, but Don Knowles, Education Service District superintendent, was there.

Some tell stories about how Ted Conn, a deceased Lakeview attorney, used to stop by and count the number of town, county, state and federal government employees. Government offices are still represented. Regular Sagehens include a trio from the county assessor's office and two post office bosses.

On birthdays, the celebrant pays for coffee and rolls.

On days when they can't pin the tab on someone else, the clan tosses for paying honors. The first round produced 10 heads and 4 tails, with the tails excused from paying. The coin flipping continued until only one person remained. When it was over Bob Alger, a businessman and town council member, was left to pick up the tab.

By 9:30 the table was cleared, the Sagehens headed back to work.

Laughed Lasater, "We solve all the world's problems." (p. 2) ❧

SOURCE: Juillerat, L. (1987, January 27). If it's 9 a.m., it's time for the Lakeview Sagehens. *Herald and News*, p. 2. Reprinted courtesy of the Klamath Falls, Oregon, *Herald and News*.

In "Razors, Opinions Equally Sharp" reporter Brueggebors (1990) focused on a barber shop in small-town Pennsylvania and the shop's role as information center.

RAZORS, OPINIONS EQUALLY SHARP

"The Price Is Right" was on the tube, but customers in Bob Park's barber shop were tuned into the man in the chair.

"And then this old bear, see, he stood right up on his hind legs and dumped that garbage bag out just like a man would do. But when he got to nosing around and didn't find nothing in it but cans, he started jumping up and down like he was taking a fit."

Everybody laughed at Charlie Welch's story—especially the barber, who never missed a snip right through the punchline.

"We talk sports and politics in here part of the time and fishing and hunting the rest," Park told a first-time visitor to his Milesburg tonsorial parlor last week. Park has been barbering in this 1,300-head Centre County community for the past 29 years. He's also borough council president—a combination of jobs he finds quite logical. "They say barber shops are information centers," he said, laughing. "We cover a lot of ground in here."

Married and the father of three, Park is a trim, buoyant man with a face lit by unquenchable good cheer. Casually dressed in neatly pressed slacks and open-neck shirt, he scissors his way through the business day, ever alert for the pulse of public opinion.

Lately, Park's rather informal barber poll has determined that:

• Penn State made a bad move in joining the Big Ten. ("People think we'll be OK in football but won't be able to compete in basketball and wrestling," he explains.)

• Pennsylvania's new "trout stamp," a $5 additional charge fishermen will pay beginning next year, stinks to high heaven. ("There's a lot of displeasure over that," the barber says, nodding his head for emphasis. "A lot of displeasure.")

• The U.S. invasion of Panama gets mixed reviews. ("Most folks think we should have gone in there to get Noreiga, but they don't think it should have taken us so long to get him out.")

Workingmen constitute the bulk of Park's clientele: the builders, carpenters, plasterers and mechanics who have lived in or near Milesburg all their lives.

On an average weekday, about 20 customers plunk down in the oversize swivel chair next at Park's work station. Just about all of them have been doing so for years.

"Probably about half of my customers are from right here in town," the barber said. "But since I'm originally from Snow Shoe, I also get a lot of people who come down from that area."

The three-term councilman's shop, a one-time justice of the peace's office, is filled with the mementos and treasures of the tonsorial trade.

A 6-foot-tall, antique barber pole stands in one corner. Two wall-mounted glass cases display Park's collection of straight razors, the oldest of which is a Civil War government issue.

A Bald Eagle Area High School sports calendar decorates the wall closest to the room's sole barber chair. Bowling trophies, American flags, a framed National Rifle Association membership and a rack crammed with "Field and Stream" and "American Rifleman" magazines take up the room's other spaces.

"We have fun in here," Park said, "and it's interesting. We don't ever seem to run out of things to talk about." (pp. A1, A12) ❧

SOURCE: Brueggebors, B. (1990, February 11). Razors, opinions equally sharp. *Centre Daily Times*, pp. A1, A12. Reprinted courtesy of Barbara Brueggebors, *Centre Daily Times*, State College, Pennsylvania.

SMALL-TOWN RELIGION

Many researchers have speculated on and some have thoroughly documented the importance of religion and the church in small communities (Larson, 1978; Levenberg, 1976). For example, in the New England towns, historically, "the minister had a powerful role to play in the town. This presence was required by law, and if a minister had not actually been a leader in the town's founding, the town made it its first order of business to bring in a suitable person" (Lingeman, 1980, p. 42). Although in the early New England towns the church and the minister, as moral guardians of the community, were part of the social hierarchy of the town and constituted a powerful judiciary, in the modern small town, the church and the minister constitute only informal sources of support, benevolence, and help for the members, or in some instances, a source of community sanction.

The church and religion took on different personalities in certain parts of the United States because of the historical forces that shaped their establishment in various geographical areas. The early Puritan churches in New England "banned music and other trappings of popishness; the congregation sat rigidly upright . . . as waves of scholarly rhetoric about divine love and eternal damnation rolled out over them from the pulpit" (Lingeman, 1980, p. 42). But not all church-life in the early New England town was easily controlled. Frequent quarrels arose over money, over the seating of parishioners, and over the degree of moral enforcement the minister could exert upon his congregation. Yet, dissenters had little choice but to conform or move away. Even after the most cruel witchcraft hunts had passed, dissenters were not viewed benevolently (Lingeman, 1980).

The southern church, however, flourished under different circumstances:

> The Settlers of New England were imbued with Puritan Congregationalist ideals; in the colony of Virginia, this traditional English village inspired by Puritanism did not take hold. They brought with them the established Church of England, with its parish and vestry, but they did not make town and congregation one, as the Puritans did. (Lingeman, 1980, p. 18)

As time went on, these initial characteristics developed into differences. New Englanders for a long time continued to legislate "sin" through the temporal laws. Blue laws were common and public morality was often linked to religion. In the South, "vices" (alcohol and tobacco, for example) were more tolerated, although Southerners were "prone to revival-meeting purgation" (Lingeman, 1980, p. 75), a tradition that is revealed in the contemporary prose of Valerie Sayers's (1987) book *Due East*. The midwestern and western church was of a different origin. Bender (1978) suggested that by the time the West began to be settled, the Ordinance of 1787 and the U.S. Constitution had established freedom of religion, so "people of a town could set up a church in any of the religious faiths they fancied" (Lingeman, 1980, p. 115). The multiplicity of faiths resulted in quarrels and discontent, but the ease with which new towns could be settled relieved the "pressure-cooker effect of . . . Puritan theocracy" (Lingeman, 1980, p. 115). As time went on, the westward movement was a community-building movement (Bender, 1978). Men and women moved west in the company of kin and friends, often from the same place of origin. Frequently, churches and other voluntary associations provided the necessary glue to hold individuals together into developing communities.

> Churches provided essentially uniform standards for behavior and community participation that could be, and were, replicated in town after town in the Middle West. . . . To a considerable extent . . . the churches were at once, centers of religious and social life, advocates of public order, and school for group and community leadership . . . (Bender, 1978, p. 97)

Many of the same religious orientations are found in contemporary small towns. The revivalist orientation of the fictitious sermon Valerie Sayers (1987c) used to show the unbending standards of a Baptist church in a southern community shows ties to that historical tradition. The many stories on Lutherans and Catholics Garrison Keillor (1985) recounted in *Lake Wobegon Days*, for example, speak of the ethnic and social ties of religious groups in small midwestern towns where the church served to preserve remnants of national or ethnic identities brought to America by European immigrants. At the same time, the church helped create almost instant local communities among people who, otherwise, would have been strangers. Being a Protestant (of one of the prevailing groups) or being a Roman Catholic gave groups within remote, yet thriving, communities an "intimate core of experience" (Bender, 1978, p. 97) that would have been hard to create otherwise. The church helped, intentionally or unintentionally, in building strong communities; however, it also helped to split them along denominational lines that often persist.

Lingeman (1980) commented that the western pioneers were prone to disputes over fine points in the Bible, a matter well illustrated by Keillor's (1985) story of his own denomination, the Sanctified Brethren, "a sect so tiny that nobody but us and God knew about it" (p. 101). Keillor told of these disputes:

> Scholarly to the core and perfect literalists everyone, they set to arguing over points that, to any outsider, would have seemed very minor indeed but which to them were

> crucial to the Faith, including the question: if Believer A is associated with Believer B who has somehow associated himself with C who holds a False Doctrine, must D break off association with A, even though A does not hold the Doctrine, to avoid taint?
>
> The correct answer is: Yes. Some Brethren, however, felt that D should only speak with A and urge him to break off with B. The Brethren who felt otherwise promptly broke off with them. This was the Bedford Question, one of several controversies that, inside of two years, split the Brethren into three branches. (p. 105)

Although the separation between Roman Catholics and Protestants is slowly fading in many small towns, such a change cannot be taken for granted. Recently, a conciliatory Lutheran pastor, addressing a local Roman Catholic congregation in a rare exchange of pulpits between a Roman Catholic priest and a Lutheran pastor in the town of Remsen, Iowa, said the following to the congregation:

> We laugh at things which hurt. And when we think seriously about the gulf that has separated this pulpit from the ones a couple of blocks away, we're more likely to weep than laugh.
>
> I still wince when I remember the sermons preached during my childhood 25 years ago. Our pastor would dish one up every now and then when our fervor was lagging. The sermon always said that the protestants were right, thank God! and that Luther had discovered the Bible, recovered the Gospel and uncovered corruption in high, holy places. The sermon was like a pre-game pep-talk, an oratory before battle. We would stand up after the sermon and sing, "A Mighty Fortress Is Our God." We sang aggressively, defiantly, and passionately. After all, it was the national anthem of heaven, wasn't it? Our battle song, for we were the good guys. (Herzberg, 1985, p. 3)

The centrality of the church as an institution must be considered and studied by local practitioners (Ostendorf, 1987).

The following excerpt from Valerie Sayers's (1987c) novel *Due East* is highly symbolic and, in many ways, a caricature of what many perceive to be small-town religion. Sayers expertly captures the tone of a revivalist southern church. The story in *Due East* is uncomplicated. Mary Faith Rapple, a 15-year-old sad and somewhat socially backward young woman, lives alone with her father, for whom she keeps house. Mary Faith's parents were religious people, Baptists, who had always conformed to the rather strict mores of their religious community. Early in the story, Mary Faith gets pregnant by an equally backward adopted son of a Roman Catholic family. The youth kills himself without knowing about Mary Faith's predicament. Jesse Rapple, Mary Faith's father, prefers to believe that the father is Stephen Dugan, another Roman Catholic who employs Mary Faith to help in adult education classes. Mary Faith defiantly claims to be immaculate and refuses to be "helped out" of her situation. When Jesse finally reconciles himself to Mary Faith's pregnancy, he wants to do what is right and what his devout Baptist wife would have done. He asks Mary Faith to get dressed up and takes her to church. Although Sayers focuses too heavily on the most punitive aspects of small-town religion, she has captured the imagery and cadences of a sermon in a revivalist small-town church.

SERVICES

Dr. Beady fussed with his big sleeves and gazed out over the congregation. He looked out of place at the front of the church—everything in First Baptist is fifties-modern, from the walnut-veneer empty cross to the walnut-veneer pulpit that looks like it was made by the Zenith Corporation after they were done making television cabinets—but Dr. Beady is straight out of the nineteenth century. He is the kind of preacher who tiptoes into choir practice, wearing a cheap black suit and his hungry rat's smile, and pulls up ten-year-old boys by the collar if he finds them acting up. That night I had a feeling he had his small black eyes directly on me, but I told myself not to play up the paranoia. I was trying to decide whether to wait for Stephen to call me. I could wait forever, with his guilt.

Finally the choir had done its bit, and Miss Christobel Hawkins had sung her solo (flipping her blond hair over her shoulder at the end of every bar), and the deacon had done *his* bit, and Dr. Beady rose to preach. The last few Sundays he had been pushing faith: faith that there would be a good tomato crop this year, faith that the building fund would grow tenfold by the end of the summer, faith that California would not fall into the sea. The bulletin board outside had given the title of the Wednesday night service—the short sermon—as "Our Duty in the Community." I was pretty sure it was another tidy way of getting at money. But as soon as Dr. Beady began to speak, I knew I was in trouble. When he was seated, listening to the choir with one finger pressed against his temple, I had had the sensation that he had picked me out to stare at. Now I had the sensation that he had picked me out to avoid. His eyes darted around and up, to everyone in the congregation but me. He started in his low nasal whine, the whine that would work up to a fever pitch.

"The sinner," he said. "What must we ask of the sinner?" All around me I could feel the electric buzz that Dr. Beady set off when he began to speak. In a few minutes, people would drift away, would stop listening to him, but for now, he had them; he had them lined up naked with their legs spread apart and they were trying to shield themselves. He loved those words *sin* and *sinner*: he sloshed them around in his mouth like wine and then spat them out, all over the congregation.

"The sinner has a debt to pay to the community," said Dr. Beady, and all the Baptists of First Baptist snuck peeks at their neighbors out of the corners of their eyes. "The adulterer." Dr. Beady went on, and we all settled in, anticipating the best. "The adulterer must go back to his spouse and beg her forgiveness." He paused. "The employee who has pilfered must go back to his employer and make restitution." Big pause. "The fornicator" (here he took a deep cleansing breath and came out of it at the other end with a bellow) "the fornicator must stop his immoral actions and begin anew on a pure path." He swallowed gasps of air, and so did the congregation. We had made it past fornicators. Dr. Beady squeezed his eyes up again to circle them over the sinners below, and again I felt that he met everyone's eyes but mine.

Suddenly he began again, off-beat, catching us off-guard. "But *what*," he said, "but *what* do we do when the sinner not only refuses to pay off this debt to those he has sinned against? What of the sinner who refused to say to the community: I am sorry? What do we do with the sinner who is proud of his low deeds? *What* do we do with the drug addict who parades his weak character through our streets?" We all tried to imagine junkies marching down River Street. "What do we do with the drunkard who will not give up his bottle?" Winos parading down River Street! "*What* do we do with the adulterer who will not return to wife and children, but goes on in his sinful ways? Or the teenager who *flaunts* her promiscuity?" I felt my father stiffening beside me. No one had drifted off this time: we all followed Dr. Beady like sheep, and he was building up for the slaughter.

He pulled in another cleansing breath. "*I will tell you what we can do,*" said Dr. Beady. "We can confront that sinner. What has become of us, in 1981, that we are afraid to confront the sinner? What has become of us that we can no longer say to those who have gone astray: 'You are wrong. You are doing e-vil. You re-pulse me.' Why can we no longer say that?" We all shrank back in our pews. "I will *tell you why*. We can no longer say that because we are afraid. Because our society, yes, our media, our schools, tell us that it is all right for our children to drink liquor, to pop pills, to engage in the sacred marriage act when they are fourteen and fifteen years old. They have *frightened* us into acquiescence." He mopped his brow, but didn't look at all acquiescent. His face had the glow of proud red anger it took on for all his sinning sermons, and the glow shone out among the congregation.

When he began again, he dropped his voice, and I could feel my father's stiff arm lean forward, as if to catch his words. All over the big white church women leaned their shoulders forward to hear how they could regain their righteousness and lose their acquiescence. "We have an example," said Dr. Beady. "We have an example," whispered Dr. Beady, "of this in-ab-il-i-ty to face sin in our community today. I mean *today*, this very day, this Wednesday, in this hot June when we are thinking of our air conditioners and our sprinklers and when we should be thinking of bigger things, of sin that must be confronted." People leaned back an inch or two: it was one thing to confront sin, but another to be made guilty about an air conditioner in Due East, South Carolina. Dr. Beady rolled on, unperturbed. "We have this very day," he said, "witnessed the local media giving coverage to, giving *encouragement* to, what it should have been deriding." There was a sucking in of breath all over the church. The local media consisted of three radio stations, two of which played country-western and one of which played easy-listening; the educational TV station on UHF that nobody ever bothered tuning in to; and the Due East *Courier*. Dr. Beady meant the Due East *Courier*. For a minute I though that even Dr. Beady couldn't do *this*, that he had never gone so far as to point a finger at an individual from the pulpit. He had hinted at those who didn't support the church, but he had never dropped hints about one who sat below his nose. About me. My father's hand had knotted into a fist. He was leaning forward again, almost to the next pew.

Dr. Beady looked around him and made a great show of relaxing his shoulders, of relaxing his whole body. We all knew this phase: when he was out of the buildup, out of the anger, and down to the conversational, I-don't-mean-to-scare-you-by-any-of-this-I'm-just-one-of-you-folks-too phase. Now his voice would be as smooth and as thick as treacle. "I don't know how many of you know exactly what I am talking about," he said. Conversational. "I'm not one of those preachers who thinks we should point the finger directly at anyone. Remember Jesus! Remember what he said about casting the first stone! Read your Bible. Read John, Chapter Eight, verses one through twelve." He laughed a little conversational laugh and hung his hands over the edge of the pulpit. "You know," he said, and now he stared directly at me, eye to eye, Dr. Beady's beady black eye thinking it was boring through me, thinking it was *scaring* me. "You know, when I was a boy, the preachers did not hold back at anything. When I was a boy, if you were caught chewing gum in church, the usher would come over and pull you up by the elbow and escort you down the aisle for all to see. Once," and he laughed again, mirthlessly, "once a young visitor to our small town upstate arrived in the middle of summer." We all of us realized we were in for a detour—Dr. Beady would take us back on a ride through his boyhood—and there was settling in all over the church.

"We were not a proud community," he went on. "Our fathers were farmers mostly, eking out a living from soybeans or peaches, but when this young visitor arrived at our church we all took notice. We were all dressed in our best—maybe not a very fancy best, maybe our shoes were run down, but they were polished; maybe our suits were worn thin, but they were pressed—we were all dressed in our best, but this young lady arrived at the front steps of our church dressed in shorts. Dressed in *bermuda* shorts." He calmed himself back into the conversational. "It was a hot day, a hot Ju-ly day, but I remember the look of my mother and the other good women of our community as they spied this young girl coming up the steps in her bermuda shorts. My mother, and all her friends, were wearing white gloves, and modest dresses with long sleeves, and their best shoes, and they blushed when they saw this young thing coming up the steps of the *house of our Lord* in her bermuda shorts. I will never forget the blushes, the shame those good women felt. When the one who should have been feeling shame bared her legs on a Sunday morning for all to see." He bowed his head in shame, and we all bowed our heads.

"I'm sure the good people of this community would blush, too," said Dr. Beady soothingly. "Even in the nineteen-eighties. Even in this day when anything goes. Even in this day of the drug addict, and the drunken driver, and the topless dancer, and the pregnant teenager." He bore down on me again. "*What do you think our preacher did?*" he roared. Then he stopped and composed himself. "This is what he did. Our minister was just arriving to enter the back of the church, but when he saw this young girl outside *the house of our Lord*, dressed in bermuda shorts, he had one of the ushers call her aside, and he took her back with him to the side entrance of the church. I suspect he told her she would have a special place for listening to the sermon, because she was a visitor. I suspect, in her pride, that she was flattered by his attention. Imagine that scene, if you will." He paused to let us all picture it. "Perhaps you can *imagine* what happened when the choir of our little church had finished singing. Perhaps you can *imagine* what happened when it came time for our minister to deliver the word of the Lord. Can you imagine it?" He let us imagine it. "Can you see our preacher bringing this young girl out in front of the congregation, and telling her what he thought of her disrespect? Perhaps you can't imagine that in 1981, but that is what happened. That is indeed what happened. Our preacher told this girl what he thought of her immodesty, what he thought—and he wasn't afraid to say it, not in nineteen *fifty-one*—what he thought of her *sin* of coming to Sunday services dressed in a pair of bermuda shorts."

Suddenly I was aware that my father had put his arm around my shoulder, lightly—not leaning me toward him or squeezing me, but just resting it there, something he'd never done before—and I saw Dr. Beady's eyes veer away from us. All the tension that my father had put into listening to the sermon, fighting the sermon, was gone. He just had his arm around me. I had never felt that sensation before, the sensation of being borne up by him. (pp. 132–137) ❧

SOURCE: Sayers, V. (1987c). In *Due east* (pp. 131–143). New York: Doubleday. Excerpt from *Due East* by Valerie Sayers, copyright © 1987 by Valerie Sayers. Used by permission of Doubleday, a division of Bantam, Doubleday, Dell Publishing Group, Inc.

The following exhibit is a report (Franklin, 1986) that shows the strong attachment to the Protestant tradition shown in many small towns as well as the concerns of those who believe differently. In the atmosphere of small towns, people can be made to feel uncomfortable and can be ostracized if they think differently. The report also reveals the nature of the tension between the strong traditions of old-timers and the concerns of newcomers in small towns.

BIBLE MARKED ABSENT IN SMALL-TOWN SCHOOL

The day she took the list of Bible proverbs off her classroom walls, Grace Wolbrink went home angry. And she hasn't felt at ease since, the 4th grade teacher says.

"I think we are heading for the perfect secular school, where there is no God and no Bible, and where there is no morality," Wolbrink complains.

Two weeks ago, Wolbrink removed such sayings as, "Let another praise you, and not your own mouth; a stranger, and not your own lips."

She and the other teachers at Allendale's elementary school also stopped using Biblical stories as literature for their 600 students.

In this small, conservative town that boasts just two traffic lights, it was a wrenching development.

After years of bitter controversy, the Allendale school board had finally decided to take the Bible completely out of the curriculum.

"Allendale had prayers and Bibles in the schools for years, and it is hard to let go," explains Ron Rotman, a school board member, over lunch in the back of his tile and carpet store.

"I guess it's time for Allendale to obey the law."

To Wolbrink, 50, and many others among the 7,000 residents of the town, the school board's action represented yet another setback for traditional values—and a surrender to "outsiders" and "local people who just want to stir up trouble."

"Disappointment" is the way Roger Rycengs, the town's elected supervisor, summed up local opinion about the changes. "There's got to be very few of them complaining," he said.

But supports of the decision say it is long overdue and is a measure of how much Allendale has changed, along with a lot of other small towns in the Midwest.

Allendale, in its 140th year, is no longer the focal point of a quiet farm community in which most people share a Dutch ancestry and worship at the local

Christian Reform Church. It now sits astride a busy, two-lane state highway, and its population is diverse.

Just down the road, there's Grand Valley State University with 2,500 students.

And there has been a steady flow of newcomers in recent years, people who commute to work in nearby Grand Rapids or to towns along Lake Michigan's shore.

Like other small Midwestern towns in which old-timers and newcomers rub shoulders—and sometimes each other, the wrong way—Allendale is being forced to take a hard new look at the values that have long defined and sustained it.

At times, it has been painful.

Wolbrink says the Biblical proverbs in her classroom left a permanent impression on the youngsters she has taught during her 12 years at the school—and created a link between herself and the students that survived their passages into adolescence and adulthood.

"They'd ask if they were still on the walls, or they would recite them," she recalls.

And when children learned to read from Biblical tales about David and Goliath, Moses, and Noah, they also developed character, Wolbrink contends.

"It's an authority for morality," she says. "In fact, it's the only authority. Has anyone come up with a better one?"

Ed Haurek, a retired sociology profession from Grand Valley State University who moved out of town two years ago, takes a different view.

"Those children who didn't know the Lord were made to feel like second-class citizens," he said.

The campaign to get religion out of the elementary school won its first victory three years ago, when the Michigan Department of Education investigated charges that teachers and students were praying in class.

To forestall state action, the school board banned prayers, the devotionals and Bible clubs on school time.

Then last month, a Grand Rapids attorney complained to the state that the curriculum that was adopted when prayers were formally halted was, in fact, permeated with religious instruction intended to "indoctrinate Protestant Christianity in all students."

The school board, which had been warned by the state in 1986 that its use of the Bible as literature posed serious problems, quickly gave in once again.

Ron Crowe was probably the most visible challenger to the use of religion in Allendale's schools.

He and his wife, Jeanne, are also the last ones left in town among the four couples who initially complained about prayers in the schools. They say the others moved away because they felt unwanted.

Some residents think it strange that Crowe, a middle-aged die maker, did not complain while his own six children were attending school.

Crowe, who hails from Baptist and Pentecostal roots in Arkansas, says he didn't think too much about the issue until the school board did not act when other parents complained about prayers.

It struck him that the parents were being "looked down on," he explains, and the situation also "hit something very basic with me: Obey the law." (p. 17) ❧

SOURCE: Franklin, S. (1986, March 6). Bible marked absent in small-town school. *Chicago Tribune*, p. 17. Reprinted courtesy of the *Chicago Tribune*.

The final exhibit, "Jews are Consigned to History in South: Proud Heritage Dies in Small Towns" (Schmich, 1987) reveals not only the sadness of a dying proud heritage in small southern towns, but also the degree of tolerance and commitment to preserving various religious traditions that have sprung up among various religious groups in those small towns.

JEWS ARE CONSIGNED TO HISTORY IN SOUTH: PROUD HERITAGE DIES IN SMALL TOWNS

Gaston Hirsch is the only surviving Jew here, and the clapboard synagogue on the town's main street has been converted to an Ace Hardware store.

The Jewish temple in nearby Morgan City, a single beige, brick building with a magnolia tree out front, is still a house of worship—but the few Jews left in town lease it to the Mormons. A big sign, "The Church of Jesus Christ of Latter-day Saints," is propped under a window shaped like a Star of David.

Last fall, when the Jewish congregation in the antebellum town of Port Gibson, Miss., had dwindled to two, a local Methodist-Catholic couple, Bill and Martha Lum, who hardly knew a Torah from a menorah but had no trouble recognizing a landmark undeserving of the wrecking ball, bought the town's red-brick Byzantine synagogue, the oldest in the state.

It was to have been sold the next day to a gas station owner who intended to raze it and install a few more pumps.

In small towns throughout the Deep South, similar stories abound—tales of synagogues converted or bulldozed, of their religious artifacts peddled as junk shop kitsch of prosperous Jewish communities reduced to two or three old people and a history preserved only in weed-throttled cemeteries.

In some towns, the only vestiges of Jewish heritage are the marquees of long gone merchants. In Canton, Miss., for example, where a funeral parlor sits on the site once occupied by the synagogue, there reportedly are no Jews in town, but the names Hessdorffer and Perlinsky remain prominently displayed on storefronts.

The explanation for the change is relatively simple.

Though Jewish communities flourish in big Southern cities such as Memphis, New Orleans, and Atlanta, the south has never been a Jewish stronghold. In Mississippi, for example, Jews make up one-tenth of one percent of the population, compared with 10 percent in New York, 3 percent in California and 2 percent in Illinois.

In the small towns, Jewish congregations were small, and once the attrition started, it fed on itself. Old people passed away and young ones moved away, usually to larger towns with more Jews and more opportunity.

"There's a great emphasis in Jewish families on going to college and a great emphasis on being part of a Jewish community," said Macy Hart, who left Winona, Miss., after high school to attend the University of Texas and is now director of the Henry S. Jacobs Camp in Utica, Miss.

"You had to leave to find those things, and once you leave you don't go back."

As a result, the Jewish presence—dwindling for the past 50 years but sustained as long as a few old residents live—will soon be extinct in many small towns that Jews helped build at the turn of the century.

Donaldsonville is a good example. Situated on the Mississippi River an hour's drive south of Baton Rouge, it is a town of about 8,000 whose chief historical distinction is having been Louisiana's capital for one day in 1830. Many of its early settlers were young Jewish men who had fled the pogroms in Europe.

While Jewish immigrants most commonly clustered near the northern ports where they landed, many headed south seeking business opportunities. In Donaldsonville, as elsewhere, young men who started out as peddlers became prominent merchants. They built themselves a stately if rustic temple in the heart of town.

"Here was the altar," said Gaston Hirsch, on a recent afternoon as he stood in the Act Hardware store and opened his arms to stacks of epoxy and cans of house paint.

"The benches were here, see." He waved toward reels of electrical wire.

"We had some beautiful windows. Let me see if they're still there," He flitted out the back door, peered up at the wall and returned shaking his head. "No, no, they're all gone."

He shrugged a deep shrug. . . . "It's a sad thing to show you what used to be a holy place."

Hirsch, born in the Alsace region of France, was a latecomer to Donaldsonville, where the Jewish population peaked in 1935 with 35 families. He arrived in 1946, with his Catholic wife and their child, after spending four years in a concentration camp.

At 79, he has outlived or outstayed every other Jew in town. Now that he has sold his men's clothing store, he occupies himself as caretaker of the local Bikur Sholim Cemetery. Like the Jewish cemeteries in many nearby towns, it was a jumble of weeds and rubble until Hirsch started taking care of it.

He also is keeper of the town's Jewish history, figuring that unless he writes some of it down, the history will die when he does. Not long ago, he and his wife spent days in the cemetery copying names, dates and birthplaces from headstones.

In Donaldsonville, as in other places in the small-town South, intermarriage between Jews and non-Jews has contributed to the situation.

In big Northern cities with large Jewish populations, it was easier for Jews to find a Jewish spouse and a community in which to observe traditional practice. In the South, young Jewish immigrants were apt to marry Christian women, with the children raised in their mother's religion.

Even larger towns are seeing their Jewish population dwindle. For example, Vicksburg, Miss., population about 25,000, used to have the largest Jewish congregation in the state.

Isadore Marcus, who is 88 and has been a member of the congregation since 1915, remembers that in the 1940s as many as 200 people attended services.

Now, though the town still has a rabbi and the temple still has a choir, only 10 or 15 people routinely show up for weekly services. Most members of the congregation are older than 60. Only one family has school-age children.

"We have 71 members total," said Marcus, "and most of those are out of town. They keep their membership because we have a nice cemetery, and they want to be buried here."

For many small-town Southern Jews, a sense of practicality overshadows regret for the past.

In Morgan City, the Mormons and Jews have an amicable agreement, in which the Jews can still use the temple on holidays.

"We take their sign in when we're using the temple," said Leonard Rocs, 83. "We may move their songbooks. And when we're done, we take our menorahs down."

In Port Gibson, Karl Weil and the one other member of the congregation decided to sell the temple because they wanted to establish a fund to maintain the cemetery when they were gone.

The shift in Jewish population away from the South's small towns has gone largely undocumented, but Macy Hart and his colleagues at the Henry S. Jacobs Camp near Jackson, Miss., are trying to change that.

Earlier this month, financed by a grant from the Plough Foundation of Memphis, they broke ground on the Museum of the Southern Jewish Experience. In addition to the museum, they are planning a synagogue furnished with the artifacts that have shown up at the camp after temples closed.

And they are establishing a program, which Hart said is the first of its kind in the country, to help dying congregations plan for their extinction.

"We'll go in and talk to them about what it's like to close down a culture, phase out an entire ethnic group," said Hart. "Then we'll go back into towns, work with the Rotary Club, the schools, teach them about Jewish community that once lived in their towns."

In the meantime, preserving the Jewish past in the South's small towns falls to people such as Gaston Hirsch. He has been collecting money to maintain the Donaldsonville cemetery after he is gone. Two young men—"Catholics but Jewish-minded"—have promised to administer the fund.

"Most of the people here came here in the condition I came here in, penniless, eager to make a living, eager to be well-received by the community," he said walking in the late afternoon sun past headstones with such names as Pforzheimer, Schoenberg, and Klein, past the plot he has prepared for himself and his wife.

"In their memory, the cemetery should be kept up." (pp. 25, 30)

SOURCE: Schmich, M. T. (1987, November 1). Proud heritage dies in small towns. *Chicago Tribune*, section 1, pp. 25, 30. Reprinted courtesy of the *Chicago Tribune*.

Small-town culture is like a map deeply embedded in the cognitive structure of those who have lived it. It has been said that place of origin might be a more important determinant of the way people think and go about managing their environments than place of residence. In the lore of many small-town folks, once a smalltowner, always a smalltowner. Yet, the dilemma for those who want to work in the small town is how to absorb its culture, to learn to appreciate its uniqueness, and to develop the needed cognitive maps. Literature is an aid in developing culture; it is an aid in helping people draw the cognitive maps they need to travel uncharted waters. The exhibits in this chapter were provided to help the reader develop a series of plans, categories, rules, norms, and other types of standards that might help him or her behave in an acceptable manner in the small town. Additionally, the exhibits should help the reader become more sympathetic to the peculiarities and dilemmas of life in small towns. In essence, for those who are familiar with small-town culture, this chapter should have reinforced what they might have known and helped develop a more critical and analytic perspective of small-town behaviors. For those who were not familiar with small-town culture, this chapter provided an introduction to developing an atlas for successful navigation.

6

SENTIMENT AND POLITICS IN SMALL-TOWN LIFE

THE INDIVIDUAL, COMMUNITY, AND GOVERNMENT

People living in small communities often are ambivalent about the role that they want government, particularly central government, to play in their lives. Since human services practitioners are citizens, they share in that ambivalence. But because they have a unique perspective on the needs of communities and provide leadership in the human services field, they have a special responsibility to review the problem carefully. The antilocal philosophy of the eclipse-of-community research paradigm was not helpful. The unexamined anticentral government perspective of inveterate locals also was not helpful. University courses in social and political science that stress economic value as the only barometer for decision making also are useless in making realistic decisions in the context of community. The problem is not an easy one.

In the recent television program "Resolved, Free Market Competitiveness Is Best for America" (Buckley, 1989), a number of leaders from the Democratic and Republican parties met at the University of Mississippi to discuss their personal and partisan differences related to the role of central government in solving the problems of the day. What did not go unnoticed to the alert listener were the often similar positions taken by those leaders. As former Senator George McGovern, one of the panelists, summarized at the end of the discussion, few surprises exist in the ranks of practical politics. Modern politicians recognize that central government must play a role; they differ in their beliefs about the degree to which government must intervene. Those differences are not so much the result of the party line but the personal judgment of the individual politician. No current political leader opposes social security; few are against nationally set minimum standards in vital health and welfare services. No one politician feels that the federal government does not have a role to play in ensuring adequate housing for all citizens, although the specifics of this role vary. Clearly, blind adherence to a partisan political perspective can no longer be the way in which decisions about the role of government are made at the community level. The role of government must be carefully and dispassionately examined issue by issue.

How can one create an atmosphere in which decisions about the role, purpose, and scope of government intervention, be it central or local, are carefully weighted issue by issue? How can one encourage practitioners in small towns, who want to consider not only economic criteria but also other criteria to make the appropriate decisions? In an editorial, exhibited as follows, Etzioni (1989), a social scientist, discusses the shortcomings of the "me first" model in research, public policy, and education. He provides a pertinent analysis of the current, erroneous paradigm of decision making that has turned practitioners into radical individualists. Etzioni suggests that the problem is not so much whether or not to enhance government but "how to rebuild the social and moral values of the community." For Etzioni, community is not coercive but balancing; in his view, a healthy community will help balance individualistic tendencies with concern for others. Although Etzioni's moral essay does not tell practitioners what decisions to make, it does highlight for small-community practitioners caught at the crossroads the various elements that must figure in the decision-making equation.

THE "ME FIRST" MODEL IN THE SOCIAL SCIENCES IS TOO NARROW

The neoclassical view predominating in both the social sciences and the public realm is that people always pursue their own self-interest. Although there is some truth in the concept, it is too narrow to explain or predict human behavior adequately. To change the concept, however, we must do more than criticize it—you cannot beat a theory (or a social philosophy) with nothing. We need to build a new, broader foundation for the social sciences, a process that is now advancing in one of the typical ways that concepts evolve.

The "me first" model is being not so much replaced as absorbed by the "I & we" model. The new model grows out of the old model's assumptions about the goals people pursue, the ways they pursue them, and the characterization of the decision-maker (is he or she a solitary person or part of a community?).

The neoclassical model assumes that people all have one overarching goal: to satisfy their own wants. Historically, those wants were depicted as materialistic. More recently, they have come to include satisfaction derived from altruistic acts, but the basic motivation remains self-centered and hedonistic. According to the neoclassical paradigm, however seemingly selfless the goal, people are always motivated by their own interests in pursuing it. Research in this tradition further assumes that a person's tastes can be neatly ordered into one unitary pattern of desire—a notion at the heart of economics.

The I & we model, on the other hand, assumes that people have a dual nature—that while they have self-serving desires, they do not pursue them mindlessly. Instead, one's "judging self" examines one's desires and evaluates them according to several criteria, the most important of which are moral and social values. A struggle then ensues. Under some conditions, desire wins out; under others, values triumph.

The significance of incorporating a moral dimension into our concept of human nature is that a sense of morality is what separates human beings from animals. Our moral commitment and our desires do not often pull us in the same direction, and much of human life can be explained in terms of the struggle between the two forces and the conditions under which one or the other prevails.

Once the conflict has been resolved and a goal chosen, how does one decide on the means to achieve it? Rationally, neoclassicists say—that is, by using empirical evidence and logical inference. But a very persuasive literature exists arguing that people do not make choices on rational grounds.

What we need is a new model of decision-making that will tell us how people do decide, rather than that they often do not do so rationally.

The idea that most people's choices are influenced heavily by their values and emotions provides a beginning. Entire categories of means to ends, whether efficient or not, are judged to be unacceptable and are automatically ruled out. For example, about a third of the people entitled to welfare benefits refuse to apply on the ground that "it's not right." While emotions and values are often depicted as distorting rationality (which they do), they also influence people against using means that may be efficient in the narrow sense but are wrong or hurtful to others. That is, our values influence both our choice of goals and the way we proceed to accomplish them.

The neoclassical model also draws on and contributes to the idea that all moral rights are invested in the individual, who is assumed to be the legitimate decision-maker. Attempts to modify the person's tastes are viewed as inappropriate interventions. For example, most government actions aimed at redirecting the individual are looked upon as coercive. In contemporary terms, neoclassicists are essentially libertarian.

The most recent philosophical conception of individuals and communities as interdependent attempts to correct radical individualism. It holds that the community has a moral status and rights of its own. While some of its proponents go so far as to neglect individual rights entirely in the name of "the motherland" or some other such cause, a more defensible position is to recognize that both individual rights and duties to the community have the same basic moral standing. For example, the I & we model recognizes both the individual's right to benefit from the savings of past generations and the obligation to save for future ones; or the individual's right to trial by a jury of peers and the individual's obligation to serve on a jury.

The voice of the community is typically moral, educational, and persuasive—not coercive. If coercion must be relied upon, it indicates that the community has been weakened, that too many of its members are engaging in activities previously considered to be unthinkable. A more effective policy than enhancing government would be to rebuild the social and moral values of the community. That shift starts with a change from the neoclassical model to one that encompasses, rather than ignores, the concept of community; that balances, not replaces, individualistic tendencies with concern for others; and that extends beyond material incentives to the role of values, particularly shared values, as long as they are freely endorsed and not imposed.

The I & we model has implications in a number of areas. For example:

• *Research*. It is productive, for explanatory and predictive purposes, to take into account both individual desires and moral commitments when studying human economic behavior. For instance, to understand compliance or non-compliance with tax laws, we need to know how high the tax rates are (a neoclassical factor) and the extent to which people consider the tax system fair or unfair. To understand why people conserve energy, we need information about changes in oil prices and about whether people believe that conservation will help their country or the environment.

• *Public policy*. Take the question of saving versus consumption, for example. Economists recommend various policies to encourage saving and reduce consumption—curtailing federal expenditures (a major source of consumption) or taxing consumption. Both policies have a cost. The first may cause a recession, which exacts huge human and economic costs; the second is regressive and imposes an unfairly heavy burden on the poor. The fact that policies have costs does not mean that they are necessarily undesirable. It does, however, point to the merit of considering other perspectives. A fuller policy would emphasize the accumulation of debt as socially undesirable behavior, behavior that undermines our collective well-being and threatens our future—the way debt was perceived until the 1950's. To bring about the change, the President, community leaders, and educators would all have a role in trying to change people's long-range perspective. Such a program would cost relatively little, is not regressive, and draws on people's values rather than imposing a solution.

• *Education*. Through textbooks, neoclassicists teach millions of high-school and college students every year a model that, as the economist Robert Solow puts it, "underplays the significance of ethical judgments both in its approach to policy and [in] its account of individual and organizational behavior." Neoclassical textbooks are replete with such statements as, "[T]he rational thing to do is to try to gain as much value as I can while giving up as little value as I can." They discuss the Bible and dope as two interchangeable consumer goods, and view both children and cars as "durable consumer goods." One wonders about the effect on the attitudes of potential parents toward children, if they are taught systematically to think of their offspring as a trade-off for other "goods," such as cars.

Studies of the educational effects of neoclassical teaching show that students become more self-oriented, just as they may become more rational in their decisions. A study of "free-ride" experiments conducted by Gerald Marwell and Ruth Ames showed that in 11 out of 12 experimental runs, most participants did not ride free and contributed from 40 to 60 percent of the resources to a group collection. However, a group of graduate students in economics contributed only an average of 20 percent.

All societies set aside certain areas as "sacred." When people are taught to think about them in cost-benefit terms, those areas are "secularized" and stripped of their moral standing, ultimately causing them to be treated as neoclassicists say they are. For example, creating a market for "rights" (such as selling permits to pollute) undermines taboos against this antisocial behavior by normalizing it.

We need to do more than document the role of moral and social values. We also need to include those factors in our teaching and public philosophy. By doing so, we will strengthen individuals who are committed to the community and encourage the development of public policies that are caring and decent. (p. A44) ❧

SOURCE: Etzioni, A. (1989, February 1). The "me first" model in the social sciences is too narrow [Editorial]. *The Chronicle of Higher Education*, p. A44. Reprinted courtesy of Amitai Etzioni, University Professor, The George Washington University, Washington, D.C.

The following exhibit is an editorial written in praise of creative government. For Milliken (1987), a former governor of Michigan, the crucial question is not whether people should have more or less government, but how people can make government more resourceful and creative. Creative government is one that unleashes cooperation between public and voluntary sectors and one that "transforms problems into opportunities." Both problems and opportunities are highly visible in small communities. Milliken's pragmatic approach to government might be a useful inspiration to small-town decision makers.

CREATIVITY IN GOVERNMENT

Teen pregnancy, environmental pollution, the homeless, school dropouts, the financial crisis in health care, AIDS—merely to list some of the major social and economic problems confronting this nation is to raise troubling questions about our ability to solve them. The current absence of creative federal initiatives contributes to a perception of government's incapacity to address intractable domestic policy issues. Moreover, the fiscal constraints imposed by huge budget deficits reinforce the notion that new and innovative federal programs are feasible.

A more encouraging—and in my view more accurate—picture of government's problem-solving capacity emerges at the state and local level. In jurisdictions throughout the country, imaginative responses to pressing social and economic needs reveal patterns of innovation with valuable lessons for other cities and states, as well as the federal government.

One such lesson is the value of relatively inexpensive preventive programs rather than costly after-the-fact remedial projects. For many years researchers have documented the long-term educational and social benefits of good-quality preschool programs. Now, in Missouri, the Department of Elementary and Secondary Education has developed a state-wide program to enhance children's development during the formative first three years of life. Seeking to prevent school failure and encourage family well-being, 1,200 trained parent-educators annually provide in-home instruction to more than 35,000 Missouri families.

Another example of this ounce-of-prevention approach is Parents Too Soon, an Illinois program to reduce the incidence and adverse consequences of teen pregnancy. Jointly managed by the state's Departments of Public Health, Public Aid, and Children and Family Services, the program provides at-risk adolescents with a variety of health-care, social, and educational services. Over the last five years Parents Too Soon has contributed to an 18 percent drop in births to Illinois teens between the ages of 15 and 19.

Many innovative government programs involve creative coalition-building among public and private agencies that have a common interest in solving a specific problem. In a program designed to recruit black families as adoptive parents, the Illinois Department of Children and Family Services established ties with black ministers and churches to encourage the adoption of one child by one family in each church. The One Church–One Child program succeeded in reducing a backlog of 700 black children awaiting adoption to fewer than 60.

The Homeless Services Network in St. Louis has also successfully developed a broad base of support for its activities. In this program, the city's Department of Human Services coordinates its services with those of the United Way, the Salvation Army, and other groups to meet the short- and long-term needs of the homeless, as well as families and individuals who are at risk of living on the street. Because of the network, St. Louis was able to shelter almost all of its estimated 10,000 homeless last year.

The use of simple technologies to solve complex problems is another hallmark of several creative state and local government initiatives. For example, the Health Department of Fort Worth, Texas, has developed a low-tech, low-cost program to evaluate and improve water quality in the city. Instead of using expensive chemical analyses to detect pollution in storm sewer water, the department tests this water by placing minnows in floating, perforated milk cartons for a day or two. If the fish do not survive, storm drain tunnels are investigated for illegally discharged contaminants.

Another common characteristic of exemplary government programs is a bold leap of imagination that transforms problems into opportunities. The Spofford Juvenile Center in the Bronx, N.Y., once renowned for drug dealing, sex offenses, and assaults on its premises, reformulated the nature of detention, using the "dead time" between arrest and trial to intervene in the lives of young offenders with counseling, medical, and school services. Officials in Arcata, Calif., have demonstrated similar powers of imagination by turning an offensive sewage dump into a park and environmental showcase.

These creative programs, and many others like them, suggest a need for fundamental changes in traditional ways of thinking about government and its role in society. Questions about the appropriate levels of taxes and public spending may be less important than analyzing long-term payoffs and the "value added" by public programs and investments. Instead of debating whether "more" or "less" government is desirable, we should encourage government to be a more resourceful and proactive catalyst for solutions. And rather than denigrating politicians and bashing bureaucrats, perhaps we should search for new ways to unleash the talents and creativity of those citizens who have dedicated their lives to public service. (p. 13) ❧

SOURCE: Milliken, W. G. (1987, October 15). Creativity in government [Editorial]. *The Christian Science Monitor*, p. 13. Reprinted by permission of William G. Milliken, former Governor of Michigan.

THE NEW ENGLAND TOWN MEETING: COSMOPOLITAN AND LOCAL CONCERNS

The following exhibits illustrate the current activities of what has become the prototype of participatory democracy in the minds of many students of small communities: the New England town meeting. Lingeman (1980) described the role of the town meeting in colonial times, a role that has not changed much through the centuries:

> At the center of the storm of doctrinal controversy and political faction that periodically raged through the towns was the meeting house on the hill—site of the town meeting. It was here that the myriad of individual interests of towns people were raised and debated; and here that these common concerns were translated into policy and governance. The town meeting spoke for the towns people as a whole and dealt much more intimately with the urgent concerns of their daily lives . . . than the remote colonial legislatures. (Lingeman, 1980, p. 47)

The traditional role of the town meeting recently has come under scrutiny. In its most traditional form, the townspeople elect leaders called Selectmen to manage municipal matters. However, the Selectmen can do little without first getting authorization from the once-a-year "all town meeting," in which everyone who lives in the town can participate. Unfortunately, many citizens can no longer devote the time required to run the affairs of state through direct, participatory democracy. Furthermore, the affairs of state, even at the local level, have become fast moving, complicated, and, sometimes, plainly cumbersome. As the first two exhibits illustrate, the viability of the town meeting has become an issue of concern throughout New England.

In some instances, allowances have been made to specialists and paid administrators, as is illustrated in the following exhibit, "Use of Ballot Changes Town's Way of Doing Business."

USE OF BALLOT CHANGES TOWN'S WAY OF DOING BUSINESS

In Rutland Town on Monday night, 39 people out of a population of 3,300 showed up for the informational town meeting. On Tuesday, Town Meeting Day, 1,206 out of 2,546 voters cast secret ballots, a 47 percent turnout.

In Pittsfield, residents held a traditional town meeting with all business conducted from the floor and with a family-style dinner of baked beans and lasagna, crab meat casserole and a half-dozen varieties of homemade pies. Attendance Tuesday was the highest ever with more than 100 of the town's 396 residents present.

The Pittsfield meeting kept Jim DuWeese, a visitor from Columbus, Ohio, who was here on a ski vacation, entertained all day. It was a meeting of civics lessons, good-natured joking and a display of cooperation among neighbors.

In both towns, slightly fewer than half the registered voters exercised their right to vote. But in most Vermont towns, fewer than 15 percent of the registered voters vote on Town Meeting Day, according to Deputy Secretary of State Paul S. Gillies.

Is the waning interest attributable to the move away from a traditional town meeting and toward the secret ballot? Some say yes and some say no.

Garrison Nelson, a University of Vermont political science teacher and longtime political observer, worries about the future of town meeting and the system of volunteer service that so many towns depend on.

He thinks that along with a decline in the number of towns now having a traditional town meeting has come a decline in participation in local politics. He also believes the attention paid to both substantive and symbolic issues has eroded in the past decade.

Some argue that during the 1980s, as global issues such as the nuclear freeze were introduced into the town meeting debate, the true meaning of town meeting was lost. Nelson isn't sure he agrees with that; he observes that in 1989, with no global issues up for a vote, the interest in traditional town meeting issues like snow plows and fire trucks has not increased.

"Town meeting has been helplessly corrupted by this time," and its "meaningful effect has been diluted," he says.

Gillies thinks differently. He says interest in town issues and budgets remains strong and that the move away from a traditional town meeting was appropriate for some communities, especially ones with growing populations.

When a town adopts the secret ballot, town meeting appears to become "less vital with smaller numbers participating," he says. But the "majority of towns in Vermont are still wedded to the idea of maintaining as much of a traditional town meeting as possible," he says.

Shrewsbury, often considered a bellwether town, did away with some aspects of the traditional town meeting last year after residents argued successfully that many . . . residents could not come to a daytime meeting and, thus, were denied their right to vote.

After much debate, residents voted to elect town officers by secret ballot but conduct all other business from the floor. Although about 75 more people voted for town officers than attended the all-day meeting, Town Moderator Arthur Patten said he did not think the outcome was any different than it would have been with a voice or ballot vote at a traditional meeting.

Patten, who prefers the old-fashioned one-day meeting with all business decided from the floor, said Tuesday's meeting showed why it is important to have people debate issues before voting.

Both the library budget and the budget for the trash-transfer station were increased through amendments introduced from the floor. The trash budget was increased by $2,500, which included $2,000 for a roadside cleanup project and $500 to increase the superintendent's salary. The library budget was increased by $500.

In Waterbury, Town Clerk Edward Finn's advice to Shrewsbury is that things will improve. Waterbury residents voted 13 years ago to elect officers by secret ballot and to conduct all other business from the floor.

Finn, who was among the last officers to be elected by voice vote, says, "Our first year it was terrible and I was against Australian ballot for electing officers. Now I'm convinced it's the way to go."

He says 225 people voted during the business meeting, and 600 voted for officers by secret ballot.

Waterbury's school budget was hashed over for more than three hours, but in the end passed, 123-88. "All the people may not have been happy with the outcome, but most were happy with the manner in which it was done," he says.

In Grafton, residents voted three to one to keep a traditional town meeting. The usual pros and cons of the issue were presented, says Town Clerk Cynthia Gibbs.

But the meeting itself was the best example of the benefits of a traditional town meeting, she says: "One man changed his mind on the issue three times." (pp. 1, 8) ❧

SOURCE: Daley, Y. (1989, March 8). Use of ballot changes town's way of doing business. *The Rutland Herald*, pp. 1, 8. Reprinted courtesy of the *The Rutland, Vermont, Daily Herald*.

In other instances, citizens still want to retain the centuries-old institution of the "town meeting" in its original form. This desire is illustrated in the following exhibit, "Business (and Pleasure) the Old-Fashioned Way."

BUSINESS (AND PLEASURE) THE OLD-FASHIONED WAY

No one was bemoaning the loss of the old town meeting spirit in Whiting on Tuesday afternoon.

Whiting is still a farming town, where there are far more silos in view than satellite dishes. With 23 working farms and only about 400 people, it is the sort of place where everyone's participation counts double, at least.

The sub-zero winds hitting the ridgeline town Tuesday would have been a good enough excuse for anyone to stay home, especially older people. But Whiting turned out, from toddlers to the town's oldest known resident. About 50 adults and 10 children—the equivalent of getting more than 2,000 people to a meeting in Rutland.

Partly, they came for the traditional noon potluck dinner. No suburban quiche cookoff, just a chance to share plain and hearty fare: scalloped potatoes, beans and hot dogs, beef and macaroni, stew.

That was fine with nine-year Town Clerk Grace Simonds. She remarked to a neighbor: "When you go to a restaurant, you order what looks good and you wonder what it is. I haven't had stew in a long time. It was good."

Off in one corner, members of the local 4-H Club were selling brownies for a quarter apiece. Karen LeRoy, nominally the adult leader, said she didn't really have the time, but the kids had understood her dilemma and had agreed to take on virtually all the work of running things themselves.

There aren't that many chances in the year for Whiting residents to gather and swap stories, and those present made the most of it:

. . . . . .

At 1:30 p.m. everyone got down to business—even the children, because it was too cold upstairs for the usual play group. There was no mistaking the seriousness of the meeting, because like many small Vermont towns, Whiting is at a turning point.

From time to time, people came in to vote by Australian ballot on two of the burning issues: whether to join the new Addison County Solid Waste District, and risk having a regional landfill sited on some of the farmland; and whether to advise the selectmen to rewrite their new and more restrictive sewage ordinance, which could preserve rural character at the expense of making it harder for the town's children to build homes.

On the floor, the first order of business was electing a new moderator, because 20-year veteran Jake Emmons has bowed out because of new business commitments.

Earlier, he had observed, "We managed to get the job done, even though it often wasn't by Roberts Rules of Order or standard parliamentary procedure."

Clarence Birchmore, already the grand juror and town agent, was nominated. He accepted, a bit reluctantly, saying, "I only heard all this 10 minutes ago." Later the voters eased his load somewhat by making his wife, Charlotte, already a justice of the peace, the new town agent. Then they made him school moderator as well.

The big hurdle for the meeting was the school budget, because cuts in state special education funding seemed to require a big tax hike. But on the strength of a report by Rep. Robert Oliver, R-Leicester, that the state would in fact pay its share, the budget went through unanimously.

Woe to a social service organization that does not take seriously the Whiting selectmen's admonition to have someone at the meeting to explain what the organization does.

Two groups had their funding requests unanimously denied for that reason, while everything else passed, just as unanimously—except the death penalty resolution, which a clear majority rejected. (p. 7) ❧

SOURCE: Barna, E. (1989, March 8). Business (and pleasure) the old-fashioned way. *The Rutland Herald*, p. 7. Reprinted courtesy of *The Rutland, Vermont, Daily Herald*.

Although many people might believe that potholes and snow removal constitute the substance of town meetings in New England villages, in reality, discussions often encompass local and cosmopolitan concerns, a matter which is itself a subject of much debate among town residents (see, for example, the article by Good, 1983).

The following two exhibits illustrate the broad scope of the business that is sometimes transacted at a contemporary town meeting. They tell the story of the ambassador from El Salvador who requested a meeting with the citizens of the small town of Weston, Vermont, after a number of towns in that state had passed resolutions asking for a ban on aid to the government of El Salvador. The stories about El Salvador's ambassador show how locals are involved in national and international concerns. Arguing for the merit of including cosmopolitan concerns at town meetings, Mary Miller, a 78-year-old resident of the town of Weston said, "International affairs have always been discussed in town meetings. . . . The first town meeting dealt with an international issue—Britain and the Colonies" (*New York Times*, 1983, p. 1). Localism in Vermont, as the ambassador learned at the 1983 meetings in Weston, is very much about thinking globally but acting locally.

EL SALVADOR AMBASSADOR TO TALK IN WESTON FRIDAY

Ambassador Ernesto Rivas-Gallont will make a plea for American military aid to El Salvador at a public forum here Friday night.

The ambassador made a request to speak here after Weston voters strongly supported a proposal to cut off aid to El Salvador and pull out American military advisors at town meeting.

Voters at that meeting expressed that such a vote was an effective way for citizens to be heard in Washington.

Rivas-Gallon will speak for 20 minutes starting at 7:30 pm at the Weston Playhouse. Following his talk a comment and question session will be held. Sam Lloyd will moderate the event.

The ambassador learned of the Weston vote in the Washington Post article which covered the town meeting and the trend all over New England to take on national issues.

Mary Mitchell Miller, who introduced the resolution at Town Meeting, feels strongly that the town meeting can be a proper form for national or international issues.

"I think it should be done in all town meetings. We might be able to stop the president from his insane course, and we should back our congressmen who aren't in favor of the aid" said Miller.

She pointed out that town meetings originally started so people could vote on double taxation which was not a local issue.

Town Clerk Gil Spaulding said he received a call from Rivas-Gallon March 9.

"He asked if he could talk to the voters of Weston. He said he wanted to give his point of view," explained Spaulding. (p. 1) ❧

SOURCE: El Salvador ambassador to talk in Weston Friday. (1983, March 16). *The Black River Tribune*, p. 1. Reprinted courtesy of *The Black River Tribune*, Ludlow, Vermont.

AMBASSADOR ARGUES FOR SALVADOR AID, BUT WESTON REMAINS UNCONVINCED

Ernesto Rivas-Gallont brought more than just a message from El Salvador with him to this town Friday; he brought citizens from throughout New England and representatives of the news media from as far away as Sweden.

Despite one small incident, when a woman shouted to cameramen to "turn off the bright lights" and the large crowd at the small Weston Playhouse threatened to become a mob, the performance, on all accounts, was remarkable.

It easily might not have been that way. There were well over 400 people in the theater and most felt quite strongly about American aid to El Salvador, and quite differently from that nation's ambassador, who sat before them. The three major television networks were there and their crews were quite evident, running around with cameras, bright lights and microphones.

Newspaper reporters from all over the nation were crowded at the front and along the sides of the auditorium.

. . . . .

Under all this scrutiny, the forum in Weston and the citizens who were part of it came out looking scrupulous and intelligent and preserved Vermont's reputation as, in Rivas-Gallont's words, "the birthplace of ideas."

On the other hand, the meeting at the Weston Playhouse was more than just another media happening, because it was first and foremost a democratic event, where integrity and respect played roles as important as opinion and sentiment.

"I expect to see the same decorum and fair play that I have witnessed here in the last 22 Weston Town Meetings that I have attended," Moderator Sam Lloyd said before turning the podium over to Rivas-Gallont. By the night's end, his wish had been fulfilled.

Wearing a dark pin-striped suit, the affable, polished, handsome ambassador looked like a prototype of a Central American diplomat and remained visibly unruffled throughout the onslaught of criticism voiced against his government and his Christian Democratic Party.

At the end of the evening, however, when the crowd rose and applauded Rivas-Gallont for several minutes, there was unmistakably the look of confusion in his eyes. He appeared not to understand this respectful tribute to him in contrast to the sharp opprobrium which had preceded it.

The source of that confusion was probably as much a cumulative effect of the night's events as it was the ovation itself, for Rivas-Gallont would probably not have come to this small town to speak in front of its people and the nation's media if he had expected his plea for American aid to lose rather than gain ground.

During his 25-minute speech the Ambassador stated his case for "a country struggling for democracy," and briefly outlined the history of his nation, its economy and the roots of the current anarchy that prevails in El Salvador.

The text was broad, directed at appealing to the crowd on a humane level, and was delivered casually.

Rivas-Gallont told jokes: "Had I known I would have been before most of the nation's media I would not have come, I would have been afraid. But with all your support, who's afraid of the media."

He praised the United States and its people: "I am not going to Weston to lecture. How can I lecture the United States from small town USA? You do not do that. You talk to the Americans. You converse with them, you hear their appeals and they will listen to your appeals. This is democracy in the United States."

He offered the crowd personal accounts as "a testimony to the will of the people of the country to survive and struggle for democracy." One story was that of his own father who cast his vote in the March of 1982 elections for the constituent assembly, despite four hours in the scorching sun.

And there were even visual aids: a map of El Salvador which nearly fit over the map of Vermont.

In general, Rivas-Gallont was able to adopt a rather folksy tone for a foreign ambassador.

The heartfelt plea was impressive diplomacy, and might have been enough to sway an undecided or uninformed audience, but Rivas-Gallont had underestimated small town USA.

While there were a number of general pleas for peace made at the meeting such as Darcy Johnson's—a mother who called for a demonstration of strength through peace not war, and who expressed fear that her son would be involved sooner or later—it was the citation of specific incidents backed by dates and statistics, that seemed to affect the mood of the audience and surprise the Ambassador the most.

He had probably not expected that so many in this audience would know so much in such detail about El Salvador, that the brothers from the Benedictine Priory would be there in force; that a physician from California who had just come back from the turbulent nation would be given the podium to tell of "another El Salvador"; or that the threat of Communism would not be enough to sway this crowd.

Larry Rosen from Boston stated that "in the past three years 35–40,000 unarmed innocent civilians have been murdered by the paramilitary and armed forces," and then asked "how many people had been brought to justice for those innocent murders?"

"The assassination of non-combatants is an event that happens in El Salvador," began the Ambassador's reply.

He went on to say that "the results of investigations usually lead to no avail."

In this case, as in many during the course of three dozen speeches, the dialogue did little to sway voters toward the need for more American aid to El Salvador's government.

Perhaps the most telling example was related by Brian Henrehan, who held up a pancho he had been given by Ita Ford, an American nun "raped, tortured and slain" in El Salvador two and one-half years ago.

"The Salvadorian sense of justice is a sham," stated Henrehan in a voice filled with anger. "May God have mercy on all of us, and your government, sir."

. . . . .

Sadness was the tone of Rivas-Gallont's short rebuttal which followed the question and statement periods.

"I don't want to leave Weston thinking that the message I brought you has gone unheard," concluded Rivas-Gallont to an audience who had appeared throughout the evening to listen to all that was said.

Perhaps it was the lopsided audience stacked against him, or the strength of the opinions with which people entered the meeting that prevented Rivas-Gallont from gaining any ground, but he evidently was quite aware that he hadn't.

After the meeting he speculated that in their opposition people were expressing dissatisfaction with the Reagan Administration; but this was certainly not the case with Henrehan, who held the pancho of Ita Ford, or Dr. Charles Clements, just back from El Salvador. (pp. 1, 9–10) ❧

SOURCE: McAffee, A. (1983, March 23). Ambassador argues for Salvador aid, but Weston remains unconvinced. *The Black River Tribune*, pp. 1, 9–10. Reprinted courtesy of *The Black River Tribune*, Ludlow, Vermont.

CONFLICT IN THE SMALL COMMUNITY

Although the integrating forces and networks of small communities have been emphasized in this book, this does not mean that conflict does not exist in local communities. Conflict is part of the small town just as it is part of the city and part of life. The following exhibits illustrate varying degrees of conflict. Surely conflict can be resolved without requiring a radical transformation of the community. Yet, sometimes conflict resolution requires more drastic measures, including the intervention of forces outside the community.

In his historical study of American communities, Bender (1978) discussed how the 19th century American community differed from its 18th century counterpart in the area of political conflict. He suggested that in the political arena, "conflict within the bounds of the local community became more prominent. . . " (p. 100). "Not all conflict," Bender continued, "was destructive of strong primary identifications with the local community. Local political conflicts could even enhance this identification simply because the local community, by providing an arena for conflict, can strengthen the sense of local bondedness" (p. 100). The political conflict illustrated in the news items that reflect the long-term debate over the election of a black mayor in the small Georgia town of Keysville is of a different nature. The small community is part of the larger theater of society in which conflict over racial equality is being played out. Inequality has been pervasive in American society and racial discrimination has been the burden of large cities and small towns. In that sense, Keysville, Georgia, or Howard Beach, New York, are just scenes in a larger and more complex play. Yet, because of their insularity, small communities are notorious for their resistance to change, particularly on racial matters. The long struggle of black citizens in Keysville, Georgia, is an example of that resistance. The white citizens of Keysville did not want to relinquish their privileged positions. Yet, the struggle of the black citizens is also an example of a group of citizens who did not give up, an example of poor people's commitment to democracy, and an example of the resiliency of an oppressed group that insists on seeing positive change in their own backyards.

The story of Emma Gresham of Keysville is a case in point. When Gresham won the mayoral election in Keysville, Georgia, on January 4, 1988, the *New York Times* reported the following:

> The small impoverished town of Keysville, 120 miles east of [Atlanta], re-established a local government that had been dormant for 54 years. The election, seen by many as a symbol of efforts by rural blacks to gain political power, marked a victory for blacks seeking more municipal services over whites who fear higher taxes. Black candidates

> won the post of mayor and four of the five council seats in a close election in the town of 300 people. Outsiders who watched the voting closely estimated that 90 percent of black voters and 80 percent of white voters cast ballots.
>
> But a court challenge to the election is continuing, brought by whites who say the town's borders were misdrawn to include a majority of black residents (Smothers, 1988, p. 14)

A federal district judge overturned the state court injunction and, in the end, Gresham became mayor. Commenting on the true meaning of the election, Ashaki Binta, development director for the Christic Institute, a group in North Carolina that aided residents of Keysville in organizing the election, said,

> This was so much more than an election. . . . Blacks are in a position to control many towns in the South but there are forces out there resistant to progress. (Smothers, 1988, p. 14)

Two editorials from *The Atlanta Constitution* praise Gresham's efforts after two successive elections, one in 1988, and the other in 1989. "Keysville Mayor Cited for Fight to Revive City Government" (Schwartzkopff, 1989) tells of Gresham's and Keysville's success in retaining gains made.

NEW DEMOCRACY TRIES TO TAKE ROOT

Here are a few clues. See if you can guess where this fledgling democracy is located:

The citizens of this land just held their first contested election in more than 50 years. They hope the new government they have chosen will help them attain some basic social services—like sewerage and water systems and police and fire protection—and help improve the quality of their lives.

Sounds like Haiti, right? Or the Philippines? How about South Korea? Wrong. The community described above is closer to home. It is Keysville, a majority-black town of 300 in east-central Georgia.

In Monday's election, a retired schoolteacher, Emma Gresham, was chosen mayor and four other blacks were picked for the town's five-member City Council. A remarkable 85 percent of the registered voters went to the polls. Although its black residents are jubilant over the election results, all is far from rosy in tiny Keysville.

White residents, who opposed the election, have vowed to continue the legal challenges, court injunctions and wrangling over boundaries that had kept the formation of a new town government in doubt for years. They say reactivation of the government will hike taxes beyond their ability to pay.

Fifty-five years ago, with the town's black community growing and its white population beginning to decline, white residents decided to stop having elections. *Just like that.* Without elections, they must have reasoned, there could be no black control. So two generations of black citizens were robbed of their right to help decide how their lives would be governed.

Even as the votes from the election were being counted, lawyers representing white residents were preparing to take the matter back to court, to try to overturn a federal judge's ruling that had allowed the election to proceed. If they succeed in getting a court to nullify Monday's election, Keysville blacks will once again be frustrated in their fight to gain enfranchisement.

Though many of us are blasé about our right to vote, having long since taken it for granted, Keysville's blacks appreciate the foolishness of such an attitude. They understand that the vote cannot be won *one and for all*, but can only be ensured by constant effort and commitment. (p. 12A) ❧

SOURCE: New democracy tries to take root [Editorial]. (1988, January 7). *The Atlanta Constitution*, p. 12A. Reprinted courtesy of *The Atlanta-Journal Constitution*, © 1988.

KEYSVILLE BLACKS CLOSER TO DREAM

In many communities, residents would look upon a local election on the day after New Year's—a time when many would still be celebrating the holiday season—as a nuisance. Not in tiny Keysville, Ga. The democratic process, with its promise of self-determination, is still too new to the town's 300 residents, most of whom are black, to be taken for granted.

Their struggle to resurrect Keysville's once-dormant government is inspiring. They are mainly poor people: Many do not have indoor toilets or running water, but they want to help themselves, to use the ballot to take charge of their own destinies and improve the quality of their own lives.

That is commendable. After all, it is the American way. They are willing to pull themselves up by their own bootstraps. They deserve the opportunity. Monday, they put the college football bowl games aside and staged only the second municipal election in Keysville since the 1930s. From the Great Depression until last year, the town's government was lapsed. Whites, who feared the growing clout of the black population, simply stopped holding elections, denying blacks a chance to participate in the political process.

On Monday, black residents re-elected Emma Gresham, the retired schoolteacher who was a driving force in reactivating the government. They chose five other blacks for the City Council. The election, the second in as many years, puts residents closer to their dream of using government as an aid in luring industry and jobs to the area and helping set up water and sewerage systems and other basic services.

Yet, even after that election, their fledgling democracy remains fragile. White residents are still adamantly opposed to the reactivation of the government. They fear that new services and a higher quality of life will cost them dearly in property taxes. They continue to use an array of legal and political maneuvers aimed at thwarting the new government, and they continue to dispute the town's legal boundaries even though a ruling by the state attorney general should have settled the issue last year.

As the election was being held, whites were filing numerous challenges against black registered voters. The courts, then, will likely have the last word on whether the wishes of the majority of the town's residents will prevail. They should.

Already, Mrs. Gresham and the City Council have made progress in Keysville. There are now regular police patrols in the community, a new post office, literacy and education programs, as well as a new day-care center. It would be a terrible shame if such a determined effort at self-improvement were short-circuited. (p. 14A) ❧

SOURCE: Keysville blacks closer to dream [Editorial]. (1989, January 7). *The Atlanta Constitution*, p. 14A. Reprinted courtesy of *The Atlanta Journal-Constitution*, © 1989.

KEYSVILLE MAYOR CITED FOR FIGHT TO REVIVE CITY GOVERNMENT

Amid comparisons to black abolitionists, Keysville Mayor Emma Gresham was honored Saturday night with the highest award given by the Georgia Association of Black Elected Officials (GABEO) for her efforts to reinstitute a city government in the small town southwest of Augusta.

Mrs. Gresham was awarded the Papa Dent Award for the Elected Official of the Year by state Rep. Tyrone Brooks (D-Atlanta), who assisted the former schoolteacher in reviving Keysville's defunct city government.

In a controversial legal battle with white residents that eventually wound its way to the U.S. Supreme Court, Mrs. Gresham helped resurrect the city government of Keysville, becoming its first mayor since 1933 on a platform promising to provide water and sewer services and police and fire departments for the town's largely poor, black population.

Under Mrs. Gresham's leadership, Keysville has a new post office and day-care center, and is working toward installing a sewage system and providing jobs for its citizens, Mr. Brooks said.

"She epitomizes hard work," he said, likening her to 19th century abolitionists Harriet Tubman and Sojourner Truth.

"It's quite a moment," Mrs. Gresham said. "I feel so humble. . . . We are committed. When we look at the children—and there are a lot of children in Keysville—that is our faith."

The battle in the tiny Burke County community began four years ago, when a grocery store owner—whose name no one recalls and who has since moved away—petitioned the County Commission for a beer license. But the commission said it had no jurisdiction since Keysville's city charter was in place, and recommended the applicant go to the city's elected officials—there were none—for the license.

No one know why Keysville, which was incorporated in 1890, stopped holding elections 55 years ago—no one who once held office is alive to explain what happened during the Depression. But the request spurred local residents, among them Mrs. Gresham, to hold an election in 1988.

Mrs. Gresham was elected mayor, and four blacks won seats on the five-member City Council, but whites quickly raised legal challenges to the outcome.

Although an Augusta Superior Court judge had ruled the election invalid, in part because the white residents raised questions about the town's boundaries and the eligibility of some voters, that order was set aside by a federal court.

Mrs. Gresham and other supporters of resurrecting Keysville's city government fought their case in Burke County Superior Court, on the steps of the state Capitol and finally before the U.S. Supreme Court.

The high court in December declined to rule on the question of whether a panel of three federal judges properly allowed the January 1988 election to proceed. It returned the case to the panel to consider whether the white voter's lawsuit should be dismissed, and the outcome remains uncertain.

This month, Mrs. Gresham was re-elected mayor by a wide margin, and blacks gained all five council seats.

Whites, who own much of the property in Keysville, say their concerns center on economics. (p. B2) ❧

SOURCE: Schwartzkopff, F. (1989, January 29). Keysville mayor cited for fight to revive city government. *The Atlanta Constitution*, p. B2. Reprinted courtesy of *The Atlanta Journal-Constitution*, © 1989.

The exhibits recounting the struggle of Emma Gresham to remain the elected mayor of Keysville illustrate what happens when local ties are used negatively to oppress and protect the interest of those who control resources and power. Despite the recognition of the merits of local attachments, not all localism is either moral or supportable. As Margolis (1981) suggested in a paper on the limits of localism, there is localism and localism. The same can be said about central government intervention in local affairs: not all federal or state intervention is inappropriate; there is intervention and intervention. State or federal government agencies have the responsibility to secure the rights of those who are being disenfranchised. In the case of Keysville, the federal courts (including the Supreme Court) had to intervene to secure the town's fragile democracy.

LOCAL EFFORTS

In a recent article in *Policy Review*, Zinsmeister (1987) discussed the phenomenon of regionalization in American culture. Zinsmeister suggested that this nation's center of gravity has shifted from the traditional dominance of New York and Hollywood toward other regions throughout the country. Although his main theme was the regionalization, democratization, and renewed traditionalism of American culture, he also observed a renewed energy that was inspiring exciting projects in many parts of the country.

A new fecundity of efforts in local communities has been noticed in many areas of endeavor. Local forces have rallied to save collapsing local economies, preserve heritage, and create employment through partnerships of government, businesses, and other collective efforts.

> "Nine years ago, after I was laid off at the dairy, I didn't think there'd be a job for me," says Gladys Baker as she adds tiny, perfect stitches to the quilt on her lap. "Most of my life I worked at Detweiler's making ice cream." When they closed down, I was unemployed for eight months before coming to work at Old Bedford Village." The hum of voices—craftspeople weaving, sewing, and crocheting—fills the warm, well-lit room where Baker sits quilting. "Now my job is to make quilts for the village shops." Old Bedford Village, a cluster of more than 40 log cabins, wooden barns, and stone buildings, is a showplace for woodworkers whose crafts predate the American Revolution. Bedford historic village is a unique solution to a problem in Pennsylvania, which has more people living in rural areas than any other state. (McMackin, 1988, p. 13)

The village was started by a county commissioner who wanted to draw on local resources and aid unemployment. Many of the local residents were skilled craftspeople; the county had an abundance of historic buildings. Sources of funding from government were tapped creatively to start the village (McMackin, 1988).

In an article about regional magazines, Wooster (1989) reported that the regional magazines, among them *New England Monthly*, *Yankee*, *Southern Magazine*, *Southern Living*, *Texas Monthly*, *Sunset*, and *California*, have experienced tremendous boom. "The content of regional magazines reflects differences in regional style and character" (Wooster, 1989, p. 13), and although one may question whether the regional archetypes portrayed by some of the magazines exist, apparently within regions some magazines also portray variety and change. For example, Wooster commented,

> If *Southern Living* stands for a carefully modified version of the Old South, *Southern Magazine* stands for the New South—a region where old racial, cultural and economic differences are much less important than in the past. (p. 15)

This type of greater social openness and renewed vigor is the form of positive localism practitioners emphasize. The following two exhibits illustrate the rekindling of local efforts, particularly those efforts that, at the same time, preserve part of the heritage of local communities. The first exhibit, an article from *The Oregonian* (MacKenzie, 1987), provides background on what has become a major economic problem for small communities: the demise of railroad lines to more remote places. The demise of the 55-mile railroad between Lakeview, Oregon, and Altura, California, would have had tragic consequences for the lumber industry autochthonous to the area and, consequently, for local employment. The community of Lakeview, encouraged by local postmaster Orval Layton, set out to save the railroad and its own future, and succeeded.

BRANCH LINES GO ON MARKET: RURAL TOWNS AND RAILROADS MAY BENEFIT FROM STRATEGY

Railroads across the country are selling off their branch lines rather than abandoning them. And that could mean good news for Oregon.

"The big change now from a few years ago is that the railroads, rather than abandoning branch lines, are selling them," said Claudia Howells, deputy commissioner of the Oregon Public Utility Commission.

"The trend has really taken hold. Not only that, but they are selling lines in packages, as well as individually."

Branch lines were originally established to feed traffic from outlying areas to the main lines. With deregulation of the transportation industry and increased competition among the various transportation modes, the major railroads have focused more of their efforts on maximizing returns from the main lines.

The initial trend was to simply abandon some of the less profitable feeder lines; now the main line railroads are looking harder at transferring the feeder lines to independent operators to keep the long haul business from shifting to other modes of transportation.

As recently as two years ago, Oregon officials were worried that potential abandonment of branch lines posed a severe threat to the economic vitality of many Oregon communities. David Astle, assistant public utility commissioner, put the problem in perspective when he announced in February 1985 that about 700 of Oregon's 1,800 miles of branch railroad lines either had been or were expected to be abandoned.

Many lines confronted eroding traffic bases and a deteriorating financial position. Part of the cause was the state of Oregon's economy, particularly the decline of the forest products industry.

The erosion also was due to government subsidies of competing transportation, networks such as the Columbia Basin waterway system and the interstate highway system. In addition, an increasing proportion of products were bypassing branch lines and being shipped directly to main rail lines or remaining on trucks throughout the entire transportation process.

In some cases, abandonment was likely to have minimal impact on the local economy served by the line because alternative modes of transportation were available at reasonable cost. In other cases, however, the potential economic impact of the abandonment was severe, particularly in rural communities with limited access to alternative modes of transportation at reasonable cost.

Mills in Lakeview, for example, reported having to wait up to six weeks to get trucks in for outbound shipments. A report by the state Department of Transportation said, "The economic ramifications to the (Lake County) area if the (55 mile Southern Pacific line between Lakeview and Alturas, Calif.) were to be abandoned were such that it would be a devastating blow to this very rural county."

Southern Pacific has sold that branch line to Lake County.

. . . . .

Some of these lines, as well as others in Oregon, are being considered for sale not because they are close to abandonment but because the major railroads believe they can be run at less cost by an independent operator while continuing to feed their business to the main line.

"Independently owned short lines are a lot more flexible in the service they can provide, they have a smaller focus on their unique geographical area, and because they are locally based they have greater customer loyalty," said Power.

Independently owned branch lines can also be less expensive to run.

"Basically, the large railroads can't operate the shorter lines as economically as the small railroads can because the smaller lines have lower labor costs," said John Dow, vice president of the American Short Line Railroad Association. (pp. D1–D2) ❧

. . . . .

SOURCE: MacKenzie, B. (1987, June 21). Branch lines go on market: Rural towns and railroads may benefit from strategy. *The Oregonian*, pp. D1–D2. Reprinted courtesy of *The Oregonian*.

In the exhibit that follows, Glover (1985) predicts the end result of the community's efforts. Volunteer efforts coupled with community proceeds from the Oregon State lottery and entrepreneurial support were the ingredients of success.

RESIDENTS OF LAKEVIEW, OREGON, FIGHT FOR THE LIFE OF THEIR TOWN: IF THE RAILROAD GOES, THE MILLS WILL SHUT DOWN

When Orval Layton came back from the Army at the end of World War II, he envisioned spending the rest of his life delivering mail to the residents of this small mountain community and fishing in the nearby lakes and streams.

And for many years, Layton enjoyed his dreams to fulfillment.

But the bubble was rudely burst last year. The 57-year-old Layton, a resident since he was 4 and now the postmaster here, has devoted all his spare time since then trying to save his adopted hometown from extinction.

Layton has been spearheading a drive opposing the Southern Pacific Railroad's proposal to abandon rail service to Lakeview, a town of 2,800. If granted, the abandonment would devastate five lumber mills here and the town in general, according to Layton and other civic leaders.

"If the train goes," Layton said, "it'll hit this town hard . . . real hard."

Twelve miles north of the California border and nestled among thick forests of Ponderosa Pine and white fir, Lakeview grew because of its timber and its means of shipping it. Now more than 600 work in the area's largest employment base: the Fremont, Lakeview Lumber Products, Louisiana Pacific, Precision Pine, and Woodgrain Moulding mills along the northern edge of town, where the "Old Perpetual Geyser" still spouts every minute or so.

(It was the geyser, along with the rich mountain landscape and timber terrain that led an earlier railroad—known as the Nevada, California and Oregon Railroad

(NCO)—to plan a run from Reno to the Columbia River with Lakeview one of several stops along the route.)

Operators of the five mills—already working reduced hours because of a nationwide slump in the lumber industry—fear that some may be forced to shut down completely. Others say one-third of their work force could be laid off if the 100-year-old rail service is discontinued.

"If the railroad goes, the mills will shut down," warned Tom Hauptman, one of the mill operators. "I don't see any alternative."

L.F. "Choc" Shelton, manager of the Fremont Sawmill Co., said his 80 employees, like the other mill workers in town, already work only 32 hours a week because of the slump in lumber sales. He predicted that at least 20 of his workers will lose their jobs if the line is shut down.

Statistics compiled by opponents of the closure indicate that 200 primary jobs will be lost if the railroad is allowed to close. That, Layton says, would mean a loss of up to $5.5 million of the $45 million total payroll in all of Lake County.

Efforts to find a company to buy the line and operate it as a short-line railroad occupy the attention of half a dozen civic leaders and organizations.

But finding a buyer hasn't been easy. The SP is asking to abandon its land on either side of the 55 1/2 miles of track and trestles, much of which needs repair. Any new owner would have to provide his own locomotives and maintain the tracks and equipment.

SP estimates total right-of-way acreage at 766 acres and has asked $700,000 for the property. The Oregon State Department of Transportation, though, estimates it at 693 acres, 207 in Oregon and 486 in California.

The furor began a year ago when the SP, which operates the branch line between Lakeview and the California community of Alturas, announced its intention to abandon the line. It filed an application with the Interstate Commerce Commission in Washington, D.C., six weeks ago.

Train service to Lakeview, the "highest city in Oregon" at 4,800 feet, began shortly after the town was founded in the late 1880s.

Robert Melbo, assistant superintendent of the SP in Portland, said in a recent interview that it "was a dream that was never to be realized."

Instead, the NCO operated the narrow-gauge route between the two communities until the 1920s, when it was purchased by the SP and converted to the wider standard gauge. It now serves as a branch off of SP's main line from Ogden, Utah, through Nevada to Klamath Falls.

Paralleling U.S. 395 out of Alturas most of the way, the Lakeview branch runs along the eastern shore of Goose Lake and through the Pit River Indian Reservation in the Modoc National Forest.

Its condition in some areas, according to a report prepared by Harold Brainerd, region right of way supervisor for the DOT, is so deteriorated that trains that travel over it twice a week are restricted to a maximum of 20 mph. The mills cannot send out full loads due to weight limitations on some of the old and poorly maintained trestles.

Already using trucks to transport the logs the 40 to 60 miles from the forest to the mills, mill operators argue that it would take two to three times more trucks than rail cars to haul the lumber from the mills. That would mean a drastic increase in the cost of the lumber and would put additional trucks onto already overcrowded and poorly maintained highways, the operators say.

Layton said he recently got a letter from SP citing cost factors. Specifically, the railroad said, rail traffic originating on the Lakeview branch generates $2.2 million but associated costs amount to $2.7 million—an annual loss of $500,000. (SP, which merged with the Santa Fe Railroad recently, declared a combined profit of $490.8 million last year.)

Ed Immel, rail planner for the Oregon Transportation Department, said his department intends to protest the closure and assist the community in every possible way. But he emphasized that "the state doesn't want to own a railroad, and it's up to the local shippers and community to find the solution."

He also pointed out that income from the newly inaugurated Oregon state lottery—income targeted for economic development—may be considered as a source to help the town of Lakeview buy the line from the SP.

Layton's committee also has talked with the operators of Rail-Tex, a firm based in San Antonio, Texas, and the Kyle Railroad of Fresno. Both have indicated interest in operating the line but not in purchasing it.

Fred Kepnew of the Great Western Railroad Museum of Klamath Falls, Ore., also was approached by the committee and said he would be interested in operating excursion trains over the line if someone else bought it. But he added, "We're not in the freight business."

The ICC has set a June 24 deadline for final arguments from both sides before it makes the final decision. (pp. 1, 4) ❧

SOURCE: Glover, M. (1985, May 5). Residents of Lakeview, Oregon, fight for the life of their town: If the railroad goes, the mills will shut down. *The San Francisco Examiner*, pp. 1, 4. Reprinted with permission of *The San Francisco Examiner*, © 1985 The San Francisco Examiner.

The following exhibit tells the end of the Lakeview railroad story. Despite the headline, the railroad is not really "private." Rather, it belongs to the county but is managed by an independent company. The combination of resources is a credit to Lakeview's spirit. The railroad is an outcome of local community efforts.

IT MAY BE SLOW, BUT LAKEVIEW'S PRIVATE RAILROAD IS A LIFESAVER

On a warm June day a year ago, about 50 residents of Lakeview brought out their lawn chairs and took their places on a flatcar of the Nevada-California-Oregon Railroad. Then they rode 15 miles in the open air to a barbecue at a park on the Oregon-California border.

The Lion's Club outing would not have happened, the train they rode on would not have existed and the tracks it ran on would have been little more than strips of rusted steel, had it not been for the efforts of Lakeview Postmaster Orval Layton. It was Layton who played a pivotal role in Lake County's purchase of the railroad from Southern Pacific in January 1986.

Layton heard in early 1985 that Southern Pacific planned to abandon its 55 mile branch line between Lakeview and Alturas, Calif. The reason, according to Southern Pacific, was a sharp decline in the volume of wood chip, lumber and mouldings being shipped on the line and the resulting heavy financial losses.

Layton went to local shippers, community leaders and government officials and argued that it was in their best interests to work together to buy the line.

"Our community, like a lot of other small communities, was headed downhill," Layton said. "I though, 'Gee, if we let this line shut down, it'll be a step in the wrong direction.' "

"I couldn't believe it," said Leonard Ugelow, one of the owners of Lakeview Lumber Products Co., when he first heard of Southern Pacific's plan to abandon the line. "I didn't believe that public opinion would permit Southern Pacific to abandon the line." If the rail line had shut down, "it might have caused us to review whether or not we wanted to operate in Lakeview." he said.

Garnering support for, and approval of, the purchase proved to be a lengthy and complicated process.

"It was like a soap opera," Layton said. "We just lived from peak to valley. One day we had it, and the next day we didn't. The whole thing from beginning to end was unusual. Nothing was routine."

Finally, a deal was cut for the state to cover 85 percent of the $555,000 purchase price out of Oregon State Lottery receipts and for four businesses operating in the area—Louisiana-Pacific Corp., Lakeview Lumber Products Co., Woodgrain Mouldings Inc. and Fremont Sawmill—to cover the balance.

Lakeview County then hired Great Western Railway of Loveland, Colo., to run the line, with the county paying Great Western a management fee and a rental fee for equipment. Although the official name of the rail line is the Nevada-California-Oregon Railroad, it's better known as the "Goose Lake 55." That's the name Molly Peterson, a local high school student, won $100 for submitting in a contest sponsored by the Lake County Chamber of Commerce.

On Wednesday, the Goose Lake 55 made one of its twice a week round trips between Lakeview and Alturas.

Jack Prasun, the general manager and engineer of the line, and Mike Chavez, the combination conductor, brakeman and fireman, boarded the cramped gray-and-orange cab of the train's diesel engine at the Lakeview depot. With the piercing sound of two long, one short and another long horn blast, the train began its trip south.

On this trip, the train was hauling eight loads of wood chips and three loads of lumber. The wood chips were en route to Crown Zellerback in Lake Oswego, the loads of lumber to Rochester, N.Y., Denver and Bayport, Minn.

Even though the Warner Mountains run alongside to the east, the run was mostly flat and straight through pasture land. It was also painfully slow, the train rarely reaching a speed more than 25 miles per hour.

Every few miles the run was interrupted by a sharp curve, where more often than not Prasun confronted groups of cows relaxing in the middle of the track. There they invariably stood, despite loud horn blasts from the train as it approached, until the engine was only a few feet away. Then they turned their heads, looked at the engineer and sluggishly moved aside.

"There are entirely too many cows," said Prasun as he slid open his side window to yell at them, "but we see a lot of wildlife, too. The other day we saw some bald eagles and about five sandhill crane nests. Then there are all kinds of ducks, geese and antelope."

As the train headed toward a black, rain-filled horizon, about five miles out of Lakeview two deer abruptly appeared out of the brush at the edge of the tracks and ran alongside for a minute or so before disappearing back into the brush. A short while later, Goose Lake appeared to the right, and the engine began to wobble back and forth as it came upon a stretch of uneven rails.

Fifteen miles out of Lakeview, without any signs or change in scenery as a signal, the train entered California, and a few miles further down the line the train slowed to a crawl. "We've got a stretch here that's only a 1 to 2 percent grade, but when we're pulling a real heavy load the engine speedometer has registered zero," Prasun said.

The train continued to lumber along through the Fort Bidwell Indian Reservation until it reached Alturas. There it dropped off its cars, picked up empties and headed back to Lakeview. (p. D2) ❧

SOURCE: It may be slow, but Lakeview's private railroad is a lifesaver. (1987, June 21). *The Oregonian*, p. D2. Reprinted courtesy of *The Sunday Oregonian*.

The next exhibit, "Keeping the Land," (Campoamor, 1989), printed in *Intercambios*, a publication of the National Network of Hispanic Women, describes how a New Mexican woman has created new jobs, kept the land in the hands of the Latinos who had worked it, and maintained the customs and traditions of the Rio Grande weavers by defending an old breed of sheep that the Spaniards had brought to New Mexico centuries ago. This article speaks of a proud ethnic heritage translated into community efforts.

KEEPING THE LAND

In the back of a remodeled century old building—the only big building in Los Ojos, a town of some 200 people in Northern New Mexico—Maria Varela sits on an old sofa in her cluttered office and defends the churro sheep, a dark, sturdy breed that the Spaniards brought to New Mexico centuries ago. "Experts thought the churro was an inferior breed and opposed our decision to revitalize it. But they were wrong," Varela asserts confidently.

Following common sense instead of conventional business wisdom, Varela runs an economic development corporation, Ganados del Valle, that in just six years has created badly needed jobs, kept the land in Hispanic hands and maintained the customs and traditions of the Rio Grande weavers.

A decade ago, Los Ojos had few jobs and one of the lowest per-capita incomes in the country. Like many rural towns, it was slowly withering away. "In one generation, many of the young people would have left to find jobs in the city. The older ones would have remained but the town would have lost its vitality," Varela explains.

Short on money but long on courage and convictions, Varela and a couple of her neighbors set out to reverse the trends and along the way created a model for small scale rural economic development. With a loan fund of $18,000 as start-up capital, they founded a business based on the skills and the culture they knew best: sheep herding and weaving. And, defying the odds, they resolved to create a market for their products rather than adapt their products to the market. So, instead of introducing other breeds of sheep, they increased their flock of churros and revived the traditional weaving patterns and colors of the Rio Grande.

Today, collectors of rugs, shawls, and other handwoven products drive two hours north of Santa Fe, up a narrow highway that winds through spectacular mountains, and mesas and valleys, to find a hand-painted sign a couple miles outside of Los Ojos announcing Tierra Wools, Ganados' most successful enterprise. A weavers cooperative that employs 23 people, most of them women, Tierra Wools last year sold $150,000, roughly 85 percent out of their Los Ojos store, which occupies the front of the old adobe building. A picture of Robert Redford (a neighbor and supporter) modeling a Tierra Wools jacket is prominently displayed on a shelf. The back of the building houses Varela's office and a large work area with looms, spinning wheels and an old wood burning stove—the only source of heating. A recently renovated side hall is used for meetings for a child's summer art program. The building embodies Ganados: a solid, artful self-contained place to work, sell, meet, care for children and pass on traditions.

And Varela herself, ironically a transplant from the East, personifies the sober grace and endurance of a northern New Mexican. A handsome, articulate woman in her forties (she does not reveal her exact age), she was born in Pennsylvania to a Mexican father and an Irish mother, educated in Catholic schools and earned a Masters degree in rural economics at the University of Massachusetts. A former photographer and founder of The Chicano Press Association, she was lured to community organizing during the sixties. Working with the civil rights movement in the South she met Reyes Tijerina, a leader in the struggle for land and water rights in New Mexico, who invited her to the state in 1967. Once there, she helped organize a clinic, married a New Mexican, Lorenzo Zuniga and had a daughter, Sabina, now 10 years old. Varela now commutes from a trailer in Los Ojos to Albuquerque—three hours south—where her husband works.

Like the characters in the movie "The Milagro Beanfield War," Varela and her neighbors' efforts grew out of their resistance to a developer's plan to turn the region into a resort area. "We had to find a way for Hispanics and Native Americans to keep their ancestral land and water rights, and use it productively, in a way that would strengthen the pastoral culture. . . . We have to find a way to keep nuestra herencia (our heritage)," she says with brimming passion.

"The Milagro Beanfield War," set in this region, renewed interest in the dispute over land ownership of the area—legal title remains in the hands of developers although residents assert their traditional rights to the land. A small pot of money from the proceeds of the premiere of the film established an endowment, aptly named The Milagro Fund, which is now held by the New Mexico Community Foundation. In the next two to three years, Varela hopes to increase the fund to $250,000. The monies will be used to help other Hispanic and Native American rural communities develop similar ventures. The fund will provide small seed grants, make loans and pay for the necessary technical assistance. Six communities have already requested help.

No one, least of all Varela, expected Ganados' quick success and relative fame. "Initially, we thought of starting a hand spinning wool manufacturing company and wholesaling the yarn out to stores. And I just thought I'd learn as much as I could about the business. Eventually the weavers in town came to us, showed us what we could do, and we simply followed," she calmly recalls.

The trick, says the seasoned advocate and organizer, was not charting a fixed path, but learning and "following the people." (pp. 18–19) ❧

SOURCE: Campoamor, D. (1989). Keeping the land. *Intercambios*, 4(1), 18–19. Reprinted by permission of the National Network of Hispanic Women, Publisher of *Intercambios*.

Social services practitioners must realize how innovative people can be in the small towns and villages. The great energy that exists in small communities can be a great asset in a variety of fields, from business to social services. Local culture can be preserved in many ways, from working with elderly people in reconstructing local history to working with artisans in traditional industries to preserve ancient crafts and jobs.

Unfortunately, in contrast with the positive local efforts depicted in the first four exhibits, consider how economic insecurity can make local communities choose courses of action that do not appear wise or safe. In many small towns across the nation, residents have accepted undesirable employment options as a result of a scarcity of jobs. Chemical plants, waste disposal stations, nuclear testing sites, plants that produce nerve gas, and other problematic industries often are located in small towns with apparently little resistance from local people. Social workers must understand that lack of options for economic survival often determines problematic courses of action in rural communities. Small-town governments often have no choice but to agree with the wishes of strong local employers who are involved in potentially harmful industries because the jobs those industries offer might constitute the only means of survival for hundreds of citizens.

In some instances, resistance and public argument to ecologically questionable projects might be strong, but often, economic incentives overshadow such arguments. The following exhibit is an example of a heated local discussion in relation to a controversial landfill project. The situation in that particular community still remains unresolved.

MOUNTAINTOP-AREA CITIZENS QUESTION PLANS FOR LANDFILL

After waiting seven months, more than 60 Mountaintop-area citizens met face-to-face last night with representatives of the company that wants to build and operate a lined landfill in their midst.

The standing-room crowd at the Snow Shoe Township supervisors' meeting in the Clarence Elementary School cafeteria, was attentive as spokesmen for Attwoods

Inc. outlined the company's plans to develop a 62-acre lined landfill on land purchased from Snow Shoe Township coal operator R.S. Carlin.

Later, though, the mood turned scrappy as audience members demanded to know everything from how the company proposed to control odors to how it would control bears.

Many in the audience laughed when J. Erik Schaeffer, manager for landfill development, said his company would "see to it" that the proposed facility was built and operated to the "most stringent rules in the county." He said it would not take hazardous, infectious or industrial waste, and that it would accept only municipal waste from Centre and surrounding counties—"not trash from Philadelphia, Trenton or New York."

Both Schaeffer and Attwoods Regional Vice President Hal Johnson said the company would be willing to negotiate agreements with the township that would govern landfill operations.

Other benefits, they said, would be 20 new jobs, a broadened municipal tax base and a "host fee" paid to Snow Shoe Township of a minimum of $1 for each ton of garbage received at the landfill.

Some in the meeting room, however, insisted that it would be difficult if not impossible for the township to know where incoming waste originated because it is generally hauled to landfills from transfer stations—collection sites for waste management companies.

Gilbert Fye, president of Citizens for a Clean Environment, drew applause and a shout of "Right On" when he asked Johnson whether Attwoods would be willing to sign a contract and post a performance bond with the township.

"Then, if you don't do what we want you to do, we can tell you to get the hell out," Fye said.

Formed shortly after the Attwoods plan surfaced last spring, CCE has pressed the anti-landfill fight with a two-pronged campaign—first, by lobbying Burnside and Snow Shoe township supervisors to draft land-use controls (now in the works) and second, by throwing a spotlight on allegations that toxic waste from central Pennsylvania chemical companies was dumped in Carlin strip mines and at his landfill in the 1960s and early 1970s.

The state Department of Environmental Resources is investigating the suspected chemical dumping but has not yet issued a report on its findings.

After the meeting, Attwoods Regional Vice President Hal Johnson said he is concerned about the DER investigation but did not expect it to affect plans for the lined landfill.

Johnson said he hopes to file the first phase of the landfill permit application with the state Department of Environmental Resources before the end of this year. The second and final phase of the application should follow in the spring, he added.

Before acting on the permit application, DER receives comment on it from both the county and the municipality.

The proposed Attwoods site lies adjacent to the existing Carlin landfill, last resting place of well over 80 percent of Centre County's trash.

Carlin, who did not attend last night's meeting, plans to close his unlined landfill before new, more stringent state regulations go into effect in April 1990. (p. A5) ❧

SOURCE: Brueggebors, B. (1988, November 8). Mountaintop-area citizens question plans for landfill. *Centre Daily Times*, p. A5. Reprinted courtesy of the *Centre Daily Times*.

The editorial "Mountaintop Sewer Woes a Catch 22" (1988) illustrates the limits of localism in environmentally wise decision making. People cannot go back on the consequences of industrialization and pollution because those problems are no longer local. Large, costly projects that attend to those consequences cannot be the sole responsibility of unaided local communities that generally lack the resources to undertake them. The analysis of the problems of small communities is a lesson in practical politics. What will be required in most cases involving controversy and political decisions in the small community is not so much a debate on whether "more" or "less" government is desirable, but an analysis of the "long-term payoffs and the 'value added' of public programs and investments" (Milliken, 1987, p. 13).

MOUNTAINTOP SEWER WOES A CATCH 22

What price clean streams?

The answer depends on who's footing the bill.

A couple of weeks ago, residents of the county's Mountaintop area learned they probably can't afford to clean up sewage-spoiled Pine Run—at least not without a public benefactor.

The problem is that the citizens of predominantly blue collar Snow Shoe borough and Snow Shoe Township have a median household income of $18,750. That makes them too wealthy to qualify for the large-scale federal grants that would allow them to build the $4.7 million sewage collection and treatment system they need so badly.

Clearly, the Mountaintop area's sewage disposal problems are serious and overwhelming.

Engineering studies show that well over half of the 450 residences and businesses in Snow Shoe and nearby Clarence—including the Clarence Elementary School and the J.H. France Refractory—either have malfunctioning septic systems or discharge wastewater directly into waterways.

But unless the proposed system service area is drastically scaled back (a notion that frankly seems silly considering the seriousness of the problem), borough and township residents aren't likely to be able to afford even to maintain and operate a public sewerage system—much less build one.

The Mountaintop area is far from alone in its dilemma.

Many other small Pennsylvania communities—particularly those in rural areas where population is scattered—share the predicament.

They're under the gun from regulatory agencies to build public sewerage systems but find it impossible to scrape together funding packages that make those systems affordable.

What's worse, the funding picture seems to be getting worse instead of better. Large-scale federal grant money is becoming harder and harder to come by. Grants currently available through the state just aren't large enough to make much of a difference.

Many in government acknowledge the paradox but have no answers for those caught in the middle.

Instead of letting existing sources of grant money dry up, state and federal officials should be finding new ways to help communities with limited funds and far-flung service areas afford the public sewer systems they need.

At the moment, those communities are caught in a Catch 22 situation that plays fast and loose with the public health. (p. A6) ❧

SOURCE: Mountaintop sewer woes a Catch 22 [Editorial]. (1988, September 24). *Centre Daily Times*, p. A6. Reprinted courtesy of the *Centre Daily Times*.

SMALL-TOWN POLITICS

Two distinct types of political activity that French statesman and author Alexis de Tocqueville observed in American society in the 19th century still exist today. In 1835 Tocqueville (1945) described the two political systems as "the one fulfilling the ordinary duties and responding to the daily and infinite calls of a community, the other circumscribed within certain limits and exercising an exceptional authority over the general interests of the country" (p. 61). One system was the local, familial, Gemeinschaftlich system of the small town, where people had always related on a personal level; superimposed on it was the most abstract and majoritarian system based on articulated rights and duties of the state and national scene.

In his historical overview of American communities, Bender (1978) observed that

> an informal, communal, essentially oral politics continued to flourish at the local level, while at the national level, and to some degree at the state levels, a formal system, abstracted from society, accepted conflict and majoritarianism in a way that was alien to local political cultures. If the local political cultures based upon shared social experience remained largely customary and trusting, the national one was contractual in the modern sense and relied upon precise articulation of rights and duties—in writing as in the case of the Bill of Rights. (p. 84)

He suggested that "the political impulse toward a purer and more homogeneous community that had prevailed at the beginning of the revolutionary crisis had been transformed into a political system that combined many small and personal local political units with one large abstract one" (Bender, 1978, p. 84). He further commented that the degree of interpenetration of the two systems had been minimal and that a doctrine of spheres seems to have prevailed in American government for a long time.

The following exhibits, all current comments on the political realities of the contemporary small town, illustrate, in a sense, the persistence of these two political spheres or paradigms. Yet, the interpenetration of the two is much more observable and pervasive today. The most abstract, contractual political system of Gessellshaft has taken over much of small-town political activity. However, the tension between the two types of ethos still exists. In the first article, "In Small Communities, It's No Contest at Election Time" (Pave, 1982), the reporter reviews the leadership crisis many small towns are facing. He offers explanations, one of which is that higher mobility and the intrusion of the contractual and often litigious ethos have rendered small-town politics stressful and time-consuming. Yet, the electoral problems black citizens experienced in Keysville, Georgia (see *Conflict in the Small Community*, pp. 184–188), seem to indicate that often formalization and litigiousness are the only way to resist the control of the informal elites.

IN SMALL COMMUNITIES, IT'S NO CONTEST AT ELECTION TIME

Last week, in the town of Northborough where 6,000 residents are registered to vote, a grand total of 186 people sloshed through the rainy weather to go to the polls.

"It was our lowest turnout ever," said town clerk Nancy Lang. But weather aside, those who stayed away from the voting booth had a good excuse: none of the offices were contested.

"I wouldn't call the lack of candidates a matter of apathy," said Lang. "It's more a matter of such a large commitment of time to hold office as a selectman, school board member or planning board member."

In Grafton, a town about the same size as Northborough, the May election features one contested race—for the board of health—while the rest of the slate is unopposed.

It is a familiar and growing scenario, particularly in small municipalities where the demands of serving on part-time boards have been exacerbated by increasingly complicated issues and laws involving finance, development and the environment.

A random sampling of a dozen towns revealed that in five—Avon, Ashfield, Barre, Peru and Whately—some offices aren't being sought by anyone, thus requiring a write-in vote.

"We've had more calls from the media and town officials this year asking if this kind of candidate drought is something we're seeing in other communities," said Daniel Soyer, a spokesman for the Massachusetts Municipal Association. "Most of the town officials we're talking to are looking for ideas or ways to stimulate more public participation."

Soyer cites as key elements in the drop in the number of candidates the growing scale and complexity—and controversy—of holding municipal office; the time factor; the fear of personal liability law suits; and the increasing mobility of families who do not maintain close ties to the community.

"Also, we've seen a greater trend of municipalities hiring town managers or executive secretaries and other people who have professional training and qualifications that the layman may not have," Soyer added. He said the membership of the Municipal Management Association, an association of executive secretaries and professional municipal managers, has more than doubled in the last 10 years.

In Grafton, for example, a charter change proposal on the ballot would increase the Board of Selectmen from three to five members and provide for the hiring of a town manager.

"The town is growing rapidly and the complexity and time demands of the jobs are forcing boards to meet two or three times a week," said Dolores Ward, a secretary at town hall and a Grafton resident for 3 years.

Or as Northborough's Land put it: "It isn't a matter of coming to a meeting for several hours twice a month anymore—you really have to devote time to study all kinds of laws and regulations and attend numerous hearings."

Time Constraints

A random sampling of communities revealed that:

• In Peru, located in central Berkshire County, the position of town auditor is open. No one filed papers for the position and a caucus was held April 4 in which two names were written in. But both, the former auditor and a former town clerk, declined to run.

"If we don't get a write-in candidate," said town clerk Mary Wheeler, "the selectmen can appoint someone or we may have to hire outside the town." The problem, said Wheeler, is that "many people, especially the younger ones, don't have the time to do the job and the older ones have served their time and are ready to retire."

• In Barre, in central Massachusetts, town clerk Alice Orszulak said the March 2 elections were "terrible" because there were nine candidates who ran unopposed, only four were opposed and there was one write-in candidate for library trustee. The turnout was not surprising: 311 out of 2,311 registered voters cast ballots.

• In Avon, 10 candidates are running unopposed and three positions have no candidates at all—a five-year redevelopment authority seat and two seats on the sewer commission.

• In Ashfield, although there are two candidates for the planning board, no one has filed papers to run for assessor and for the board of health.

And the beat goes on: In Bernardston's May 2 election, 10 of 13 offices have but a single candidate. In Mendon, 10 candidates are unopposed. In Bolton, 17 of 19 candidates face no opposition, while in the recent Whately election, no one ran for the board of health (216 write-in votes were cast) and, aside from the selectmen's race, the rest of the positions were unopposed.

Soyer said the towns with this problem fit no particular geographical pattern. He said the association has had calls from throughout the state, "and the majority seem to be smaller communities."

Said Whately town clerk Virginia Allis, "Some of the positions have become quite demanding and this could explain why so few people choose to run for office. Last year there was only one new person elected to office here." (p. 17) ❧

SOURCE: In Small Communities, It's No Contest at Election Time, by Marvin Pave, April 14, 1982. (Reprinted courtesy of *The Boston Globe*.)

The following exhibit, a column by Welch (1987), contrasts with Pave's (1982) "In Small Communities, It's No Contest at Election Time" in that, in encouraging citizens to participate in local government, Welch, like one of his informants, stresses the joy, the personal aspects, and the personal satisfactions of the job.

GO AHEAD, RUN

Seeking and holding public office at the local level is not the trial-by-fire that some think it to be. In fact, to hear some State College area office-holders tell it, the experience is downright enjoyable.

"I stress the joy of the job," a longtime member of Borough Council told participants in a League of Women Voters program last weekend. "It's so interesting," she told the 60 participants in the how-to-run-for-public-office workshop, "because every decision you make affects you personally, as well as your friends and neighbors."

Said another Council member, "I wish I'd gotten in 30 years ago. Serving on Council has been a fabulous learning experience."

What makes this form of community service so rewarding?

"It's an experience for personal growth," said a school board member.

It offers a chance to "develop a vision and move it forward," said a township supervisor.

Despite the many "plusses" of service in local government, many potential candidates for office see only the "minuses."

There's no question that working in the public eye can have its rough spots.

Borough Manager Peter Marshall noted, "Sometimes it's exciting to a fault," adding, "You make a mistake and everybody reads about it in the newspaper."

On balance, however, the positives far outweigh the negatives. That's especially true in our area, where graft, power politics and the like just aren't on officials' agendas.

"This is a unique place to be a public official, because of the people," said a township official, alluding to the lack of such misbehavior.

And yet we shouldn't be too quick to pat each other on the back. While our area enjoys a fine reputation for honest and open government, all it takes to shove the pendulum in the opposite direction is for key positions on policy-making bodies to fall into the hands of persons whose interests are selfish, not public-spirited.

A workshop participant made the familiar point that "all that is necessary for evil to triumph is for good men to do nothing."

Another participant offered a Harry Truman quote along the same lines:

"The stench that surrounds politics could be removed if enough good citizens would run in the party of their choice."

So, good citizen, why don't you run for public office?

The time is now: Tuesday is the first day to circulate and file nominating petitions for the May 19 primary election; March 10 is the last day.

The election cycle can be complicated, with its deadlines and regulations. Similarly, campaigning—who to contact when, how to raise money—can pose seemingly impossible challenges for those who've never been through the process.

Don't be deterred by the apparent difficulties. The important step, as one official said at the workshop, is to "choose to participate and all the rest will follow from that."

Party officials, the League of Women Voters, elected officials can provide you with the information and advice you'll need for your campaign. If you don't know any of those folks, feel free to give me a call. I'd be pleased to put you in touch with someone who can help you along the road to elected office.

Throw your hat in the ring. Your community, and the future, will be grateful. (p. B2) ❧

SOURCE: Welch, B. (1987, February 15). Go ahead, run. *Centre Daily Times*, p. B2. Reprinted courtesy of the *Centre Daily Times*.

The following article, by Cawthon (1988), is a personal note. Although in theory the national political system demands abstraction and impersonality, in the reality of many small towns, the process is still personal.

WAY OUT IN THE COUNTRY, SUPER TUESDAY MUCH MORE THAN A VOTE-AND-RUN AFFAIR

Super Tuesday marked a new milestone in our voting process. It also marked a new milestone in *my* voting process. It was the first time in 20 years that I had not voted in my regular, bustling metro-Atlanta precinct; the first time I would cast a ballot in the country.

I vote relentlessly, sometimes for candidates whom I later discover I shouldn't have voted for and on issues about which I am not as informed as I should be. But as a youngster, a ballot, to me, represented entrance into the glorious world of adulthood and its responsibilities. I longed to vote more than I longed to be invited to the prom. (Well, I was always stepping on my date's toes.)

My first voting was done on those giant, impressive machines with levers. I never adjusted to these little cards you punch. They seem undignified, and when I remove the card, I always do so with the dark suspicion that those holes I put in it aren't where they are supposed to be.

I didn't have to worry about those holes this time.

I stopped by the country store in search of a ballot, a straw hat and a loaf of bread. Stella and Raymond Sidwell rose from their rockers with smiles and provided the last two, but elections were no longer conducted at "the voting house," a tiny brick structure on their property. They had been moved to the volunteer fire department.

In all those 20 years of voting at the same urban precinct, George and I never saw anyone we knew personally; just faces vaguely familiar from previous elections. It's different in the country.

Inside, next to the red fire engine and in charge, were: Col. Joe Price, retired military man who is now commander in the war against conflagration in our countryside; his wife, Jean, whose family lineage includes the people buried in my backyard, and Eunice Tory, a tall, gracious black woman living up the road from me.

When they asked if I wanted a Republican or Democratic ballot, I realized when I had asked for one party or another before, my choice was anonymous. Now folks you actually *know* can pretty well figure out how you vote, if they set their minds to it.

There was no line and only two booths. But they were hung proudly with red, white and blue curtains, and inside were no stylus and punch card but a pencil and an old-fashioned ballot. I don't know that I trust a pencil (which easily can be erased) any more than I trust a nameless punch card, but I did see for whom I voted, and I do trust polling officials who are also upstanding neighbors. I dropped my ballot in a cardboard box.

Later, Col. Price informed me (with, I thought, some satisfaction) our little precinct already had passed the percentage of persons who had been estimated to cast ballots. Between voters, the three manning the polls, ever more willing to do their civic duties, weeded an area for a new flower bed around the fire station.

Not everyone won on Super Tuesday. I did. (p. 2B) ❧

SOURCE: Cawthon, F. (1988, March 10). Way out in the country, Super Tuesday much more than a vote-and-run affair. *The Atlanta Constitution*, p. 2B. Reprinted courtesy of *The Atlanta Journal-Constitution*, © 1988.

In the next article, Walburn (1987) reveals a variety of political tensions in small-town government, not the least of which is the traditional male reluctance to accept female leadership. However, as reporter Walburn suggests, even that reluctance is softening.

WHERE GOVERNING IS "WOMEN'S WORK"

There have been times during the past 1 1/2 years, when Mayor Lona Johnson was on the p.m. side of a 10-hour workday, that she used to push her chair away from her desk at City Hall and consider her salary of $52.09 per month.

"If it were not for the extra nine cents, I believe I'd just quit," she would mutter.

But things have gotten better. Nowadays, she usually works two six-hour days a week. And she gave herself a raise to $60 a month, payable at the end of the year, provided there is any money left over after all the city's bills have been covered.

Money has not always been left over here. In fact, when Mayor Johnson took over, the biggest concern was where the money was. There were outstanding bills dating back to 1982 and the matter of $18,000 that, to this day, cannot be traced.

Compared to what goes on in big cities such as Atlanta—accusations of cocaine use in governmental circles, fist fights between security and taxi drivers in the mayor's reception room, local government drifting in and out of favor with the business community—the job of leading a Middle Georgia hamlet of 1,000 citizens and tracking down an elusive $18,000 may not seem like such a big deal. But duck if you say that around Mayor Johnson.

"We have the same city problems that a town like Atlanta has, but on a smaller scale," she says.

When she took office in December 1985, there hadn't even been a city government for three months. That came about after a big blowup at a City Council meeting (the council went into executive session, and nobody has been willing to say what went on there) when two members and the clerk resigned. Since it was impossible to assemble a quorum, city functions came to a standstill.

So, Lona Johnson decided to run for mayor, basically for three reasons. A bright 34-year-old widow of means who drives a beautifully appointed Mercedes and plays the stock market, she had some free time. Two, she figured that since her daddy had once owned the water works, a grocery story and a logging company here, she needed to make a contribution back to her town. Three, nobody else wanted the job.

"Politics hasn't been a barn burner here in quite a few years," City Attorney Joseph Boone says. "Just not much interest in it."

In fact, in Irwinton where the Wilkinson County government is also located, politics is apparently viewed chauvinistically, for the men have just about conceded all elected positions as being "women's work."

Not only is the mayor female, except for a black man, Mack Robinson, the four-person City Council is composed of females. Over at the county courthouse that sits at the junction of highways 441 and 57, most of the elected positions are filled by women.

Hilda Brunner is tax commissioner, Mary Reece is county extension agent, Cinda Bright is clerk of court. Nina Maxey is county clerk and Hazel Green is probate judge and chief magistrate. The City Council includes Cornelia Byington, retired teacher; Lynn Mason, waitress at the Dixieland Restaurant; and Elizabeth Eubanks, vice president of the Wilkinson County Bank and owner of a Merle Norman store in Dublin, Ga.

Ronnie Chambers, who runs the service station that sits diagonally across from the courthouse and parallel to Maebob's, where the meat loaf is worth driving long distances to get, thinks he knows why so many women are running the city and county governments here.

A tall, lean man whose wife, Mary, was mayor a couple of administrations ago, Chambers spat a stream of tobacco into a receptacle and mused, "Women just seem to take more interest in the towns. Besides, by the time a man works all day, it just isn't worth it to him."

In a way, Mayor Johnson wasn't even elected formally. She qualified a month before the scheduled election, and it so shocked the 200 registered voters that nobody ran against her. It was the first time anybody could remember that somebody had qualified before the final day.

"She just up and qualified and left for the Georgia-Florida football game," according to one resident, shaking her head with the same amazement that might have been exhibited in Atlanta in a discussion of Mayor Young's latest excursion to Zimbabwe.

Since she was unopposed, the townfolk called off the election as too expensive under the circumstances, circumstances including, as previously mentioned, the missing $18,000, and a drawer full of unpaid bills. By July of last year, Irwinton, which derives income from property taxes, franchise taxes and beer and wine licenses, was broke. Mayor Johnson and Rep. Kenneth Birdsong arranged a $7,500 grant from the governor to tide them over until taxes were collected.

Now, the city is on sound financial footing, and something of a false sense of security has settled over the town, according to the mayor. Irwinton is in the middle of kaolin county with its high-paying mining jobs, and there is plenty of work in the lumber industry. Also, the town is close enough to Macon and Milledgeville for commuters to take advantage of economic opportunities there. The townspeople have escaped most of the economic problems associated with rural Georgia, even if the government hasn't.

Mayor Johnson points out that either Irwinton must get some new business inside its city limits, or she will have to push for a tax increase.

"But when I tell people that, they just say, 'We're really not interested. Irwinton is just fine the way it is.'

"If we could just get one liquor store [it would take a special referendum and probably cause a whirlwind of controversy] or a little shirt factory, it would make a big difference in our tax base," says Mayor Johnson, who in addition to her other work, is a one-person industrial development authority.

"We had a man from over in Dublin who wanted to put up a 7-Eleven-type store, but nobody would sell him any land for it. Another man wanted to build a Dairy Queen, but, again, nobody would sell their land. We are going to have to do something or go up on taxes."

Shortly before the lunch rush last week at the Dixieland Restaurant, Councilwoman Lynn Mason took a drag on her cigarette and tried to put it all into perspective. Mrs. Mason, 27, came to government along with Mayor Johnson and is considered to be the council's loose cannon. She is a free spirit whose tongue launches verbal volleys the moment her mind loads the ammunition.

"What it was," she says, "is the men really had this town screwed up."

The first thing the new administration did was present the case of the missing $18,000 to District Attorney Joe Briley over in Milledgeville, but it has been a year now, and there has been no report of impropriety.

"It aggravates me a little bit," Mayor Johnson says, "but on the other hand, I'm afraid of what he might find. If any wrongdoing was turned up, it would split this town right in half, and I don't want that."

Also, admits Mayor Johnson, the money could simply have been lost in the complexity of installing an expensive water system without adequate bookkeeping procedures.

When the Johnson administration took over, the water department was in shambles, according to Mrs. Mason, who became chairwoman of the department.

"We were $20,000 in the hole, and there hadn't been a bill paid since the previous July. There were leaks all over the system, and we discovered there were 45 houses connected whose owners weren't even being billed. All told, we were losing revenues on half the water we were pumping," she says.

"The previous administration had put in a $1.2 million water line, and nobody was connected except in the middle of town. And there weren't any records to even tell us where the lines were laid.

"Me and Lona rode in sleet and rain and cold looking for valves and screwed up meters and such. But we got the danged thing straightened out."

Prior to her ascent to governmental leadership, Mayor Johnson's closest brush with politics had been the 4-H club. She needed help.

Mayor George Israel of nearby Macon came over with his financial director, Bob Loveland, helped set up a budget and showed her how to take in revenues. The state Department of Community Affairs contributed advice, and the Human Resources Department sent engineers to help salvage the water system.

Less than two years later, Irwinton's government is in the black, even though it collected just $10,996 in taxes last year. They also shared in a countywide one-cent sales tax and received $14,000 from Georgia Power through franchise fees.

Additionally, Mayor Johnson is learning how to tap other sources. With help from Rep. Birdsong, $250,000 was obtained from the state for a new library.

But not all efforts have been successful. Just trying to get the driveways widened at the fire station for the 1962 and 1971 model trucks has gotten entangled in so much red tape with the state Department of Transportation that Mayor Johnson has just about given up. But she is still looking for grant money to replace the aging chariots.

Recently, Mayor Johnson fought the good fight for a $148,000 community development block grant from the federal government. In order to compile the volumes of information needed to fill out the application, she and two volunteers almost became their own census bureau, traipsing through town compiling information from every resident.

"After all that, we didn't get it," Mayor Johnson says with a sigh. "We wanted the money to extend the water lines to a predominantly black area of town, but they [government officials] said they were into big cities this year."

Nevertheless, Mayor Lona Johnson keeps plugging away on behalf of her little town. A random sampling of voter attitudes at lunch revealed support or, at least where there wasn't a commitment, blessed apathy.

Clerk of Court Cinda Bright, for example, says that Mayor Johnson is a shoo-in because "she's the only one who will chew out Wilkinson County Cablevision when the picture gets messed up."

But among certain enclaves of male voters, the issues are not so clearly defined. Three men standing on the grocery store side of the downtown crossroads are asked what they think about Mayor Johnson.

"I don' know no Mary Johnson," says one.

"He's talkin' about Mayor Johnson," explains one of his companions.

"I don't know him either," is the reply. (pp. B1, B4) ❧

SOURCE: Walburn, L. (1987, May 11). Where governing is "women's work." *The Atlanta Constitution*, pp. B1, B4. Reprinted courtesy of *The Atlanta Journal-Constitution*, © 1987.

Conflict is a normal condition in human interaction. Whether internal or external to the individual, whether intrapsychic or societal, conflict exists all around. Institutions have been created to maintain conflictual situations within boundaries that permit creative resolutions. Government is one such institution. Critical to the political or governmental process, however, is public sentiment that reflects the way people feel about and use the institutions they created to resolve conflict. The exhibits in this chapter provided the reader with a close view of the ways in which small-town people look at government and the political process.

Because governmental institutions, as gatekeepers of conflict, often have been needed more where large numbers of people are found, the tendency has been to regard formal governmental structures as more of an urban phenomenon. The exhibits in this chapter should have made the reader aware of how governmental institutions, whether local or central, have a creative role to play in the small town. Governmental institutions play a role not only in conflict resolution (witness Keysville, Georgia), but also in responding to the creative endeavors of citizens (witness Lakeview, Oregon) and in pushing the barriers of change (witness Irwinton, Georgia). Governmental institutions in small towns are close to the grassroots and, as such, are personal. Yet, governmental institutions clearly are growing too complex and aloof and thus creating conflict and tensions for the citizens. The sentiment of small towns might not always be where the institutions are; the institutions are often more "centralistic" and bureaucratic than the citizens might want. Yet, tension can be creative and lead to change among the citizenry. This tension, however, cannot become too great because those who have created government as gatekeeper of conflict, namely, the citizens, will react and modify the institutions to keep that tension at a manageable level.

PART 3
FUTURE DIRECTIONS FOR THE FIELD

7

The Small Community and Social Work Practice

Practitioners in traditionally community-oriented positions and generalist social workers need to view the small community in a different and more positive way. The local community has often been a neglected variable in social work practice. Social workers often have relegated thinking about the community dimensions of practice to those who specialize in community organization or community work. Yet, community variables affect all fields of social work: case management, gerontology, child welfare, advocacy, and psychotherapy. Local communities are not utopian settings where all ills are resolved; however, practitioners should recognize how community, particularly in small, local settings, has been a forgotten dimension that, if better understood and appreciated, can become a major asset in practice.

MOVING TOWARD COMMUNITY-ORIENTED PRACTICE

Many practitioners and academicians have felt more at ease emphasizing vertical rather than horizontal ties, national rather than local organizations, and outside rather than communal relationships. In general, because social work practice relates to the current major social problem, practitioners have sought solutions from central systems: the federal or state government and national plans of voluntary organization, for example. Because of the nature of the problems social workers confront, solutions often have had to be centralistic and large scale, sometimes leading to the assumptions that central solutions are always better than local ones.

Generally, central or bureaucratic solutions often are more universal and standardized than Gemeinschaftlich or local responses, which tend to be more personal. Also, bureaucratic responses are less nepotistic and have fewer strings attached to them. Nevertheless, no one level of organization, whether central or local, has a monopoly on positive or negative attributes. Not all central solutions are universal and egalitarian, nor are all local efforts fraught with difficulties or nepotism or punitive of particular groups. Centralistic solutions are needed in many areas. Yet, with centralistic policies often come centralistic administrative demands and bureaucratic practices. These demands and practices curtail the autonomy of social workers and other practitioners to respond to local needs in ways that are congruent with and sensitive to unique local environments. Even when practitioners themselves understand the small community and want to relate to it differently, bureaucratic demands prevent them from doing so. Although efforts at decentralization that started during the Nixon administration have moved administrators, politicians, and practitioners in the direction of examining carefully locality and local solutions, more in-depth examination is required. Even in designing local solutions, people today often have duplicated the ethos of centralistic ones.

In discussing the origins of centralist policies, Hadley and Hatch (1981) wrote the following, which relates to the British social services but also applies to the American situation:

> For some historians centralist policies are simply the corollary of collectivism, and collectivism is the product of industrialization. Clearly the major economic, social and political changes that were taking place in the nineteenth century posed new problems which neither the old paternalism nor the new individualism could cope with. Rapid increases in population, urbanization and the shift from an agricultural economy to an industrial economy greatly inflated the problems of unemployment, poverty, public health, law and order, and led to important shifts in power within the country towards the new middle and working classes. The development of organized public action (or collectivism) to deal with such problems has been a common response in the history of all western countries as they have gone through the phase of industrialization.
>
> But the history of other industrializing countries by no means bears out the second part of the thesis, to show that collectivism necessarily leads to centralism. In Belgium, Holland and Germany, for example, substantial public funds are devoted to the provision of social services, but within the framework in which independent voluntary organizations play a large role, and in which central control and direction is much less developed. (p. 6)

In the United States, central government measures have been essential to the development of a welfare system. In social security, public assistance, and mental health, for example, standardization and strong central government involvement have been essential. Yet, these positive and essential central policies often have been accompanied by an ethos or attitude that equates central with high status and advanced thinking and local with lower status and lower creativity. Because of this misconception, local areas often have been drained of the people who could have energized them and made localism work for all.

> By concentrating power in the center and by implication attracting the best politicians and administrators to work in national government [or other central bureaucracies], a climate is created in which *ipso facto* those involved in local government are regarded as second rate. This neatly provides those at the center with the grounds for recommending still more centralization. (Hadley & Hatch, 1981, p. 16)

Social workers and other human services providers have not been and are not immune to the same type of thinking. It is more difficult for social workers to take an entirely new look at the local community in the midst of societal misconceptions. However, by caring for people, some of these misconceptions can be corrected. Practitioners often can energize locals through the concept of helping. Local leadership can be developed and new strengths and human resources unearthed to create a new chain of events.

The idea that "nonlocal" is better also has affected counseling. Emphases on objectivity—sometimes bordering on depersonalization and anonymity that results in unrealistic demands for confidentiality—and on professionalism, which undervalues the help provided by nonprofessionals, are but a few of the common attitudes that are detrimental to local community involvement. In relation to anonymity and confidentiality, for example, Moore-Kirkland and Vice-Irey (1981) suggested:

> To define confidentiality only in relation to the one on one psychotherapeutic process between worker and client places unnecessary limits on social workers. The definition of confidentiality must deal with people in their social environments—the very relationship the social work claims as its unique focus. Social workers cannot view individuals in their relationship to workers apart from the social context. The issue of confidentiality within the social context is especially acute in rural environments. In small towns and communities, social workers and clients must function not only in therapeutic sessions but also in daily interactions within circumscribed social systems. (p. 319)

Most social workers are used to accomplishing their aims within the confines of agencies. Professional standards have been set using the agency or organization and not the local community as the framework of reference. The problems inherent in this approach are apparent in small communities, where the more intimate scale of living makes it difficult not to redefine certain practices and standards. Professional commitments to anonymity, definitions of confidentiality, and reliance on lay helpers all require modification in the less formal and bureaucratic context of small towns. In relation to the use of lay people in the context of community, Hadley and MacGrath (1980) commented:

> The compartmentalism and rigidity of the bureaucratic structure reinforces the emphasis on qualifications and narrow interpretation of professionalism held by many social workers. It encourages a view in which care is seen as the prerogative of the professional, in which the unqualified should be relegated wherever possible to routine tasks and in which volunteers should be confined to marginal, dogsbody roles. (p. 7)

Particularly in small towns, a different kind of practice has always been required, although this practice has not been systematically taught or regarded as bona fide in many circles. This practice involves the provision of care by members of the community, to each other, in mutually supporting relationships and by social workers and other human services personnel working in the community, in partnership with friends, neighbors, and volunteers. This practice involves the reinterpretation of confidentiality to suit the context; the use of nonprofessional helpers in many varied tasks; and greater reliance on neighbors and churches. These principles constitute the basis of community-oriented social work, a concept that has reached greater popularity in the United Kingdom and other parts of Europe but that has not been as yet fully addressed in the United States.

The case for community social work, according to the 1980 Barclay Working Party, which was set up in Britain by the secretary of state for social services to study the role and tasks of social workers, "rests upon our understanding of the nature of community and the meaning of social care" (National Institute for Social Work, 1982, p. 199). The Working Party's report defined community "as a network, or informal relationships between people connected with each other by kinship, common interest, geographical proximity, friendship, occupation, or the giving and receiving of services—or various combinations of these" (p. 199). The Working Party defined *social care* as "the sum of helping (and when need be, controlling) resources available to people in adversity, whether provided informally by community networks or formally by the public services" (p. 199) or, as would be the case in the United States, whether provided by the formal services—public, voluntary, or private—or by other informal networks of kin and friends.

The Working Party further suggested that community social work was not so much a specific technique or method but, rather, that it depended on "an attitude of mind in all social workers, from the director of the department or agency to front-line workers, which regards members of the public as partners in the provision of social care" (National Institute for Social Work, 1982, p. 198). Community-oriented social work depends on an attitude of mind that sees community as a potentially nourishing and important source of support and identity to its members. The notion that community nourishes its members is not commonplace. It probably is not an idea that is in the forefront of consciousness when social workers help clients make decisions. Although community-oriented social work is important, there is no single recipe that those involved in using and providing social care should follow.

> Each statutory and voluntary agency must consider the geographical area and the nature of the people and the communities it serves before deciding upon the particular forms and combinations of community social work it wishes to develop. (National Institute for Social Work, 1982, p. 198)

In discussing the concept of community-oriented services or community care, Abrams (1980), an analyst and generally a critic of the model, suggested that community-oriented social work can develop in four possible ways—these ways describe the types of relationships that emerge between the formal system of agencies and organized services and the informal system of kin, neighbors, and friends, caring for each other "in community." The four possible alternatives are (1) domination, (2) appropriation, (3) incorporation, and (4) coexistence.

Abrams (1980) suggested that *domination* exists when the governmental or voluntary agencies "merely impose their own preferred hierarchies and control on local systems. . . . " (p. 20). The formal system tends to dominate in most projects where the formal and the informal operate in the community. For example, in a "friendly neighbor" scheme one practitioner examined in a rural village, local citizens operated a telephone line to arrange for rides for elderly citizens when they needed them and friendly visits to people who were lonely, to answer question from neighbors, and to provide neighbor-to-neighbor advice. The informal group contacted a government agency to secure answering machines for some of the neighbors' houses to help them refer calls from one neighbor to another when one of the neighbors was unavailable to take a call. The formal system with its resources came to the rescue but, with the answering machines came a number of suggestions on how to operate the system "more efficiently." For example, off-times for answering were suggested, when the point of the scheme had been to provide ready responses when people needed them, regardless of time. The group was encouraged to organize formally and establish a hierarchy of officers, when they had been operating on the basis of collective responsibility. Although many of the suggestions from the formal system were practical and increased efficiency, the formal system was imposing its structure and consequent tendency toward professionalization.

Appropriation occurs when boundaries are not just drawn, but drawn so that they redefine previous perceptions of the formal and informal systems (Abrams, 1980, p. 20). The informal becomes an extended part of the formal. "The advantages of appropriation are the advantages of bureaucratic tidying up and control. Unfortunately . . . the administrative gain is in practice usually the informal sector's loss" (p. 20). This situation frequently occurs when innovative services that were started as lay community efforts seek funding, for example from United Way. In many small towns, women's centers that emerged as places where neighbors helped each other informally and outside the organized service structure had to become, out of necessity, formal organizations when they tried to partake of the organized community funding efforts.

Incorporation occurs when the formal system makes significant efforts to respect the "untidiness" of the informal system and actually tries to incorporate some informality into its own formal structure. For example, during crises, communities may respond informally to a given threat and the formal system then tries to follow up on those responses. The formal system often realizes that it cannot succeed by applying its own bureaucratic system and that it must limit its bureaucratization. For instance, during the farm crisis in some midwestern states, support groups that had begun as informal, neighborly gatherings often were incorporated into the structure of mental health services. It became apparent to the system that the "untidiness" and integrity of the informal efforts had to be respected even if unorthodox approaches had to be used (Blundall, 1987). One social work student who had worked in a basic needs project that had been started initially as an informal effort by a local group but that had been incorporated into the formal structure of a voluntary counseling service described the methods that she had needed to use:

> Some of the things that . . . I did seemed to me to be unorthodox at first. I could not really explain them from a social work perspective but, when I thought about my experiences in a project I did with real citizens in the community and when I thought of the ways in which Bell and Newby . . . described primary relationships in community, I felt justified in what I did. I often exaggerated certain client characteristics or understated others to get help from specific groups. If I needed help from a church, my clients' religious merits would be emphasized while their "spiritual" shortcomings were deemphasized. . . . At first, I was concerned that what I was doing was not technically quite right; but then, I thought about my ways as using what I knew about gemeinschaftlich relationships in community to help my clients.

The only viable alternative for a healthy orientation to the community is *coexistence*. According to Abrams (1980),

> What I have in mind is sufficient strengthening of the informal sector to enable it to deal intimately but on equal terms with agencies in the formal system. Co-existence would differ from incorporation not only in the extent in which informal and formal social care were closely meshed together but in the fact that in a relationship of coexistence, the values, norms and relationships of the informal sector would be brought

> forward and sustained as a basis for social policy in their own right and not as re-made to suit the administrative or other purposes of the formal system. This means that instead of patronizing or colonizing the local community, the existing statutory and voluntary agencies are going to have to learn to live with it as an equal. . . . Some serious surrender of powers is unavoidable if one really wants any significant measure of social care to be provided within neighborhood social networks. (p. 23)

Abrams's model of *coexistence* implies the need for a different and fuller understanding of community. To achieve community-oriented practice, social workers must correct their neglect of community and nurture a more sympathetic view of the forces that make up small communities. They must understand how Gemeinschaftlich relationships, values, and norms influence (whether supporting or contradicting) practice principles and behaviors.

INFLUENCE OF GEMEINSCHAFTLICH RELATIONSHIPS, VALUES, AND NORMS ON PRACTICE BEHAVIORS

If one views community as "an alternative to emphases on individualism, self-sufficiency and mass society ordered by comprehensive legal, rational authority" (R. Buck, personal communication, October 20, 1982), then the relationships in community will emphasize local ties, will be personalized, will be based on affectivity, and will be more public than anonymous or confidential. Social workers need to conceptualize and appreciate the effects of local ties, community values, anonymity, confidentiality, and accountability on their practice behaviors.

Local Ties

Social workers who are perceived by others as too attached to local ties often are viewed with a great deal of condescension. One social work student who worked in a basic needs program in a small town commented in her diary:

> I noticed, among some of the more "esteemed and established" social workers who led the traditional agencies in [Town X], an attitude that was quite condescending. Many of them felt sorry for my clients not only because they were poor and couldn't get out of poverty, but also because they seemed destined to spend their entire lives in [Town X or] the closest neighboring communities. At the time, this condescension made me feel edgy but I couldn't place why. Talking about "pride of place" in class helped me understand better why this discussion of pity made me angry beyond the obvious "looking down on the poor" it implied.

Apparently, some social workers in Town X could not readily think of any strengths in those clients' local relationships or never thought the clients actually might be attached to their communities. Attachment to locality is just not an outstanding consideration in American mobile society or in professional culture. Clearly, the student faced an inner struggle to reach the conclusion that "living in [Town X] for all one's life would not be the worst a person could experience." It is not easy for human services workers to be cognizant of attachment to locality as an important dimension in people's lives, particularly in small towns. Generally, attachment to locality is only considered in relation to elderly people and, often, as an impediment to making appropriate living arrangements for people who can no longer manage independently. Although it is essential that attachment to locality should be considered in this regard, can it also be used as a positive force to propel young clients to improve their current situations?

Attachment to locality and the need for an often intertwined set of local relationships often become apparent when, for example, clients who have housing difficulties refuse to move "alone" even to nearby communities. Social workers often surmise unhealthy dependence among neighbors or families that must be overcome. Yet, people with limited resources often value more keenly the proximity of their communal networks of support. What surprises workers is that the people in those networks are often themselves highly needy. In this context, it is essential to understand the nature of networks in communities. Johnson (1983) noted that community "networks are not developed; they emerge" and that "networks seem to emerge around an exchange or reciprocity in terms of limited resources" (p. 28). Real networks of support are likely to increase in importance as availability of resources decreases. The older, or less mobile, or poorer the client, the greater the importance of his or her local networks. The following case example illustrates a network. Four only distantly related families always moved as a "block." They lived in rented trailers but always moved together even if only one family was dissatisfied or was experiencing problems with housing arrangements. Although the relationship among the four related families on the surface may have appeared as too dependent and limiting of their individual possibilities for employment or housing improvement, they derived great support from their tight network. The four families represented to each other a supportive community.

The social worker who practices with an orientation to the community needs to be not only particularly sensitive to natural networks among people but also willing to surrender a great deal of power and control to enhance those networks. Because professionalism is often seen as control, imposition of structures, and formalization of the networks, it is viewed as destructive to networks (Sarason & Lorentz, 1979). In *domination* and *appropriation*, professionals may destroy networks perhaps because professionalism has often been blind to the autochthonous language and culture of a community. The inability to appreciate the different ways in which ordinary people secure help and support can be potentially dangerous to practitioners. However, the community-oriented practitioner can be supportive to networks once he or she has learned to appreciate them for what they are through incorporation and coexistence, in which the professional accommodates the informal system. The practitioner will sometimes serendipitously facilitate the development of informal networks, which may turn out to be effective, provided they are not discontinued only because the formal system discovers it is not necessarily doing what it set out to do. One practitioner related such an example:

> The agency had what was called a "budgeting class" which was supposedly devised to teach poor people in the small town how to budget their money. I was annoyed and politically opposed to the class because, although it was open to anyone who wanted to come, I knew that those who came were likely to be our poor clients who were probably being "encouraged to come" by various agencies. Surprisingly, I soon began to discover that a steady group came of their own volition. Many were not even clients. The class was clearly an excuse for people to get together, discuss money matters and network.

In this case, the agency or the social worker running the budgeting class was serendipitously but successfully strengthening networks. As long as no one was upset about whether the clients learned precisely about budgeting or not, the effort was an effective—albeit indirect—way of strengthening community and informal networks. Social workers must become cognizant and positive about what they are doing, even if the serendipitous results need to be reported differently.

Another important but seldom-used way of strengthening natural community ties is for the formal sector to provide appropriate financial support to people who help each other. Wenger (1984) found that although neighbors are often prepared to support old people with day-to-day help in their homes (for example, cooking extra for them or taking them shopping), they often are unable to do so because of costs. Unfortunately, few agencies are willing to provide even the smallest financial help to those neighbors because they are concerned about accountability and legal risks. Yet, in many small communities, it could be possible to redefine accountability in ways that do not preclude more flexible arrangements among people. Wenger (1984) suggested that although in government agencies accountability might be rigidly defined, in the voluntary sector, particularly in working with elderly people, there are many opportunities for redefinition of accountability, giving more weight to the negotiating of informal arrangements and stressing creativity in the use of funds to support those arrangements.

Other concerns are related to the social worker's application of local community ties versus that of the people in the community. In many small towns, the *local*, the person who has lived in the town all or most of his or her life, is respected as an authority by other locals. Yet, this same person might be treated with little deference by the professional who does not understand the town's history. This value difference might inhibit communication. Locals might be clients, but they also might be volunteers, friendly neighbors, or board members. The community-oriented social workers needs to know a great deal about these residents and their unique claims, not only because they are often part of the power structure, but because they are also part of the community's fibers. Often people in local communities judge outsiders (or for that matter, service providers) by their decorum or conventional observance of the community's rules. Insiders might be more readily able to criticize locals (or any other characteristic of the community) than outsiders would.

Jacobsen (1980, 1988) identified three models of community work, (1) locality or community development, (2) social planning, and (3) social action. *Locality or community development* is

> "a process designed to create conditions of economic and social progress for the whole community with its active participation and the fullest possible reliance on the community's initiative" [according to the United Nations]. Community development practitioners tend to assume that social change can best be pursued through broad participation of a wide range of people at the local level. (Jacobsen, 1988, p. 313)

Social planning usually addresses specific issues or problems of the community. Goals are often more important than process for the social planner. Planning seems to be an essentially pragmatic approach to community problems. Representatives of the community are usually involved in advisory capacity. The overriding goals of *social action* have been basic changes in the community's institutions. The social action practitioner tends to see the community as structured through power and privilege; it is that very structure that the social action practitioner sees as target (Jacobsen, 1988). Of the three models, locality development and social planning are more likely to be applied in the context of small communities because in locality development and in planning, powerful locals are viewed as important collaborators of the practitioner; in social action, they often are viewed as part of the power structure and, thus, as target for action. This is not to say that the power structure might not benefit from change, but change in small communities more often than not needs to be the collaborative endeavor of many inside forces. Even if the insiders wish to change the power structure, efforts of the outsider will not be viewed kindly. Outsiders often will be accused of polarizing and "meddling."

In community-oriented social work, practitioners also will need to be particularly sensitive to the language and needs of locals—whether the locals are decision makers or not—because locals are legitimizers of the social worker in the community. Particularly in small communities, the language of the local will be different from that of the outsider or the cosmopolitan, not only because of its context, but also because of the referents used. For example, regardless of where people live, people often navigate the geography of places and towns by mental maps. Those maps depend on the age of the person, and his or her relationship to the locality. That sort of generational local geography exists in most communities, but it is particularly tale-telling in small towns. How people orient themselves in the community is important; the hidden meaning of the referents they use in navigating the locality will tell a great deal about clients and social workers. For example, one young social worker who worked with elderly people in a small town that was changing rapidly told a practitioner about clients who used to direct her to their houses by landmarks that no longer existed. "I live upstairs from the cinema," an elderly client would say, when the cinema was no longer there. Although the social worker thought it was the peculiar way of elderly people, this mapping process tested the social worker's wits as well as her ability to rely on other locals to decipher the directions.

Understanding local community ties fully is an important element of community-oriented practice. The way in which the worker conceptualizes and appreciates those ties will affect his or her understanding of events and situations, determine his or her views and behavior toward local people, and influence his or her ways of serving people.

Community Values and Practice

One of the major concerns of social workers who have been used to functioning in fairly large and anonymous agency settings is the difficulties of maintaining anonymity or confidentiality in small community settings. Both anonymity and confidentiality are closely intertwined in the small community.

Anonymity

Anonymity refers to the state or situation of wanting a name. A client in a large city might, on occasion, meet an agency worker on the streets or in the market, but relationships generally can remain anonymous, not because people do not recognize one another occasionally, but because when they do, people and names will seldom be put together in a way that is meaningful to anyone. In the small community, faces and names are always put together in more meaningful ways. People often move to small communities because they do not want to remain anonymous. They enjoy doing business in highly personalized ways. They value being recognized and treated as people with names at the grocery store, the school, or the playground. Whether liked or disliked, small-town dwellers are seldom anonymous. The attaching of names to specific preferences, situations, and problems worries social workers in small communities. It is impossible for a person to remain anonymous in the small-town agency setting. The secretary who greets the client at a social agency will recognize individuals by name and attach the act of coming to a social agency to a known person, not to an anonymous case. Even before the issue of confidentiality of the professional contact becomes a concern, lack of anonymity has become a worry.

However, lack of anonymity also is a positive dimension too often ignored. Perhaps the more significant issue to be analyzed in the context of small communities is the value of anonymity to clients and social workers. People who grew up in small towns generally value personalization or at least are more used to handling highly personalized community encounters than are social workers. For elderly people, the lack of anonymity of the small community is usually a safeguard or asset and can be transformed into a major component of care in the community. Consider, for example, Stella Jones, an 89-year-old who always gets her hair done on a Monday. She did not show up at the hairdresser's one Monday—everyone noticed. What agencies and social workers who care for elderly people try to do is develop networks of community support and channel their knowledge of the lives of elderly people into appropriate action. What social workers want to achieve in these situations is a response from the network, whether it be calling Stella Jones, visiting her, or calling the social worker. Of course, it might well be that Stella Jones never liked to be missed in such a highly personal way, but that she still lives in the community makes it unlikely that she would be upset when people "check up on her." It is possible that she counts on such "checking up." It has become fairly accepted that a social worker interacting with elderly people in the community context will try to capitalize on the lack of anonymity of small community behavior.

Yet, the behavior of social workers is quite different in other fields of practice. Social workers often get upset and do not know how to handle comments from people who have noticed that children are no longing living at home or that an alcoholic person is once again drinking. The problem seems to be that human services providers and the social services system have been able to make lack of anonymity positive in certain situations but not in others, perhaps because of the stigma attached to particular services (for example, services to elderly people are acceptable but child welfare services are not). The challenge of community-oriented social work in relation to anonymity is not to control what people notice—social workers cannot do that—but rather to see how public knowledge can be used in helpful ways. Social workers who deal with public knowledge of issues can afford to be more relaxed about confidentiality. In small communities, clients themselves often reveal problems to friends and neighbors. For example, in the *People v. Hawkrigg* decision regarding a person with acquired immune deficiency syndrome (AIDS) who had disclosed positive test results to a roommate and to a local volunteer fire department, the judge stated that "once the condition has been disclosed, there is no longer any reason for the privilege" (Schwartz, 1989, p. 224).

One social worker who works in a mental health center in a midwestern state told a story in which "what everybody knows" was used to help save lives during the farm crisis of the 1980s. A small-town veterinarian, during his rounds, noticed that many of the farmers with whom he was interacting were depressed because of the stresses they were experiencing. As a result, he formed a group of people who cared about their neighbors and were willing to become "active listeners" as they went about their daily rounds. The country vet consulted the local mental health agency for pointers on how to listen, but other than that, the group of approximately 12 people was never formalized. One day, the vet went into the town's feed store and noticed that the manager was looking glum. He chatted with the manager, who "joked" about pulling in front of a tractor or taking all his heart medication at once. Not knowing exactly what was happening, the "active listener," as a neighbor, called the manager's wife. Later that day, the feed store manager entered the local mental health center for treatment for depression. His wife had convinced him to go.

The notion of partnership of all community members in caring for each other transforms lack of anonymity into a privileged knowledge community members have of each other. What is important is to help the community use this knowledge as a privilege for positive action. Many public service campaigns are predicated on this same principle on a more massive scale. For example, campaigns against drunk driving rely on the fact that people who know someone has had too much to drink will not allow that person to drive. Not allowing someone to drive when he or she has had too much to drink is not an indictment of the individual's character but an act of community responsibility. An important element of community-oriented services is reciprocity (Martinez-Brawley & Blundall, 1989). If the social worker is successful in helping people see that their care for others might one day result in care for them, then stigmatization might be reduced.

The idea that certain groups are the clients of social work, however, often stresses to some social workers the differences between the social worker and the community and, thus, may minimize the importance of the partnership. In a study of community-oriented social work in Britain, Harrison (1989) found that many community-oriented social workers had trouble with the term "client." Community-oriented workers did not "want the people with whom they worked to be dependent objects of their interventive efforts" (p. 74). "Clientizing" people was a process they were trying to avoid. Yet, community-oriented trends of practice might be more appropriate to the postindustrial society in which individuals face complex and rapid changes, with consequences so "widespread and the needs for interdependence and assistance so great that a concept of clienthood to distinguish a troubled minority may be obsolete" (p. 74).

In a recent study of farm families' perceptions of the personal social services (Martinez-Brawley & Blundall, 1989), farm families, despite their concern about the families' reputation in the community, wanted social workers to visit with them, to talk about their concerns and problems, and to talk about their options before any services were required. Those families were suggesting community-based prevention efforts that must be part of community-oriented social work. Those same families would be much more willing to participate in services if they viewed them as something in which recipients and providers shared jointly. A family in the same study, referring to the lack of anonymity in small communities, commented that it was impossible for people "not to know" what was going on. The family suggested that it might be best for family and social workers to confront those situations directly, so that they might be able to help instead of gossip (Martinez-Brawley & Blundall, 1989). The first step in dealing with concerns about anonymity is to confront them and decide on their importance. Is the lack of anonymity a problem? If so, can it be transformed into an asset? If not, what can realistically be done about it? How important is anonymity to the people involved in the transaction? The answers to these concrete questions might form the bases for decisions. These questions will be particularistic; the answers will apply to specific instances and will be different in each situation. Particularistic responses might make for more appropriate answers to the problem of lack of anonymity than broadly based rules or guidelines.

Confidentiality

Another major concern of social workers considering a more community-oriented practice in small towns is safeguarding confidentiality. *Confidentiality* means that the disclosure of information disclosed by a patient or client to a social worker or therapist will not be revealed by the social worker or therapist to others except under certain circumstances, and then only for the purpose of helping him or her (Reynolds, 1976). The National Association of Social Workers (NASW) *Code of Ethics* (NASW, 1980) suggests that the social worker's primary responsibility is to the client and that the social worker should hold in confidence all information obtained while rendering professional services. Yet, the NASW *Code of Ethics* also acknowledges that social workers should share with others confidences revealed by clients, without their consent, for compelling professional reasons. In the 1976 California court decision of *Tarosoff v. Regents of the University of California*, the court stated that "the right to privacy ends where the public peril begins" (Schwartz, 1989, p. 225). In child welfare cases, the courts have rules that the privilege of protecting confidential communications must yield to the duty of the courts to protect the welfare of the child. In cases where reporting to central registries is mandated by state laws, social workers also must disclose information. The matter of confidentiality is highly complex and depends on the particular situation.

Unfortunately, discussions of confidentiality that portray communication "as a simple dyadic exchange in which the worker guarantees the privacy of the client" (Moore-Kirland & Vice-Irey, 1981, p. 319) have been most common in social work classes and even in the early literature. Yet, the model of the dyadic exchange is inappropriate to the small-town practice setting.

> To define confidentiality only in relation to the one-to-one psychotherapeutic process between worker and client places unnecessary limits on social workers. The definition of confidentiality must deal with people in their social environments—the very relationship that social work claims as its unique focus. Social workers cannot view individuals—including individuals in their relationship to workers—apart from the social context. (Moore-Kirkland & Vice-Irey, 1980, p. 319)

The problems of the traditional dyadic way of interpreting confidentiality have become apparent in the limitations and dilemmas experienced by social workers who treat elderly people or people with AIDS. The futility of the dicta in the public context of the small communities is another example of the need for considering confidentiality beyond the classic dyadic model.

The lack of anonymity that exists in the small community social context requires that matters of confidentiality be examined differently (see, for example, "Our Town in 1981" on pp. 123–124). Threats to confidentiality are generally thought to be external forces associated with technological changes, such as computer systems or even written records that social workers or agencies may not know how to protect. Legal concerns about records being subpoenaed and concerns about privileged communication often constitute the crux of decisions about confidentiality. Yet, the concerns of practitioners in small communities about confidentiality are more basic and related to what is truly private and what becomes public information in the events of small towns. Concerns about protecting confidentiality in small towns focus on the social workers' inability to deal with the lack of anonymity or public nature of relationships, a matter that is at times a positive and useful attribute and at times a hindrance.

> Consider a social work client, Mr. M, whose family has lived in a small town for three generations. His wife's family has lived there even longer. Mr. M's alcoholism is common knowledge in the community, which began to observe the disintegration of Mr. M and his family long before he was sent to a treatment center out of the county. The neighbor's sheltered Mr. M's wife when her husband became violent and have occasionally provided financial assistance for the family. Church members and school teachers cluck with concern over the plight of the children and are already predicting that the 12-year-old son, always a problem in school, will turn out just like Dad. No one can understand—yet everyone speculates—why Mr. M, whose parents are pillars of the community, has turned out this way, though they know that he and his father get along poorly. Mr. M's neighbors, work associates and children's teachers all know of his hospitalization and will view his return to the community from the perspective of their own relationship with the family, their own understanding of alcoholism, and their own opinion about the prognosis. These expectations will shape the community's behavior toward Mr. M and toward each family member. These expectations are an integral part of the social context with which Mr. M and his family must cope. His return home is thus a social event, not a private affair, and the question is not whether the community knows about the problem but what blend of information and misinformation has evolved. Speculation will fill in the gaps. (Moore-Kirkland & Vice-Irey, 1980, p. 320)

Confidentiality in such instances must be examined in relation to what the client, the agency, the social worker, and even the community are trying to achieve. How will withholding or correcting information affect the well-being of clients and the achievement of goals? What are the clients' views and preferences on the situation? Are they being given the opportunity to assess the realistic limits of confidentiality in their case? Are they being presented with all the alternative scenarios, or are they just given a single one, the one in which the agency battles to protect information that the community probably already has?

There are cases in which confidentiality might be more important to the agency or social worker than to the client. There are instances when although the professional might assume that certain information is confidential, the client behaves otherwise. For example, one case involved a chronic alcoholic who periodically spent time in a state hospital. During a ride back to his native small town upon discharge from the hospital, the following event occurred. A well-meaning social worker who was driving the man asked the client where he wanted to be left, because going to his home necessitated a ride the entire length of Main Street and she was driving a clearly marked state vehicle. The social worker was assuming that the client wanted an inconspicuous return that could not be achieved in a marked state car. She was surprised when the client responded that he wanted to be taken all the way home, regardless of the route. The social worker was further surprised when the client rolled down the window and greeted all passers-by on the way along Main Street. Obviously, the strength of that particular client's network did not depend on his keeping his hospitalization secret. The social worker obviously would have to reconsider keeping the incident confidential and rather help the client and community use their knowledge for positive ends and mutual support. Speck and Attneave (1971) suggested that perpetuating the existence of "secret information" among networks of people often leads to pathological or destructive social relationships. Secrets, alliances, and collusions might need to be corrected for change to occur in those networks. In some cases, helping people reveal "false secrets" might have positive consequences.

Social workers in small communities where strong networks already exist might sometimes need to manage information to change potentially harmful alliances into beneficial ones. Confidentiality must be examined in relation to the roles of manager, advocate, mobilizer, or resource and friendly neighbor. Although professionals need a set of standards—general moral values or specific principles—to guide their behavior, in relation to confidentiality, "there will be no single, definitive answer to tell the confused practitioner what to do" (Wilson, 1982, p. 338). Resolving concerns over confidentiality requires consideration of each instance in its unique social and statutory context. In working with the community, issues of confidentiality take on an additional dimension. The social worker will not only need to be cautious about the effects of revealing or not revealing information, but also conscious of his or her role as interpreter of the client's situation to a community that already has relevant and irrelevant information. The social worker also will have to be mindful that his or her relationship with clients involves not only confidentiality but trust. Likewise, his or her relationship with community members involves trust.

Social workers must be careful that they do not offend the trust of clients or community members. For example, a minister in a small town once called a social worker to ask where to complain about "the offensive" behavior a child welfare worker in his community had exhibited to him. He indicated that he had referred a teenager to the agency because of his concerns about her present and future. He had recognized that the teenager's problems required more than his guidance and had convinced the young woman to seek the agency's specialized counseling. The minister later encountered the agency social worker in the market and had asked her whether the young woman had gone to the agency. He said he was curtly told that agency information was confidential. The minister felt that his helpful efforts had been rebuffed; he only wanted to know whether the young woman had followed up on her decision because he was concerned about her well-being. In this particular instance, the social worker had taken refuge behind the shield of confidentiality and not addressed skillfully the real issue of how to appreciate community support without divulging confidential information. Even if the social worker had been skillful in handling the minister at the informal level, she still would have faced a confidentiality dilemma: deciding the extent to which she could involve the minister. In this case, there was the antecedent of a condition that had already been disclosed by the client to the minister. Such disclosure, a review of pertinent state laws and their interpretation, consultation with the client, examination of agency practices, and legal counsel are all useful sources of information that provide guidelines to reach satisfactory decisions. However, perhaps the most frequently ignored sources in the decision-making process are consideration of the social context in which the interactions occur and consideration of the consequences sharing or not sharing information will have for clients.

Levy (1976) suggested that

> the social worker has the ethical responsibility to make provision for the consequences that his own professional acts may generate and to determine a priority ordering of the alternatives at his disposal and of the values affecting them that may be in conflict with one another. (p. 88)

In certain instances, the values of the community and the values of the social worker might be in conflict. In those instances, Levy's principle of ethical responsibility can provide guidance. Perhaps the offense of the minister might have been alleviated had the social worker honestly told him that she was faced with a dilemma that required more than spontaneous action. She needed to draw on the more collective wisdom to reach a decision and determine the extent of the minister's involvement. That case also illustrates the need to prevent potentially embarrassing situations by ensuring that when working in the context of small communities, the social worker discusses the sharing of information (and consequently, any related procedures) initially. Particularly, when clients are referred by other community members, the social worker's dual responsibility to the client and to the referring source must be discussed and clarified immediately. In small communities and particularly for groups (such as elderly people or children) that might profit from communal responses, discussions with the client about what type of information must remain confidential at all costs, what type of information could be shared, what type of information must be shared according to the statutes, and what type of information is already essentially public must be discussed initially. In addition to solving practical matters, such honest discussions will help in delineating and establishing the parameter of trust among social worker, client, and community members. Essentially, the social worker is not boxed into behaving in a particular way in relation to ethical decisions or to decisions affecting confidentiality. Hall (1952) suggested that it is impossible to reduce conduct in all situations to simple rules. What the social worker is obliged to do is to consider the alternatives at his or her disposal. In the case of community practice, the social worker must consider his or her alternatives in the light not only of the proper legal framework but also of the nature of the professional responsibility to community networks of support.

A current problem is a keen awareness that litigation can cloud a practitioner's common sense and judgment. Yet, given the numbers of people served by social workers and social agencies, cases ending up in litigation either against agencies or social workers are relatively few and relate first to instances of sexual impropriety, second to incorrect treatment, and third to breaches of confidentiality (NASW, 1989). Furthermore, statistics that can help determine whether litigation is common in rural communities are unavailable. The stress of rural practice for the social worker (particularly the new social worker) comes not so much because the social worker worries that he or she might divulge confidential information given to him or her by the client in a formal office setting, but because the social worker does not know how to handle immediate judgment calls on confidentiality. Consider the friendly neighbor who stops the social worker because he has seen him or her visiting an elderly lady down the street. The neighbor wants to know what is wrong. How can he help? Should he go in to see the elderly person? More complicated situations than this exist, such as the one involving the return of a patient from a psychiatric hospital, when the patient before admittance had been gloomy, moody, and often aggressive toward community members. What should the social worker do to create a more favorable atmosphere in the community and among neighbors when the patient returns? Clearly a negative atmosphere will make adjustment difficult or impossible. Some social workers would try community meetings to create a more favorable environment (Thomas, 1976). Others might opt for working only with the patient and strengthening his or her coping capabilities, but such an activity would not be orienting the social worker's practices to the community, which, in addition to helping the patient, might benefit from the knowledge acquired as a result of the client's interaction with the social worker. Furthermore, the ethical responsibility of the social worker (versus that of the psychiatrist or psychologist) is to correct misinformation in the social environment that might adversely affect the client (Moore-Kirkland & Vice-Irey, 1981). An example of a situation in which the community has misinformation that is potentially harmful to a person is portrayed in "A Pretty Girl" (p. 151).

Unfortunately, the recent tendency among professionals has been to ignore the duality of the social worker's ethical responsibility. Yet, if social workers are to practice community-oriented social work and recognize the strengths of the communal system, then the duality of the responsibility must be considered as social workers negotiate the nature of their confidential agreements with clients. Levy (1976) suggested that social workers must use client confidences for them, not against them. Although risks are inherent in determining the long-term consequences of any action, social workers need to secure permission from clients to be able to operate with good judgment within given parameters. The courts have been helpful in this respect:

> To constitute a waiver, there must be a clear relinquishment of a known right (*Community Service Society v. Welfare Inspector General*, 1978). No particular form (or indeed any form at all) is necessary in drafting a release; all that is required is an expression of present intention to renounce a claim or discharge an obligation (*Pratt Plumbing and Heaving v. Mastropole*, 1979). However, obtaining a written release is the safest practice because it helps forgetful clients recollect that they authorized such release. (Schwartz, 1989, p. 224)

In the context of community-oriented work in small towns, it is essential that social workers be aware of the parameters within which they exercise sound judgment and discretion in using information for the benefit of the client. Agencies need to discuss their policies in light of local community strengths and resources and also need to be guided by the experiences social workers and clients have had in a particular community. Clients must be made aware of potential benefits to be accrued from community networks as well as of drawbacks from the more public knowledge of private concerns common to small towns.

Moore-Kirkland and Vice-Irey (1981) challenged the profession to examine the concept of confidentiality in a more realistic and applicable way to serve those who practice in small communities. Their challenge is doubly important to social workers who practice with a community orientation. Although statutory provisions that govern the behavior of social workers are sometimes clear, in the fields that are most amenable to a community orientation (for example, work with elderly people and child welfare), decisions are still a matter of careful judgment and adjustment to the local context.

Accountability

Social work services that are community-oriented must make appropriate use of all of the resources, formal and informal, that exist in the small community. However, the closer practitioners get to altering their ways of caring to the patterns of the informal system, the more they encounter problems of accountability. *Accountability* is not only the concern of the formal sector—whether public, voluntary, or for-profit—but also a genuine preoccupation of the voluntary and private sectors, although often the mechanisms through which practitioners account for what they are doing differ from sector to sector. In the public sector, accountability is generally seen as a bureaucratic process through which the public becomes cognizant of what elected officials and public employees do and monitors the use of tax monies. Accountability in the voluntary sector is the way in which organizations justify to their sponsors how they are carrying out their mission and using their resources. Despite the mystique that often surrounds the concept of accountability, whether in rural or urban areas, in the public or the private sector, or at home or in business, social workers must explain and often justify the way in which they have used resources because resources are finite and require the setting of priorities.

Carter (1983) suggested that accountability measures fall into two categories: efficiency and effectiveness. *Efficiency* refers to output in relation to resources, for example, the number of clients served by each social worker. *Effectiveness* refers to the achievement of goals, for example, the number of elderly people who were in danger of becoming institutionalized but who are not within a year after the start of a home-help program. Efficiency stresses how much one gets for his or her money; effectiveness stresses how well one is doing one's job.

One of the concerns of service managers and social services providers in small communities and rural areas is that criteria of efficiency often are inappropriate because of the size of the population. Often, small communities cannot afford to provide certain services because the number of people served, used as a single criterion, does not justify the expense. The generalist and community-oriented approaches can address this problem. Community-oriented services can make use of resources that already exist in the community. However, those resources often need nurturing or support and social workers find themselves unable to give this because such indirect support does not meet efficiency criteria. For example, research with elderly people shows that rewarding caring behavior from kin and friends is important and maybe even essential to maintaining those networks. Yet, kin and friends are seldom defined as the "client" and social workers often are unable to spend time with them. Resources—whether time or money—often need to be spent not on the client, who is being cared for by the network, but on the community networks themselves. Natural networks, like people, can become exhausted. Social workers and other human services providers doing community-oriented work need to play an active role in ensuring liaison between all who provide care. Wenger (1984) addressed this point in relation to services to elderly people. In community-oriented work with senior citizens, she suggested that

> accountability to the social service agency will still be important to social workers, especially in statutory work; much social work with the elderly is non-statutory. This presents opportunities for much redefinition of accountability giving more weight to agreements reached between helpers, clients and social workers rather than strict responsibility to the agency. It may also need to include access to discretionary funds for social workers in order to make such negotiations practical. (p. 193)

Clearly, the type of accountability that gives the social workers the opportunity to exercise their discretion in the use of funds—even small amounts—is creative but hard to secure. Yet, to strengthen the informal sector, the social worker might need to use resources in discretionary ways. For example, a researcher visiting a small town in an agricultural county needed to talk with people who were community carers but not necessarily participants in any organized form of voluntary organization. The researcher wanted to talk with true natural carers: the neighbor who visited elderly people who lived alone, or with the one who cooked for a neighbor when he or she was not well. Almost everyone knew who these carers were, but three neighbors were identified by the local social worker as being important to the village's caring scheme. The three neighbors were elderly and not mobile themselves, thus they did not participate in any organized efforts. Yet, each visited or kept an eye on a neighbor, and one lady had routinely cooked for an even more elderly friend next door once a week for many years. The social worker had tried to encourage these elderly people and to reward them. What she thought they would enjoy most was an occasional meal out with her. Yet, she had no discretionary funds for such needs. When she found that the visiting researcher was searching for conversation and willing to have lunch with these elderly people, she was delighted. Yet, nourishing these informal carers on a regular basis through informal interactions such as lunch should not have been left either to the personal resources of the social worker or to the serendipitous arrival of a researcher. The use of discretionary funds in this instance would have made for justifiably effective community-oriented social work.

Social services providers often rely on formalized ways of helping people because these give them more control (for example, they can standardize and control the menu of centrally prepared "Meals on Wheels" programs but cannot exercise the same degree of control if they provide monetary help for natural carers to cook for their elderly neighbors). Yet, the interaction of a neighbor-to-neighbor cooking arrangement for an elderly person can enhance the quality of life of that elderly person more than the well-balanced but somewhat antiseptic meal delivered by strangers. Social services providers need to weigh many factors in choosing solutions. If their goals are related to the need for ongoing interaction for the elderly person more than to strict dietary controls, then the less formal arrangement might be the most efficient and effective.

In small communities, once goals are set, it is easier to explain and establish relationships among various factors, including community factors, that may have gone into achieving those goals. Effectiveness criteria are common sense to people in small contexts. Carter (1983) suggested that "the accountability measure employed varies according to where an individual is located in the decision-making process. The closer a staff member is to the actual delivery of services to clients, the more likely he/she is to use effectiveness as a criteria" (p. 20). Unfortunately, however, more frequently administrators, constrained by policymakers, tend to emphasize efficiency rather than effectiveness. Recent review of "efficiency and effectiveness criteria used at the state level illustrates that effectiveness measures are not often assigned much importance" (Carter, 1983, p. 20). To analyze the types of measures that legislators and other policymakers take to respond to accountability questions, cost measures (that is, the number of clients served) were systematically collected and used, but effectiveness measures were gathered only on a special one-time study basis (Carter, 1983). This "ethic of intrinsic goodness," according to Benton

(1981), arose because of the philanthropic origins of social services and the symbolic commitment of society to do good. "As a result, the extent of the society's commitment has traditionally been measured in the size of the investment in programs to meet the economic and social needs of deserving individuals, families and communities. That is, the more we would spend on social programs, the better" (Benton, 1981, p. 1)

The "ethic of intrinsic goodness" may have been just one factor that prevented the full use of effectiveness measures; but, the public seldom spent enough money on social programs on a long-term, consistent basis to conclude that resources have been spent on ineffective programs, despite the negative visions of social programs politicians made public in the early 1970s (Brawley & Martinez-Brawley, 1988). Many other factors prevented the full use of effectiveness measures, among them, the state of the art in program evaluation and the reluctance of practitioners to accept and use those measures. During the Nixon years, when the "accountability crisis" (Newman & Turem, 1974) reached its peak, the state of the art in program evaluation could rarely show tangible evidence of effectiveness. Nevertheless,

> the issue of accountability had to be taken seriously and conscientious efforts were made to apply the most rigourous evaluation tools to all aspects of social intervention, from direct social work practice to broad-scale social programmes. These efforts were less fruitful than was anticipated. It became clear that there was an enormous gulf between policy-makers, programme administrators and practitioners on the one hand and researchers and evaluators on the other. The former complained that research and evaluation studies did not tell them what they needed to know and the latter complained that their findings were not being used. The "crisis of accountability" was accompanied by a "utilization crisis." (Brawley & Martinez-Brawley, 1988, p. 393)

Although program evaluation, like accountability, has been surrounded by an aura of mystique, and although practitioners have associated program evaluation with complicated measures, charts, and figures, program evaluation can be simple and commonsensical. Program evaluation traditionally has used, among other measures, goal attainment measures to explain success or failure of programs. Program evaluation measures, many of which are descriptive and easy for practitioners to follow if done on a continuous basis, can help collect and provide to policymakers ongoing information on the effectiveness of programs. One of the advantages of program evaluation is that descriptive information on community networks, for example, how they are helping to care for people, can be incorporated into accounts. Unique approaches that defy rigid efficiency measures can be documented through the program evaluation approach.

Cox (1977) suggested that program evaluation studies tend to focus on one-time instances and therefore lack historical continuity, a focus that may have been true in the past. Clearly today, "to change the perceptions of administrators and/or legislators it is important to have a long enough history of consistent information" (Carter, 1983, p. 27). Consequently, to document community-oriented approaches to caring for people within the context of smaller environments, it might be more essential than ever to use the program evaluation methodology, ensuring that it includes not only efficiency but, most important, effectiveness measures of accountability. If used routinely, a history of consistent information on community-oriented efforts can be compiled and provided to policymakers. In addition to using this information for founders, it can be used to communicate to the community what the agency is doing and to secure its cooperation and support (Brawley, 1985/1986).

Program administrators in small environments need to play an active role in stressing the importance of effectiveness measures when their programs are reviewed. As long as they comply with the demands for efficiency measures that are inappropriate in the context of their organizations, they will reinforce policymakers' reliance on those measures to the exclusion of other measures. Bureaucracies have tended to emphasize mechanistic forms of accountability that often are inappropriate to the more flexible conditions of the small environment (Aldridge, Macy, & Walz, 1982). One major advantage of decentralizing administrative structure is possibly to stress the compatibility of certain types of measures of accountability in certain environments and the lack of compatibility of others.

In her research on business organizations, Woodward (1965) classified firms into mass production firms and small batch firms and showed how different organizational structures and approaches were appropriate for the two different types. Woodward and other contingency theorists "make clear that an effective organization can run the gamut from traditional bureaucracy to a highly organic, constantly changing structure" (Lewis & Lewis, 1983, p. 83). Contingency theories minimally can offer administrators and social workers a means for clarifying their ideas about their own organization and designing ways of functioning and measures of accountability that are appropriate for their milieu.

> If human service professionals were to use contingency theories to determine the best way to structure the work of their programs or agencies, they would, as a first step, identify the most salient characteristics of their services and settings. Following Woodward's example they would need to ask whether their agencies were in fact mass production firms or small batch firms. Human service workers who viewed themselves as technicians offering consistent services to a wide range of clients might be able to use mechanistic organizational structures, but such designs would be inappropriate for professionals attempting to deliver multifaceted services based on community. (Lewis & Lewis, 1983, p. 83)

Weinbach (1990) discussed the relationship between the proliferation of bureaucratic activities and the degree of hostility from outside forces that some organizations face. The more hostile the environment in which an organization functioned, the more rigid and bureaucratic its procedures became. One of the advantages of community-oriented approaches is that they help decrease the level of outside hostility, and thus decrease the perceived need for bureaucratic forms of accountability that are designed solely to protect the organization.

> A business or corporation exists to make a profit. Consequently, it is "efficiency driven." Any activity that will reduce the cost of production of a product has the potential to increase profit. . . . If after a reasonable time, efficiency methods cannot generate a profit, the product will be dropped. . . . The decision is purely an economic one. . . . Sentiment and concerns over fairness rarely enter into the decision to drop a product or division. They may play a role only in treatment of employees who are displaced, require retraining, or are otherwise negatively affected by the decision. In contrast, a social agency and the managers who must make decisions within it must attempt to balance efficiency and equity. A social agency cannot ignore efficiency. It must pay utility bills, salaries and address the other expenses incurred. But is must also meet professional obligations to client service and cannot afford to develop a reputation for being overly preoccupied with efficiency. (Weinbach, 1990, pp. 31–32)

Certainly, in orienting services to the community, effectiveness, responsibility, and ethics should dictate more than efficiency. The more community oriented that services are, the more that services involve the local networks of support and the more that constituents will rise to their defense. After all, one of the pleasures of working in small communities is that constituent support can be quickly translated into pressure on policymakers. The persuasiveness of a supportive and involved community is often the most powerful argument in resolving conflicting positions in relation to social services.

ASSUMPTIONS OF COMMUNITY-ORIENTED SOCIAL WORK

Community-oriented social work is clearly predicated on a different understanding of the local community and on the interweaving of the formal and the informal systems of care. Community-oriented social work is predicated on the notion that caring for people is the common task of professionals and laypeople in their roles as friends and neighbors and necessitates the development of a truly cooperative and egalitarian relationship among all caring systems in the community. Thus, community-oriented social work presupposes a power shift in the professional relationship. Community-oriented social work also presupposes that the professional is open to different ways of accomplishing goals, despite that the professional often is constricted by standards and particular techniques of helping and the layperson is not. From the interweaving of different ways of doing, new approaches will emerge. For example, the accountability of the professional has been to the agency and to the profession; the accountability of a natural helper has been to a code of norms that govern community interactions. In community-oriented social work, these two ways will have to mesh harmoniously and borrow from each other.

Community-oriented social work emphasizes a more egalitarian environment in which local people help plan and participate in providing services. Such an environment might open professionals and agencies to closer scrutiny and, potentially, criticism, but also might open them to the possibility of attaining the local support they never had before. Social workers and other professionals need to be prepared to handle these situations. Community-oriented services are as much an attitude as a collection of techniques. Because communities and local people vary, community-oriented social services will have their own unique aspects in each local community.

However, community-oriented social work and greater reliance on community networks do not deny the importance of the services of the professional. It only means that the professional will perform a different, but necessary role in direct care. According to Wenger (1984), even in the most caring community, "often people will feel inhibited from helping where an offer of help might be construed as a slur" (p. 193). For laypeople, "it is easier to offer to cook a meal than to suggest cleaning up the house and unlikely that many feel confident enough to suggest washing or bathing a neighbor except in a crisis situation" (Wenger, 1984, p. 193). Professionals still will need to carry responsibilities that are beyond the boundaries of communal interactions. In community-oriented social work, though, social workers will find that they rely on the help of natural caregivers—primarily women. This is a concern because women often see their horizons limited by their caregiving roles. Nevertheless, those people in essential caring roles without the support or recognition of the professional establishment might be encouraged through recognition, support, and the provision of occasional additional resources to carry out their tasks.

Community-oriented social work presupposes a great deal of knowledge of the local community. It requires knowledge of local people and strong diplomatic techniques. It requires the ability to interpret events not only in the language of the agency but also in the language of the policymaker, the politicians, and the local citizen.

REFERENCES

Abrams, P. (1980). Social change, social networks and neighbourhood care. *Social Work Service, 22*, 12–23.

Aldridge, M., Macy, H., & Walz, T. (1982). *Beyond management: Humanizing the administrative process*. Iowa City: University of Iowa School of Social Work.

Alinsky, S. D. (1971). *Rules for radicals*. New York: Random House.

Allemand, E. L. (1976). The ideal for the nation: Josiah Royce's view of community. *Intellect, 105*, 47–48.

Anton, T. J. (1963). Power, pluralism and local politics, *Administrative Science Quarterly, 7*, 448–457.

Arensberg, C. M. (1955). American communities. *American Anthropologist, 57*, 1143–1162.

Arnow, H. (1949). *Hunter's horn*. New York: Macmillan.

Bachrach, P., & Baratz, M. (1962). The two faces of power. *American Political Science Review, 57*, 947–952.

Bachrach, P., & Baratz, M. (1970). *Power and poverty: Theory and practice*. New York: Oxford University Press.

Badillo Ghali, S. (1977). Cultural sensitivity and the Puerto Rican client. *Social Casework, 58*, 459–461.

Banfield, E. C. (1961). *Political influence*. New York: Free Press.

Barna, E. (1989, March 8). Business (and pleasure) the old-fashioned way. *Rutland Herald*, p. 7.

Bell, C., & Newby, H. (1972). *Community studies: An introduction to the sociology of the local community*. New York: Praeger.

Bell, W., Hill, R. J., & Wright, C. R. (1961). *Public leadership*. San Francisco: Chandler.

Bender, T. (1978). *Community and social change in America*. New Brunswick, NJ: Rutgers University Press.

Benson, E. F. (1977). *Make way for Lucia*. New York: Crowell.

Benton, W. (1981, August). Keynote address to the International Council on Social Welfare, Ontario.

Berger, B. M. (1981). *The survival of a counterculture. Ideological work and everyday life among rural communards*. Berkeley: University of California Press.

Blundall, J. (1987). *Dealing with the human pain of the rural condition* [Mimeograph]. Spencer, Iowa: Northwest Iowa Community Mental Health Center.

Bokemeier, J. L., & Tait, J. L. (1980). Women as power actors: A comparative study of rural communities. *Rural Sociology, 45*, 238–255.

Bragg, M. (1969). *The hired man*. New York: Knopf.

Brawley, E. (1985/1986). The mass media: A vital adjunct to the new community and administrative practice. *Administration in Social Work, 9*, 63–73.

Brawley, E. A., & Martinez-Brawley, E. E. (1988). Social programme evaluation in the U.S.A.: Trends and issues. *British Journal of Social Work, 18*, 391–413.

Brueggebors, B. (1988, November 8). Mountaintop-area citizens question plans for landfill. *Centre Daily Times*, p. A5.

Brueggebors, B. (1990, February 11). Razors, opinions equally sharp. *Centre Daily Times*, pp. A1, A12.

Buckley, W. F. (Producer). (1989). Resolved: Free market competitiveness is best for America [Firing Line series]. Southern Educational Communication Association.

Byler, W. (1977). The destruction of American Indian families. In S. Unger (Ed.), *The destruction of American Indian families* (pp. 1–11). New York: Association of American Indian Affairs.

Campoamor, D. (1989). Keeping the land. *Intercambios*, *4*(1), 18–19.

Caplow, T., & Chadwick, B. (1979). Inequality and life-styles in Middletown, 1920–1978. *Social Science Quarterly*, *60*, 367–386.

Carter, R. K. (1983). *The accountable agency*. Beverly Hills: Sage.

Cawthon, F. (1988, March 10). Way out in the country, Super Tuesday much more than a vote-and-run affair. *The Atlanta Constitution*, p. 2B.

Christie, A. (1950). *A murder is announced*. New York: Dodd, Mead & Co.

Christie, A. (1963). *The mirror crack'd*. New York: Dodd, Mead & Co.

Clark, D. C. (1973). The concept of community: A reexamination, *Sociological Review*, *21*, 397–416.

Columbia Broadcasting System (Producer). (1974). *Autobiography of Miss Jane Pitman* [Film].

Conklin, C. (1980). Rural community care givers, *Social Work*, *25*, 495–496.

Constantini, E., & Clark, K. H. (1972). Women as politicians: The social background, personality and political careers of female party leaders. *Journal of Social Issues*, *28*, 217–236.

Cook, W. J. (1989, December 18). Lisbon. *U.S. News & World Report*, pp. 64, 65.

Cox, G. B. (1977). Managerial style: Implications for the utilization of program evaluation information. *Evaluation Quarterly*, *1*, 499–508.

Curtis, R. F., & Jackson, E. F. (1966). *Inequality in American communities*. New York: Academic Press.

Dahl, R. A. (1961). *Who governs? Democracy and power in an American city*. New Haven: Yale University Press.

Daley, Y. (1989, March 8). Use of ballot changes town's way of doing business. *Rutland Herald*, pp. 1, 8.

Darley, G. (1978). *Villages of vision*. London: Granada Publishing.

Davis, P. (1982a). Getting there. In *Hometown: A contemporary American chronicle* (pp. 9–20). New York: Simon & Schuster.

Davis, P. (1982b). *Hometown: A contemporary American chronicle*. New York: Simon & Schuster.

Dean, L. R. (1967). *Five towns: A comparative community study*. New York: Random House.

Delafield, E. M. (1931). *Diary of a provincial lady*. New York: Harper and Brothers.

Delgado, M. (1977). Puerto Rican spiritualism and the social work profession. *Social Casework*, *58*, 451–458.

Dewey, J. (1930). *Individualism old and new*. New York: Capricorn Books.

Donahue, P. (1982, November 30). [TV Interview with "Tough Love" member].

Edelman, J. M. (1977). *Political language: Words that succeed and policies that fail*. New York: Academic Press.

El Salvador ambassador to talk in Weston Friday. (1983, March 16). *The Black River Tribune*, p. 1.

Etzioni, A. (1989, February 1). The "me first" model in the social sciences is too narrow [Editorial]. *The Chronicle of Higher Education*, p. A44.

Fabricant, M. (1985). The industrialization of social work practice. *Social Work*, *30*, 389–395.

Fenby, B. L. (1978). Social work in a rural setting. *Social Work*, *23*, 162–163.

Frankenberg, R. (1957). *Village on the border*. London: Cohen and West.

Frankenberg, R. (1966). *Communities in Britain, social life in town and country*. Baltimore: Penguin Books.

Franklin, S. (1986, March 6). Bible marked absent in small-town school. *Chicago Tribune*, p. 17.

Freeman, J. (1973). The origins of the women's liberation movement. In J. Huber (Ed.), *Changing women in a changing society* (pp. 30–49). Chicago: University of Chicago Press.

Freeman, L. C., Fararo, T. J., Bloomberg, W., & Sunshine, H. (1968). Locating leaders in local communities: A comparison of some alternative approaches. In W. D. Hawley & F. M. Wirt (Eds.), *The search for community power* (pp. 189–199). Englewood Cliffs, NJ: Prentice-Hall.

Freilich, M. (1963). Toward an operational definition of community. *Rural Sociology*, *28*, 117–127.

Fuson, K. (1988a, May 22). It's a new day in State Center, but what will life be like at dusk? *The Des Moines Register*, pp. 1A–8A.

Fuson, K. (1988b, October 16). Lack of teamwork hinders State Center's fight to survive. *The Des Moines Register*, pp. 1A–4A.

George, A. J. (Ed.). (1904). *Complete poetical works of William Wordsworth*. New York: Houghton Mifflin.

Giardina, D. (1987). *Storming heaven*. New York: Ivy Books, Ballantine.

Ginsberg, L. (Ed.). (1976). *Social work in rural communities: A book of readings*. New York: Council on Social Work Education.

Ginsberg, L. (1981). Social work among the rural disadvantaged. In T. M. Cassidy, M. Gordon, & A. Heller (Eds.), *The mountains and valleys are mine: A symposium on rural mental health* (pp. 92–103). Ridgewood, NY: Bren-Tru Press.

Glass, R. (1966). Conflict in cities. In A. DeReuck & J. Knight (Eds.), *Conflict in society* (p. 148). London: Little and Churchill.

Glover, M. (1985, May 5). Residents of Lakeview, Oregon, fight for the life of their town: If the railroad goes, the mills will shut down. *The San Francisco Examiner*, May 5, pp. 1, 4.

Goist, P. D. (1977). *From Main Street to State Street: Town, city, and community in America*. New York: Kennikat.

Good, J. (1983, March 26). Vermont Spoilers. *The New York Times*, p. 23.

Goode, W. J. (1957). Community within a community: The professions. *American Sociological Review*, *22*, 194–200.

Greenwood, E. (1961). The practice of science and the science of practice. In W. G. Bennis, K. D. Benne, & R. Chin (Eds.), *The planning of change: Readings in the applied behavioral sciences* (pp. 73–82). New York: Rinehart & Winston.

Guru followers has edge in Oregon election. (1982, November 3). *Washington Post*, p. C8.

Hadley, R., & Hatch, S. (1981). *Social welfare and the failure of the state*. London: Allen & Unwin.

Hadley, R., & McGrath, M. (1980). *Going local: Neighborhood social services*. London: National Council of Voluntary Organization, Bedford Square Press.

Hall, E. T. (1981). *Beyond culture*. Garden City, NJ: Anchor Books.

Hall, L. K. (1952). Group workers and professional ethics. *The Group*, *15*, 3–8.

Harrison, W. D. (1989). Social work and the search for postindustrial community. *Social Work*, *34*, 73–75.

Herriot, J. (1985). *All creatures great and small*. New York: St. Martin's Press.
Herzberg, M. (1985, January 25). Prayer for Christian Unity. Sermon presented at the Remsen Lutheran Church, Remsen, Iowa.
Hillery, G. A. (1955). Definitions of community: Areas of agreement. *Rural Sociology*, *20*, 111–123.
Hillery, G. A. (1969). *Communal organizations: A study of local societies*. Chicago: University of Chicago Press.
Hobbs, G. (1985). Harriet Arnow's Kentucky novels: Beyond local color. In E. Toth (Ed.), *Regionalism and the female imagination* (pp. 83–91). New York: Human Sciences Press.
Hunter, A. (1978). Persistence of local sentiments in mass society. In D. Street and Associates (Eds.), *Handbook of contemporary urban life* (pp. 133–162). San Francisco: Jossey–Bass.
Hunter, F. (1953). *Community power structure: A study of decision makers*. Chapel Hill: University of North Carolina Press.
Hurston, Z. N. (1935a). [Chapter 1]. In *Mules and men* (pp. 23–34). Philadelphia: J. B. Lippincott.
Hurston, Z. N. (1935b). *Mules and men*. Philadelphia: J. B. Lippincott.
Iowa's small towns crumbling in wake of dismal economy. (1987, November 17). *The Des Moines Register*, pp. 1B, 6B.
It may be slow, but Lakeview's private railroad is a lifesaver. (1987, June 21). *The Sunday Oregonian*, p. D2.
Jacobsen, M. G. (1980). Rural communities and community development. In H. W. Johnson (Ed.), *Rural human services* (pp. 196–202). Itasca, IL: Peacock.
Jacobsen, M. G. (1988). Working with communities. In H. W. Johnson (Ed.), *The social services: An introduction* (pp. 308–323). Itasca, IL: Peacock.
Johnson, L. C. (1983). Networking: A means of maximizing resources. *Human Services in the Rural Environment*, *8*, 27–31.
Jones, G. (1980). Nature makes no leaps. In H. Roger & M. McGrath (Eds.), *Going local: Neighborhood social services* (pp. 16–28). London: National Council of Voluntary Organization, Bedford Square Press.
Juillerat, L. (1987, January 27). If it's 9 a.m., it's time for the Lakeview Sagehens. *Herald and News*, p. 2.
Kanter, R. M. (1972). *Commitment and community: Communes and utopians in sociological perspective*. Cambridge: Harvard University Press.
Kaplan, S. (1981, February 19). Population pendulum is swinging. *Los Angeles Times*, pp. 1–15.
Keillor, G. (1985). *Lake Wobegon days*. New York: Viking.
Keillor, G. (1987). *Leaving home: A collection of Lake Wobegon stories*. New York: Penguin Books.
Keyes, R. (1973). *We, the lonely people: Searching for community*. New York: Harper & Row.
Keysville blacks closer to dream [Editorial]. (1989, January 7). *The Atlanta Constitution*, p. 14A.
Klapp, O. (1969). *The collective search for identity*. New York: Holt, Rinehart & Winston.
Kuhn, T. S. (1962). *The structure of scientific revolutions*. Chicago: University of Chicago Press.
Larson, O. (1978). Values and beliefs of rural people. In T. Ford (Ed.), *Rural U.S.A.: Persistence and change* (pp. 91–112). Ames: Iowa State University Press.
Levenberg, S. (1976). Building consultative relationships with rural fundamentalist clergy. *Professional Psychology*, *7*, 553–558.

Levine, R. (1988). City stress index: 25 best, 25 worst. *Psychology Today*, *22*, 52–58.
Levy, C. S. (1976). *Social work ethics*. New York: Human Services Press.
Lewis, J. A., & Lewis, M. D. (1983). *Management of human service programs*. Monterey, CA: Brooks/Cole.
Lewis, R.W.B. (1955). *The American Adam: Innocence, tragedy and tradition in the nineteenth century*. Chicago: University of Chicago Press.
Lewis, S. (1920a). [Chapter 9]. In *Main Street* (pp. 131–143). New York: Harcourt, Brace.
Lewis, S. (1920b). *Main Street*. New York: Harcourt, Brace.
Lingeman, R. (1980). *Small town in America: A narrative history, 1620–the present*. New York: Putnam.
Logsdon, G. (1986). Amish economics. *Whole Earth Review*, *50*, 74–82.
Long, K. (1987, November 20). Clubs: Small communities in the big city. *The Atlanta Constitution*, p. 38.
Loomis, C. P. (1960). *Social systems*. Princeton, NJ: D. Van Nostrand.
Lyford, J. (1962). *The talk in Vandalia. The life of an American town*. New York: The Friend for the Republic.
Lynd, R. S., & Lynd, H. M. (1929). *Middletown*. New York: Harcourt Brace Jovanovich.
Lynd, R. S., & Lynd, H. M. (1937). *Middletown in transition: A study in cultural conflicts*. New York: Harcourt Brace Jovanovich.
Macdonald, F. J. (1983). *Crowdie and cream: Memoirs of a Hebridean childhood*. London: Futura Publications.
MacIver, R. M. (1924). *Community*. New York: Macmillan.
MacKaye, B. (1962). *The new exploration: A philosophy of regional planning*. Urbana: University of Illinois Press.
MacKenzie, B. (1987, June 21). Branch lines go on market: Rural towns and railroads may benefit from strategy. *The Oregonian*, pp. D1, D2.
Madge, J. (1963). *The origins of scientific sociology*. London: Tavistock.
Magill, R. S., & Clark, T. N. (1975). Community power and decision making: Recent research and its policy implications. *Social Service Review*, *49*, 33–45.
Margolis, R. J. (1980). *At the crossroads: An inquiry into rural post offices and the communities they serve* (Report No. 052-062-00034-9). Washington, DC: U.S. Government Printing Office.
Margolis, R. J. (1981). The limits of localism. *Working Papers for a New Society*, *8*, 32–39.
Marin, P. (1970, November 8). *The greening of America* [Book review]. *The New York Times*, pp. 3, 58.
Marquand, J. P. (1949). *The point of no return*. Boston: Little, Brown.
Marshall, Texas, Marshall, Texas: A walk through the 20th century with Bill Moyers [Film]. (1984). Produced by Corporation for Entertainment Learning and Bill Moyers.
Martinez, C. (1977). Curanderos: Clinical aspects. *Journal of Operational Psychiatry*, *8*, 35–38.
Martinez-Brawley, E. (1981). *Seven decades of rural social work*. New York: Praeger.
Martinez-Brawley, E., & Blundall, J. (1989). Farm families preferences toward the personal social services. *Social Work*, *34*, 513–522.
May, J. A. (1979, February 21). Village life—In crisis or clover? *The Christian Science Monitor*, p. 23.
Mazer, M. (1976). *People and predicaments*. Cambridge: Harvard University Press.
McAfee, A. (1983, March 23). Ambassador argues for Salvador aid, but Weston remains unconvinced. *The Black River Tribune*, pp. 1, 9–10.

McMackin, R. L. (1988). Out of the woods: New frontiers for rural communities. *Penn State Agriculture*, Winter, pp. 12–21.

Meenaghan, T. M. (1976). Clues to community power structures. *Social Work, 21*, 126–130.

Mermelstein, J., & Sundet, P. (1978, March). *Education for social work practice in the rural content*. Keynote address given at the Conference on Educating for Social Practice in Rural Areas, Fresno, CA.

Merton, R. K. (1949). *Sociological analysis*. New York: Harcourt, Brace.

Merton, R. K. (1957). *Social theory and social structure*. Glencoe, IL: Free Press.

Milliken, W. G. (1987, October 15). Creativity in government [Editorial]. *The Christian Science Monitor*, *79*, p. 13.

Moore-Kirkland, J., & Vice-Irey, K. (1981). A reappraisal of confidentiality. *Social Work*, *26*, 319–322.

Morganthauw, T., et al. (1981, July 6). America's small town boom. *Newsweek*, pp. 26–37.

Mortimer, J. (1984). *Paradise postponed*. New York: Penguin–Viking.

Mountaintop sewer woes a catch 22 [Editorial]. (1988, September 24). *Centre Daily Times*, p. A6.

Narvaez, A. A. (1987, July 22). Two rebellious Essex towns, upset over big tax jumps, seek sympathizers. *New York Times*, pp. B1, B4.

National Association of Social Workers. (1980). *Code of ethics*. Silver Spring, MD: Author.

National Association of Social Workers. (1989). *Malpractice claims against social workers*. Silver Spring, MD: Author.

National Institute for Social Work. (1982). *Social workers: Their roles and tasks* [Barclay Report]. London: Bedford Square Press.

New democracy tries to take root [Editorial]. (1988, January 7). *The Atlanta Constitution*, p. 12A.

Newman, E., & Turem, J. (1974). The crisis of accountability. *Social Work*, *19*, 5–16.

Nichols, J. (1974). *The Milagro beanfield war*. New York: Holt, Rinehart & Winston.

Nisbet, R. (1953). *The quest for community*. New York: Oxford University Press.

O'Brien, M. (1988, November 30). A paradox of intellectual life since the 60's: We are cosmopolitan; our scholarship is not. *The Chronicle of Higher Education*, pp. B1–B2.

Oldenburg, R. (1989). *The great good place: Cafes, coffee shops, community centers, beauty parlors, general stores, bars, handouts and how they get you through the day*. New York: Paragon House.

Ostendorf, D. (1987). The church and the covenant of the land. In K. Schmidt (Ed.), *Renew the spirit of my people* (pp. 2–10). Des Moines, Iowa: Prairiefire.

Pahl, R. (1966). The rural-urban continuum. *Sociologia Ruralis*, 6, 299–329.

Park, R. E. (1952). *Human communities*. Glencoe, IL: Free Press.

Pave, M. (1982, April 14). In small communities, it's no contest at election time. *The Boston Globe*, p. 17.

Pearson, T. R. (1985a). *A short history of a small place*. New York: Ballantine Books.

Pearson, T. R. (1985b). *Mayor*. In *A short history of a small place* (pp. 251–303). New York: Ballantine Books.

Pearson, T. R. (1987). *Off for the sweet hereafter*. New York: Ballantine Books.

Pelly-Effrat, M. (Ed.). (1974). *The community: Approaches and applications*. New York: Free Press.

Petersen, W. (1968). The ideological origins of Britain's new towns. *Journal of the American Institute of Planners*, *34*, 160–170.

Pierson, G. W. (1964). The M-factor in American history. In M. McGiffert, (Ed.), *The character of Americans* (pp. 118–130). Homewood, IL: Dorsey Press.
Piven, F. F., & Cloward, R. A. (1977). *Poor people's movements: Why they succeed, how they fail*. New York: Random House.
Piven, F. F., & Cloward, R. A. (1982). *The new class war: Reagan's attack on the welfare state and its consequences*. New York: Pantheon Books.
Polsby, N. W. (1960). How to study community power: The pluralist alternative. *Journal of Politics*, *22*, 474–484.
Powers, R. C. (1967a). Power actors and social change, Part 1. *Journal of Cooperative Extension*, *5*, 153–163.
Powers, R. C. (1967b). Power actors and social change, Part 2. *Journal of Cooperative Extension*, *5*, 238–273.
Redfield, R. (1941). *The folk culture of the Yucatan*. Chicago: University of Chicago Press.
Reese, M., & Malamud, P. Our town in 1981. (1981, July 6). *Newsweek*, p. 28.
Reich, C. (1970). *The greening of America*. New York: Random House.
Reynolds, M. (1976). Threats to confidentiality. *Social Work*, *21*, 108–113.
Richards, B. (1985, June 7). Forget the newspaper and TV—Local cafe is where the news is. *The Wall Street Journal*, pp. 1, 13.
Richards, R. O. (1978). Urbanization of rural areas. In D. Street and Associates (Eds.), *Handbook of contemporary urban life* (pp. 551–591). San Francisco: Jossey–Bass.
Riesman, D. (1955). Some informal notes on American churches and sects. *Confluence*, *4*, 127–159.
Rivera, F. G., & Erlich, J. L. (1981). Neo-Gemeinschaft minority communities: Implications for community organization in the United States. *Community Development Journal*, *3*, 189–200.
Ross, M. G. (1955). *Community organization: Theory and principles*. New York: Harper & Brothers.
Ross, M. H. (1989). The demise of the melting pot model. *Bryn Mawr Alumnae Bulletin*, Spring, 1–3.
Roszak, T. (1969). *The making of a counter culture: Reflections of the technocratic society and its useful opposition*. Garden City, NY: Doubleday.
Roszak, T. (1978). *Person/planet: The creative disintegration of industrial society*. Garden City, NY: Anchor Press/Doubleday.
Royce, J. (1908). *Race questions, provincialism and other problems*. New York: Macmillan.
Royce, J. (1916). *The hope of the great community*. New York: Macmillan.
Salvador furor comes to town in Vermont. (1983, March 20). *New York Times*, pp. B1, 16.
Sarason, S. B., & Lorentz, E. (1979). *The challenge of the resource exchange network*. San Francisco: Jossey–Bass.
Sayers, V. (1987a). A pretty girl. In *Due east* (p. 1). New York: Doubleday.
Sayers, V. (1987b). *Due east*. New York: Doubleday.
Sayers, V. (1987c). Services. In *Due east* (pp. 131–143). New York: Doubleday.
Schattschneider, E. E. (1960). *The semi-sovereign people*. New York: Holt, Rinehart & Winston.
Schmich, M. T. (1987, November 1). Jews are consigned to history in South: Proud heritage dies in small towns, *Chicago Tribune*, section 1, pp. 25, 30.
Schumacher, E. F. (1973). *Small is beautiful: Economics as if people mattered*. New York: Harper & Row.
Schwartz, G. (1989). Confidentiality revisited. *Social Work*, *34*, 223–226.

Schwartzkopff, F. (1989, January 29). Keysville mayor cited for fight to revive city government. *The Atlanta Constitution*, p. B2.

Scroggins, D. (1988, January 26). Alpharetta cafe stands test of time: Alpha soda hub of activity, symbol of small-town values. *The Atlanta Constitution*, p. C1.

Segal, J. (Ed.). (1973). *The mental health of rural America* (DHEW Publication No. (ADM) 73-9035 or 760349). Rockville, MD: National Institute of Mental Health.

Sills, P. (1975). Power and community groups. *Community Development Journal*, *10*, 24–28.

Simmel, G. (1950). The secret and the secret society. In K. Wolff (Trans.), *The sociology of Georg Simmel* (pp. 307–379). Glencoe, IL: Free Press.

Slater, P. (1976). *Pursuit of loneliness: American culture at the breaking point*. Boston: Beacon Press.

Smith, P. (1963). *As a city upon a hill: The town in American history*. New York: Knopf.

Smothers, R. (1988, January 6). Vote puts small-town blacks on top. *New York Times*, p. 14.

Speck, R. V., & Attneave, C. (1971). Social network intervention. In J. Haley (Ed.), *Changing families* (pp. 312–332). New York: Grune & Stratton.

Statistical Abstract of the United States: 1980 (101st ed.). (1981). Washington, DC: U.S. Government Printing Office.

Steckler, P., & Bell, A. (Producers). (1985). *Hands that picked cotton* [Film]. Distributed by PBS.

Stein, B. (1976). Whatever happened to small town America? *The Public Interest*, *44*, 17–25.

Stein, M. R. (1960). *The eclipse of community*. Princeton, NJ: Princeton University Press.

Suttles, G. D. (1972). *The social construction of communities*. Chicago: University of Chicago Press.

Tarkington, B. (1900a). *The gentleman from Indiana*. New York: Grosset and Dunlap.

Tarkington, B. (1900b). The great Harkless comes home. In *The gentleman from Indiana* (pp. 346–384). New York: Grosset and Dunlap.

Taylor, J. B. (1977). Toward alternative forms of social work research: The case for naturalistic methods. *Journal of Social Welfare*, *4*, 119–126.

Thomas, N. (1976). Network intervention in the small town. *Human Services in the Rural Environment*, *1*, 19–20.

Tocqueville, A. (1945). *Democracy in America* (2 vols.). New York: Random House. (Original work published 1835)

Towns—coming and going [Editorial]. (1987, August 17). *The Christian Science Monitor*, p. 15.

Twain, M. (1900). *The man that corrupted Hadleyburg and other stories and essays*. New York: Harper and Brothers.

Vidich, A. J., & Bensman, J. (1968). *Small town in mass society: Class, power and religion in a rural community*. Garden City, NY: Anchor Books.

Walburn, L. (1987, May 11). Where governing is "women's work." *The Atlanta Constitution*, pp. B1–B4.

Walker, A. (1982). *Community care: The family, the state and social policy*. Oxford: Basil Blackwell.

Walker, A. (1983). *In search of our mothers' gardens*. San Diego: Harcourt Brace Jovanovich.

Warner, W. L. (1963). *Yankee city*. New Haven, CT: Yale University Press.

Warren, R. L. (1963). *The community in America* (3rd ed.). Chicago: Rand McNally.

Warren, R. L. (1966). *Perspectives on the American community: A book of readings*. Chicago: Rand McNally.

Weinbach, R. W. (1990). *The social worker as manager: Theory and practice*. New York: Longman.

Welch, W. (1986, October 4). Your view of town may depend on your age. *Centre Daily Times*, p. B4.
Welch, W. (1987, February 15). Go ahead, run. *Centre Daily Times*, p. B2.
Welch, W. (1988, October 23). Small change. *Centre Daily Times*, p. B4.
Wellstone, P. (1978). *How the rural poor got power: Narrative of a grass-roots organizer*. Amherst: University of Massachusetts Press.
Wenger, G. C. (1984). *The supportive network: Coping with old age*. London: Allen & Unwin.
Wilder, T. (1938). *Our town*. New York: Coward McCann.
Wiley, D. (1986, March 30). We won't roll over and die: Hawkeye is a small town fighting back. *The Cedar Rapids Gazette*, pp. 15A, 16A.
Williams, W. M. (1964). Changing functions of the community. *Sociologia Ruralis*, *4*, 299–314.
Wilson, S. J. (1982). Confidentiality. In S. A. Yelaja (ed.), *Ethical issues in social work* (pp. 338–355). Springfield, IL: Charles C Thomas.
Wilson, W. J. (1973). *Power, racism and privilege: Race relations in theoretical and sociohistorical perspectives*. New York: Free Press.
Wirth, L. (1938). Urbanism as a way of life. *American Journal of Sociology*, *44*, 3–24.
Wolfe, T. (1929). *Look homeward angel: A story of the buried life*. New York: Modern Library.
Wolfinger, R. E. (1960). Reputation and reality in the study of community power. *American Sociological Review*, *25*, 636–644.
Woodward, J. (1965). *Industrial organization: Theory and practice*. London: Oxford University Press.
Wooster, M. M. (1989). A nation divided: The regional magazine boom, *Public Opinion*, *11*, 12–15.
Zablocki, B. (1971). *The joyful community*. Baltimore: Penguin Books.
Zinsmeister, K. (1987). The revolt against alienation. *Policy Review*, *2*, 60–68.

INDEX

A

B

C

D

H

I

J

K

L

M

N

O

P

ABOUT THE AUTHOR

Emilia E. Martinez-Brawley, EdD, ACSW, is Professor of Social Work at The Pennsylvania State University, University Park. She received her MSS at Bryn Mawr College and her doctorate at Temple University. She is the author of the books *Pioneer Efforts in Rural Social Welfare*, *Seven Decades of Rural Social Work*, and *Rural Social and Community Work in the U.S. and Britain* and of numerous articles that have appeared in *Social Work*, *Journal of Education for Social Work*, *Social Casework*, *Arete*, *Community Development Journal*, *The British Journal of Social Work*, *Human Services in the Rural Environment*, *Sociology and Social Welfare*, and *International Social Work*, among others.

In addition to her extensive involvement in research on rural communities in the United States, Dr. Martinez-Brawley has carried out international research on rural services in Canada, Latin America, Great Britain, the Republic of Ireland, Australia, and Spain. She has been a Visiting Lecturer at the University of Regina, Saskatchewan, Canada; a Visiting Fellow at the School of Economic and Social Studies of the University of East Anglia in Norwich, England; and a Fulbright scholar at the University of Western Australia in Perth and at Bar-Ilan University in Israel. She has been a consultant on rural and evaluative issues for the European Centre for Social Welfare Research, an arm of the United Nations in France and Spain; a guest faculty member at the "Consejo Superior de Investigaciones Cintíficas" in Madrid, Spain; and a consultant on rural development for projects in Murcia, Navarra, and Catalonia, Spain. She has been the recipient of a research fellowship from the "Comité Conjunto Hispano-Norteamericano." She was also the recipient of a Hispanic Leadership Fellows Award sponsored by the American Council on Education, the New Jersey Commission on Higher Education, and the Woodrow Wilson Foundation and of an Ida Beam Award from the University of Iowa.

Dr. Martinez-Brawley has been a member of the National Board of the National Association of Social Workers and of the Commission on Accreditation of the Council on Social Work Education.